Pehr Osbeck, Olof Torn

A Voyage to China and the East Indies

Pehr Osbeck, Olof Torn
A Voyage to China and the East Indies
ISBN/EAN: 9783743385269
Manufactured in Europe, USA, Canada, Australia, Japa
Cover: Foto ©Andreas Hilbeck / pixelio.de

Manufactured and distributed by brebook publishing software (www.brebook.com)

Pehr Osbeck, Olof Torn

A Voyage to China and the East Indies

A VOYAGE
TO
CHINA AND THE EAST INDIES,

By PETER OSBECK,
RECTOR of HASLOEF and WOXTORP,
Member of the ACADEMY of STOCKHOLM, and of the
SOCIETY of UPSAL.

Together with A VOYAGE TO SURATTE,
By OLOF TOREEN,
Chaplain of the GOTHIC LION EAST INDIAMAN.

AND

An Account of the CHINESE HUSBANDRY,
By Captain CHARLES GUSTAVUS ECKEBERG.

Translated from the GERMAN,
By JOHN REINHOLD FORSTER, F.A.S.

To which are added,
A FAUNULA and FLORA SINENSIS.

VOL. II.

LONDON,
Printed for BENJAMIN WHITE,
at Horace's Head, in Fleet-street.
MDCCLXXI.

PETER OSBECK'S

VOYAGE to CHINA.

October 24th.

TO-DAY I had another opportunity of gathering plants near the watering-place:

Utricularia bifida [Tab. iii. fig. 2. *a. b.*] is a plant which looks very like our *Swedish Utricularia vulgaris*, but is somewhat less. It grew in a valley in low swampy ground, which however was not under water. As this plant had never been found before, I immediately drew up the following description: the *calyx* is diphyllous: the *foliola* are oval, excavated, persistent: the *corolla* is ringent: the *upper-lip*

lip is without incisions, oval, with reflected sides: the *lower-lip* is bifid, with deflected sides: the *mouth* is elevated: the *nectarium* conical: the *capsule* is egg-shaped, and is dehiscent on the sides: the *seeds* are numerous: the plant in length is an hand's breadth: the *root* is fibrous and ramose: the *bracteae* are very small, oval, alternate: the *peduncles* grow alternately, and are compressed: the *flowers* are small and yellow. It grows in wet places.

Phyllanthus Niuri. The *corolla* is monopetalous, sexdentated, and white: the *capsule* is sixlocular: the *root* is fibrous: the *stem* is erected, undivided.

Hypericum Chinense differs from the *Hypericum quadrangulum* in the following particulars: *Hypericum Chinense* is much less, and lies on the ground. The segments of the *calyx* have five veins, and are somewhat longer than the flowers: the *petals* are narrow, lanceolated, excavated, erect, and of the length of the *calyx*: the 13 *filaments* are filiform: the *antherae* globose and very small: the *germen* is egg-shaped, and with three filiform *styli*: the *stigma* is obtuse; and the *capsule* egg-shaped: the *seeds* are numerous, oblong, and small: the *leaves* are oval, coming out of the *stem* from the angles: the *peduncles* bear but one flower

flower each, and grow at the top of the *ſtalk*. It is found on ſteep hills.

Scutellaria Indica grew in ſhady places, on an earthen wall, and was a great rarity. I have never found it any where elſe. On a curſory view it looks very like the *Glecoma hederacea, Ground-ivy,* which in our apothecaries ſhops is ſold by the name of *Hedera terreſtris.* This plant not yet being deſcribed by any botaniſt, I have here drawn up an accurate deſcription of it:

The *calyx* is divided into two equal ſegments, very ſhort; it has behind an elevated, ſpoonlike, ſharp-pointed ſcale, whoſe margins are bent down, and cloſe after the flower is withered: the *corolla* is ringent: the *tube* is cylindrical, or almoſt quadrangular: the *upper-lip* is trifid: the middlemoſt *lacinia* is emarginated, and inflated: the *laciniæ* on the ſides bend towards each other, and cover the *ſtamina* with their ſides which are bent inwards: the *lowerlip* is divided into four *laciniæ*, expanded, excavated, and the *laciniæ* on the ſides dotted: the four *ſtamina* are covered by the *upper-lip:* two of them are ſhorter, and are the length of the *ſtylus:* the *antheræ* are round and ſhort: the *germen* is divided into four parts: the *ſtylus* is filiform, and the *stigma* is entire: the four *seeds* are uncovered, small, and round. The plant lies on the ground, and has the appearance of *ground-ivy* (*Glecoma hederacea*): the *root* is fibrous: the *stalk* is quadrangular, somewhat rough, ramose: the *branches* are composite, and stand at the top: the *flowers* grow on short *peduncles*, commonly by pairs: the *bractea* are small, lanceolated, oval: the *leaves* are opposite, cordated, oval, crenated, petiolated, pilose, except the small leaves coming from the corners of the greater ones, which are kidney-shaped. I found in a shady place no more than two single plants of this kind. The *Chinese* call it *Tim-gam-sa*.

Hedyotis herbacca? the *calyx* is quadrifid, short, with pointed, reflected segments: the *corolla* is monopetalous: the *tube* is cylindrical, very short: the *limbus* is quinquefid, cylindrical below, bearded in the inside, with equal reflected *laciniæ:* the four *filaments* are shorter than the *corolla*, bearded, and rest on the incisions between the *laciniæ:* the *antheræ* are of equal breadth, of the length of the *filaments*, erect, simple: the *germen* is almost round, and below the *corolla:* the *stylus* is filiform, bearded, longer than the *corolla:* the *stigma ma* is double, club-shaped, trigonal. It grows on dry places.

Croton sebiferum. A little tree, which the *Chinese* call *O-ka-o*, and at first sight looks like an *asp* or *aspin* (*Populus tremula*). The male flower. The *calyx* is very small, bidentated: the *corolla* is wanting: the *filaments* are numerous, very short: the *antheræ* are double, almost round, erected: the female flowers sit below the male ones, six, seven, or more together, on common peduncles: the *calyx* is trifid, with pointed, erected *segments*: the *germen* is oval: the three *styli* are somewhat reflected. The tree is very branchy, and as high as a man: the *branches* are round, smooth, with buds of leaves: the *leaves* are alternate, smooth, and like those of the Black Poplar-tree (*Populus nigra*): on the inferior side they are somewhat woolly, and have long, filiform, softly striated *petioli*, or foot-stalks. The *leaves* have about twelve veins, which on the lower side are stronger: the *flowers* are yellow, stand at the top; the male and female in a *corymbus*. This tree is to be met with on the shores and ditches, though but seldom. *Du Halde* says, the fruit of the *Candle-tree* is covered with an hard, lignous, smooth, triangular shell; these shells contain three little seeds of the size of peafe, pease, each of which is surrounded with a white tallow-like skin. When the fruit is ripe, the shell opens into three parts. For my part, I have never seen the fruit of the *Croton*, and therefore cannot be sure whether it is the same tree of which the *Lappt-yacks* candles are said to be made, as I have been told.

Chrysanthemum Indicum grew here and there, both on the mountains and on the walls of *Canton*, and likewise before the rooms of the *Chinese* in flower-pots. The flowers not only serve as an ornament, but are used instead of tea. The *Chinese* call it *Kock-fa*.

Lattsa is the *Chinese* name of a little tree which here grew on a high field, and looked like the *Yew-tree*; but the leaves were ornamented on the inferior side with white stripes, running length-ways as in *Pinus balsamea*, or the *Phalaris picta*, known among us. It seemed to be *Taxus nucifera Fi, vulgo Kajo. Kæmph. Amæn.* 814.

Briza elegans? spicis oblongis, valvulis carinatis, an exceeding fine grass, which grew near the highest plantations.

Daphne Indica. The *calyx* is wanting: the *corolla* is quadrifid: the *laciniæ* are all of an equal

equal breadth: the eight filiform *ſtamina* are as long as the *corolla,* or the *piſtillum:* the *antheræ* are ſmall, almoſt round, and ſtand on the ſides: the *germen* is oval and rough: the *ſtylus* pointed: the *ſtigma* entire: the *branches* are round and axillar: the *leaves* are oppoſite, petiolated, oblong-oval, ſmooth, without inciſion. The plant is of a ſpan's length. It grows in high places.

October the 25th.

THIS day I took a journey to the watering-place, after the ſermon, and from thence proceeded to the *European* burying-place, on the *Daniſh Iſland.* I obſerved the following natural curioſities:

Celoſia argentea grew as a weed on the potatoe fields.

I found tendrils lying every where in the low grounds hereabouts; they were like the *Hydrocotyle Aſiatica,* but had no parts of fructification.

Adiantum flabellulatum. The *ſtalk (ſtipes)* is triquetrous, and ſtriated on one ſide: the *branches* are alternate: the *leaves* are unequal, and form semicircles, quadrants, or octogons. The *Chinese* call it *Siag mao quang.*

Sambucus nigra looked like a shrub, and was wreathed with the *Cassytha.*

A sort of *moss*, which was like our *Lichen parietarius*, lay dry on the hills by the side of the plantations, but without the parts of fructification.

A climbing plant with white berries was found on the *Chinese Pine-trees* and stones.

Hedysarum maculatum on the hills.

Hedysarum (styracifolium) foliis simplicibus cordato orbiculatis, retusis, supra glabris.

Holcus (latifolius) glumis trifloris, flosculo primo inermi, duabus margine aculeatis, foliis subovatis. The *stalk* is smooth, and scarce a foot high: the *leaves* are very broad, and almost oval, with broad striped *vaginæ:* the *panicula* consists of simple branches like rods: the *flowers* stand alternate, single, on hair-like peduncles: each flower is oblong and oval: the *calyx* is shorter than the flower, and consists of two skins, and contains three flowers; of these the first is smooth, but the second and third

third are armed on the upper margin with crooked spines.

Ko-su, or *Yam ko-sua*, is the name which the *Chinese* gave to the great trees which grew near the plantations.

Palamm is the name of the leaves with which they covered their fruit baskets.

Paulinia Asiatica was planted round the wall of a little spot of ground. If this shrub would grow in our country, it would make the best hedges about our gardens, &c. for in case any one should attempt to pass through it, he would scarce escape without marks in his hands and cloaths from the sharp-pointed hamated thorns of this plant.

Olom-sio was the name given to a certain great tree. Its *leaves* were pinnated, smooth, with opposite *foliola*. A rosin came out of the tree, very much like the *Gum arabick*.

Polypodium varium.

Trichomanes Chinense.

Smilax China. This little shrub grew but sparingly on this island. Its *root* is universally known amongst us by the name of *Radix Chinæ,*

China, and is annually brought from thence to *Sweden* in great quantities.

Smilax Saſſaparilla.

Saccharum Chinenſe grows in the river like reeds. The *Chineſe* call it *Mao*.

The 29th of *October*.

Quong-fong, or *Chineſe* waſps (bees), often tormented us in great numbers, both in town and on board the ſhip. It is *Apis lævis flavo fulvoque varia, abdomine, lineis tranſverſis undatis nigris*.

I took another journey to *Canton* to-day. Near the firſt cuſtom-houſe grew *Hibiſcus mutabilis*, which began to bloſſom in the beginning of this month, and ſtill continued to do ſo. Enquiring for the name of this tree, I was anſwered, that it was called *Fa*, which ſeemed a much too general denomination, for *Fa* denotes a flower. It is poſſible that the *Chineſe* have impoſed upon me on this and many other occaſions; but it is indifferent which is the true *Chineſe* name of a plant, ſince we can do better with the *Latin* name.

The

The *calyx* is like the head of a hat squeezed together. On the entrance towards the house a fine *Pomegranate-tree* was planted, which was then in fruit. Both this and *Rosa Indica*, together with *Rubus parvifolius*, are tokens of the taste this nation has for all sorts of plants to adorn their habitations. You will scarce meet with a family either in town or in the boats without some herbs or trees in flower-pots, if not for use, yet for the sake of pleasure.

Kow-sonn is the *Chinese* name of white long roots, of the thickness of *Parsneps*, the extremes of which had been cut off, and with which a sampane that passed by was quite filled. They were tied into bunches with their ensiform leaves, and were offered to sale.

The *Feast of Lanthorns* began this day, and was to be celebrated for three successive nights, in honour of the god of fire, *Fa-kong*, which is done in the following manner: Many hundred lanthorns made of skins were so hung up, that they together made a sort of arches over the street; and besides these, many chandeliers in form of trees were made use of. Before the houses on the outside they had placed

great

great paper-men, and horses; commonly all the rooms in the houses were flung open, and were every where illuminated. The musicians were in the rooms towards the street, and played on instruments which I had never before heard. I was met by three sacrificing priests, who walked about in the house sacrificing and burning incense. They were cloathed in long, wide, red robes, and wore high caps. The *Chinese* said that they thus annually prayed for security against fire.

The 30th of *October*.

BASELLA *rubra*, which is here called *Tand-foy*, climbed up the walls of the factory of the merchant *Soyon-quas*. It had flowers and fruits at present. The spots which the berries make in white linen are very hard to be got out.

November 2d.

[a] SITTA (*Chinensis*) *palpebrâ inferiore purpureâ*. (*Diff. Chin. Lagerstr.* 6.) The *Chinese* call it *Kow-kay-konn*. This bird was somewhat longer

---
[a] This bird is not in the Syst. Nat. Edit. 12.

longer than a gold-finch. It sometimes sung a little, and was beautifully marked. A couple of these were sold here at half a piastre. Its description is as follows: the *back* from head to tail is dark, ferrugineous, with bluish downs: the *breast* and the *belly* are white; but toward the throat it is black: the *bill* and *head* are black: the *crest* consists of black feathers, and is longer than the bill: near the eyes is an oblong, small, scarlet spot, and close to this a large one as white as snow: from the temples to the throat runs a black line: the *chin* (*mentum*) and the *throat* itself are white, but this white is encompassed with black, except a white line in the middle of the breast, which joins the white of the throat with the snowy breast: the *uropygium* is yellow at the top: the nineteen *quill-feathers* have ferrugineous dark coverts: the twelve blackish *tail-feathers* have white tops: the *feet* have four toes: the *hind-toe* is the length of the toes on the sides: of the *fore-toes* the middlemost is the longest.

THIS bird is kept in *China* more for the sake of its beauty, than for its fine song. It is fed with boiled rice.

The

The 3d of *November*.

We dined to-day with the merchant *Tantinqua*, at whose house tea was packing up for us. Here again the high value which the *Chinese* set upon flowers planted for ornament was observable. Before the dining-room was a fine garden, laid out with stones, and in it was:

Quaisa, a tree about six yards high, with small, white, sweet-scented flowers, whereof three or four were in one *Involucrum*. The tree belongs to the *Tetrandria* class.

Laan-fa, a tree with yellow, corymbose flowers, and pinnated leaves.

Dracæna ferrea, the *iron-tree* [b], which in the *Chinese* language is called *Tat-fio*, was higher than the preceding; and for this reason I could not reach the flowers, which were at the top in bunches. The branches were sup-

---

[b] (*Dracæna ferrea*, Linn. *Syst. Nat. Ed.* 12. p. 246.) D. S. remarks that it is called *Asparagus terminalis*, in *Species Plantar.* and *Terminalis alba* by Rumph. *Am.* vol. iv. p. 79. tab. 34, but *Linnæus*, in his new system, page aforementioned, calls that species of *Asparagus*, *Dracæna terminalis*. F.

ported by *Bamboo* sticks. What follows is its description: the *calyx* is monophyllous, bidentated: the *corolla* is monopetalous: its *tube* filiform, shorter than the *limbus*; which is sexfid, with oblong *laciniæ*, of which the exterior ones are somewhat larger, and include the *filaments*; which are shorter than the *corolla*, and fastened at the base of the *limbus:* the *antheræ* are oblong, narrow, erected: the *pistillum* is longer than the *filaments:* the *germen* is oval, and rests on the tube of the *corolla :* the *stylus* runs into a point: the *stigma* is entire, and inflected. The tree is more than twice the height of a man. The *stem* is very ramose, uncovered, rough: the *branches* are bent, naked, and have bunches of leaves at their ends: the *leaves* are lanceolated, sword-shaped, only grow at the top, are numerous, reddish, with striated foot-stalks, or with revoluted margins : the *flowers* grow at the top, in form of *Corymbi*; each of them is small and red.

Epidendron ensifolium was planted in flower-pots. Its flowers had an exceeding fine scent, especially after sun-set.

Chrysanthemum Indicum. About 30 plants of this species were put into each flower-pot. They

They were difposed in circles one about another, and each had a little *Bamboo* stick to support it. The *flowers* were as large as thofe of the *Tagetes patula*, commonly called *Flos Africanus*, white, double, or full, and each by itfelf, as well as all together, like a round brufh.

In the corner of the garden was fomething which refembled an altar, compofed of pebbles; on it was placed a little vafe, in which fome fmall ftones and fome rubbifh lay, which were all as wet as if they were continually immerfed in water. I did not learn its ufe; but perhaps it ferved to water the *Bamboo-tree*, which ftood between the ftones and the wall.

The 7th of *November*.

I went by water to *Sto-namm*, but was forced to take the interpreter, or *comprador*, with me; who greatly circumfcribed my pleafure by being in fuch hafte to return. I found no new things, except

Nyctanthes hirfuta.

Lycium barbarum, a fhrub on the road.

Juffiæa

Jussiæa repens, in a ditch, with a *Lemna.*

Carpesium abrotanoides, in a shady place.

The 9th of *November.*

CAMELLIA *Japonica,* (its *Chinese* name is *To-kai*), a tree which was carried about and exposed to sale in the streets. I bought one of a blind man in the street, which had fine double white and red flowers. But by further observing it in my room, I found that the flowers were taken from another tree, and one *calyx* was so neatly fixed in the other with nails of *Bamboo,* that I should scarce have found it out, if the flowers had not begun to wither. The tree itself had only buds, but no open flowers. I learned from this instance, that whoever will deal with the *Chinese,* must make use of his utmost circumspection; and even then must run the risk of being cheated.

I HAD a mind to see the situation of the environs of the suburbs, in that part where I had not yet been; and was forced to go by myself for want of company. As soon as I had passed the usual trading streets, the boys gathered about me in thousands, throwing sand, stones, and dirt at me, and shouted all together *Akia, aque ya, quailo*; and with this music they followed me through the whole town. At the end of the suburbs begins a plantation with *Sagittaria bulbis oblongis* close to the houses. A large, low, clayey field was employed in the culture of this plant. And as I stopped here, and only gathered now and then a plant, my disagreeable company stopped their noise, especially when I turned to them. Here was no road which carried directly into the country, nor did I venture any farther; but returned whence I came. However, in the afternoon, I went out of town in a *palankin*, by this means avoiding my disagreeable forenoon companions. Returning again, I went on foot about the wall of *Canton*, on the side from the country, and there found *Chrysanthemum Indicum*, *Urtica nivea*, little clumps of *Fern*; and other plants between the stones, but they were out of my reach.

When we came to the first city-gate, towards the side of the *European* burying-place, a *mandarin*, with a whip in his hand, joined us to accompany us about the city. Near this gate was a *Chinese* inn, where brandy and tea were

were fold. The people flood by the fide of the round-houfe on the wall, and flared at us; however, we got by without hurt, though not without fear, becaufe we remembered that a perfon was fome time before pelted with ftones from this very place. When we approached nearer to the fuburbs, we every where, and almoft clofe up to the wall, found houfes; they were all full of men, and efpecially children and youths, who fang their old fong, of which they were put in mind by the grown people, if they did not begin it themfelves. Yet we likewife found an old reverend man who had more fenfe than the others, and made his children or grandchildren greet us civilly. The perfons of rank in this country teach their children from their earlieft years the dictates of virtue and honefty, and fpare no expences towards a good education: but the common fort of people train their children up with their dogs; for which reafon neither of them can bear ftrangers. We afterwards paffed by many gates, and over a little canal into a lane along the fide of the wall, in which *China-oranges*, *Plaintains*, *China-olives*, or *Packia*, and many other fruits, were fold. An intolerable ftench, and the noife and clamour of the populace, obliged us to make hafte to the *Swedifh* factory.

The 17th of *November*.

To-day I went to the ship, and afterwards to the *Danish Island*, on which some *Chinese* oyster-shells had been thrown.

Of these shells I have seen an entire wall of a garden made, on the other side of the river near *Canton*. The shells were in substance like ours; but larger, longer, and narrower at one end. The *Chinese* call them *O-a*, or *O-ha*.

The 21st of *November*.

Cloudy sky, and drizzling rain.

On account of the sands which are in the river, the *European* ships are obliged to go somewhat lower towards the mouth of the river, before they take in their full cargoe; which we did to-day, after we had taken a pilot on board. We now anchored at *South-Haven*.

The 22d of *November*.

In the fore-noon we went on further against the tide, as far as the first bank, or bear, as our sailors call the sands. In the afternoon we had an agreeable country, with villages and woods, on our left; but along the river side a narrow rice-field, and in the river two small islands. We sailed very near the most outward of the two, by means of the sampanes keeping always at an equal distance: but we afterwards steered off from it, as if we were going full upon a little house on the right, surrounded with trees: but before we had quite reached the middle of the river, we went strait on again, and were said to have passed the first sand. Somewhat nearer the *Lion-tower*, (which we saw on our right) we approached the shore on the left hand, in expectation of another sand. We lay at anchor all night.

The 23d of *November*.

In the morning we passed the *Lion-tower*. We kept near the shore on the left, to escape the third bank, which is faid to be 1500 fathoms in circumference. Having got paft the river which goes to *Little Canton*, by the help of 16 fampanes (whence the water for the voyage homeward is fetched with more conveniency than from *Bocca Tiger*, where the water-tubs muft be rolled a good way in deep clay), we anchored not far from the great rice-field on the left; where already two *French*, a *Danifh*, two *Dutch*, and two *Englifh* fhips, were at anchor.

The people brought an unpalatable fruit from the watering-place, which was almoft round, larger than an apple, and contained great dry rhomboidal feeds, which grew narrower towards the bottom.

The 24th of *November*.

We lay in a very bad birth here, and were expofed to ftorms and to the cold air of the fea. Here we learnt that though the *Chinefe* winter is but juft cold enough to produce an ice in the night, which is melted away in the day-time; yet the air about this feafon is very fharp and piercing.

WE

We were now almoſt as far again from *Canton* as in our firſt ſtation, at leaſt we were forced to pay a double price in order to go thither. It was not poſſible to go on ſhore, on account of the great rice-fields, which occupied both ſides of the river. In theſe rice-fields we every day ſaw ducks, and great long-legged white birds, but they were too far off for us to know their *genus*. I viſited the *Daniſh* ſhip, which was full laden, and had a far greater number of men than ours: the cabbin of the chaplain, *Lawrence Hercks*, was one of the fineſt and largeſt in the ſhip. This perſon told me, that the *Daniſh* ſea chaplains had, beſides their ſettled income, a conſiderable contribution from the ſhip's company; and that accordingly their income was reckoned treble to that of the *Swediſh* chaplains. But they are ſufficiently rewarded in our country if they can gain the love of their audience.

CHINESE *turtle-doves* were bought for our return, and we kept them alive a good while aboard the ſhip. Their characters are theſe: the *bill* is red: the *upper jaw* is the longeſt, and has a protuberance like a nail: the *tongue* is triangular: the *body* and the *wings* below are ferrugineous: the *head* and the *neck* are darker at the top: the *back* is marked near the wings with reddish yellow spots; but a little farther on it is red, verging towards black, where likewise two black lines run over the edges of the feathers: they have twenty-two *quill-feathers* whose coverts change from green to gold; and eleven feathers in the *tail*.

The 27th of *November*.

To-day the *Danish* ship sailed for *Europe*. The *Danes* hasten their departure, but lose more time in the refreshments they take on their voyage. On their going to the *Indies* they choose an agreeable port which our ships pass by; for they stop at the *Cape of Good Hope*, where they can purchase the finest wines at low prices, besides the pleasure of visiting a people who adorn their bodies with what would turn our stomachs but to hear of: I mean the *Hottentot* girls, who twist raw guts about their legs to shew that they are beauties; and have many other strange customs, as travellers relate.

For want of other diversion, I described the following fishes, which were caught here:
Clupea

Clupea Myſtus: the *membrana branchioſtega* has ten rays: the *dorſal-fin* is oblong, directly oppoſite to the ventral-fins, and has thirteen rays, of which the firſt is the ſhorteſt: the *pectoral-fins* have ſeventeen rays, of which the ſeven upper ones are divided, and of ſuch a length as to reach beyond the anus: the *ventral-fins* are oval, and have ſeven rays: the *anal-fin* has eighty-ſix linear rays, and reaches from above the middle of the fiſh to the tail: the *tail* is ſharpened, and has thirteen or fourteen rays: on the *belly* are 43 little teeth (*denticuli*): the *body* is narrow, compreſſed, the hind-part decreaſes very much: the *upper jaw* is the longeſt, and ends in a prominent, ſerrated beak, ſhaped like a ſword: the *mouth* is in the form of a rhombus, and large. The fiſh is of a ſpan's length, and white.

Perca Chinenſis. The *dorſal-fin* reaches from the head almoſt to the tail, is lower in the middle, and has thirty-ſix rays, of which the ten firſt are ſpinoſe, and the ninth is the ſhorteſt, and unarmed: the *pectoral-fins* have eighteen rays: the *ventral-fins* have ſix unarmed rays: the *anal-fin* has ten rays, of which the two firſt are ſpinoſe: the *tail* is oval, and has ſeventeen rays: the *mouth* is oblong, the
teeth

teeth are in the *branchiostega*. The fish has the outward appearance of the *Perca fluviatilis*, but is less. The *linea lateralis* is bent. The fish is pale yellow: the *lower jaw* is shorter than the upper.

Clupea Thrissa. The *membrana branchiostega* has seven rays: the single *dorsal-fin* takes up the middle, and has 16 rays, of which the last is double the length of the rest: the *pectoral-fins* have fourteen rays: the *ventral-fins* have seven rays, and are very small: the *anal-fin* has twenty-four rays; it does not begin quite in the middle, and reaches to the tail: the *tail* is furcated, and has 24 rays: the *mouth* is large, oblong: the *lower-jaw* is the longest, and dotted with black towards the top: the *body* is narrow, white: the *denticuli* on the belly are thirty in number.

THE *Mandarin fish, Sparus nobilis.* The *membrana branchiostega* has three rays: the first *dorsal-fin* has four, and the other nine rays: the *pectoral-fins* have sixteen rays: the *ventral-fins* have six rays: the *anal fin* has twelve, and the *tail* twenty-four rays. The length of the fish is hardly a foot: the *body* is narrow, the *scales* are white: the *head* is egg-shaped, and round:

round: the *mouth* small, globose: the *upper-jaw* is the longest: the *eyes* are small, near the upper margin of the *mouth:* the *opercula branchiostega* consist of three bones.

SNOW-WHITE Dolphins (*Delphinus Chinensis*) tumbled about the ship; but at a distance they seemed in nothing different from the common species, except in the white colour.

THE next day I again went to *Canton.*

The 11th of *December.*

THIS day, which is the sixth in the eleven month of the *Chinese*, or *Shienghio*, is very remarkable among them; if it is clear, it foretells a good year to come; but when beginning with rain, they expect a sterility of crop. They bring sacrifices to their idols, in order to be preserved from the dearth. It was fine weather all the day along, whence they prophecied a plentiful year.

The 17th of *December.*

IN the forenoon I buried the Purser *Hubin,* who died yesterday of the dysentery. He was
born

born in *France*, and brought up to the Roman Catholic religion: he afterwards embraced the *Lutheran* religion at *Gothenburgh*, and poſſeſſed great knowledge in both religions. He kept his good-humour on to a great age; and indeed it never forſook him to his death. In the afternoon I gave him the ſacrament, and immediately after he departed peaceably. To bury him, we paſſed the river to a peninſula, and afterwards through a great canal, over which many bridges were made, till we at laſt arrived at the burying-place, which had been bought for him in an incloſed place on the left. The *Chineſe* took ſix *tale* for the grave. Near the burying-place was a number of coffins above the ground, as I have already remarked elſewhere.

THE mob was very riotous, and we made haſte to finiſh the ſervice. Afterwards we went to the aforementioned *pagode*, which lies on the other ſide of the canal, in *Honang*. In the fields hereabouts were little holes here and there, in which ſeeds were put and covered over with aſhes. A ſpot, on which according to the account of the *Chineſe* a medicinal herb was planted, was covered with mats, which were expanded a yard high above the ground.

ground. This plant was as yet so small, that I could not tell whether it was or was not the *Amaranthus tristis*. I was shewn, but at a great distance, how the high fields about *Bocca Tiger* were green with a plant out of whose seeds the *Chinese* press their oil, which they call *loam*. It is said they have a trick of boiling the seed before they sell it. It is most probably *Sesamum*. We visited their sail-cloth manufacture of *bambou* splints on which *bambou* leaves are laid. They call it *Tiock-yee*. The ropes are likewise made of *bambou* threads. Here also was a place where both great and small boats were built; and rudders, and several mills to grind rice, &c. were made. On the fields the *Poa Malabarica* was growing; and near the pales and enclosures a sort of reed, which the *Chinese* call *Luta*, and looks like *Arundo donax*. I at last got for a piastre twenty-five kinds of pot-herbs.

The 21st of *December*.

I AGAIN returned to the ship, and met the ship chaplain *Toreen* in the bancshal; he had buried a sailor on the *French Island*, who died of a pain in his side aboard our ship.

SCOLOPENDRA

SCOLOPENDRA *pedibus utrinque viginti* was here found near the bancfhal.

THE fhips prepared for their voyage home, except the *Dutch* commodore fhip, which was to ftay till *March*, and bring the fhips accounts into order.

The 25th of *December*.

CLEAR, calm weather.

OYSTERS, which the *Chinefe* called *Hao*, were fold quite frefh to us. It was a different fpecies from thofe whofe fhells have been aforementioned; they were rounder, five or fix, or more of them grew together, and are extremely difficult to open: for the purpofe of opening, the *Chinefe* always have a proper piece of iron about them when they fell *Oyfters.* Some of them were faftened to great ftones, and on them the *Sertularia confervæ formis* was faftened. It was plainly vifible that they came out of a clayey bottom. They were very like our oyfters, but larger, in particular the animal in them; which the *Chinefe* take

out,

out, put into water, and thus sell them to their countrymen without the shell.

SPARUS *Chinensis*, or the *Little mandarin fish*, which is like the *Sarfe* (*Cyprinus Erythrophtalmus*) were here caught in plenty, and by the *Chinese* called *Kya-yo*. The following is its description: the *membrana branchiostega* has five rays: the first *dorsal-fin* has four simple rays, of which the hindmost is quite soft; this fin has a lanceolated appendage on each side: the second *dorsal-fin* is not armed, has eleven divided rays, and is of the length of the former: the *pectoral-fins* have 14 rays: the *ventral-fins* have six rays, they have on both sides and in the middle a soft appendage: the *anal-fin* has twelve rays: the *tail* is furcated, and has sixteen and more rays: the *head* is narrow, flat; the *mouth* is small; it has no teeth: the *eyes* are near the mouth: the *irides* are white: the *body* is narrow, and lanceolated: the *linea lateralis* does not appear: the *back* is blue, and the rest white: the *opercula branchiostega* consist of two entire leaves. The length of the fish is scarcely a span. The *scales* are white rhombs.

GOBIUS

Gobius *Eleotris*, by the *Chinese* called *Sinnhas*, is a greenish, almost round fish, which is somewhat less than the preceding. The *membrana branchiostega* has five rays: the *dorsal-fins* have from six to eleven rays: the *pectoral-fins* have eighteen rays: the *ventral-fins* have eight rays, and are joined together into one infundibuliform fin: the entire *tail* has twelve rays: the *body* is almost round, covered with little rhomboidal green scales: the *lower-jaw* is the longest: the *teeth* are fixed in four rows in the mouth, are small and very sharp: the *eyes* are in the upper part of the head.

The 27th of *December*.

In the afternoon I went in the sloop along the shore, and passed by the *Lion-tower*. Here was a great mountain on the shore where a reddish sand-stone appears, which is here squared, and afterwards sent to *Canton* and other places hereabouts for coffins, flags, stone-dykes, walls, &c. The workmen had erected a number of little houses in the quarry, which made the mountain on the side towards the sea look like a little town. The mountain was covered

covered with *Chinese* (as an ant-hill is with ants) from the top to the bottom. At the summit was a little redoubt, and paved roads led towards the shore. On the fields where rice had been growing, some shallow furrows were made to keep the fishes back in them when the water ran off. I would have landed with the sloop, but it was out of my power. One might have made a pretty collection of fossils here. We were astonished to see that the *Chinese*, who had put their nets into the water, shot continually without aiming at any thing: but upon enquiry we were told that they were forced to watch their fisheries continually, and to frighten away the ducks, who would else empty the nets sooner than men could. I never saw such fearless and numerous flights of ducks as here: one flight after another came, notwithstanding the noise that was made on all sides, and endeavoured to settle near the nets; but were always hindered in the above manner: these wild ducks were not quite like ours, as will appear from the following description:

Anas (Chinensis) regione oculorum maris viridi. The male: the wings have about twenty-eight quill-feathers, of which the first ten are

are the longest, and ash-coloured; their upper margin is black, and the ground grey: the four or five next are ash-coloured, with green upper margins and white bordered tops: the four hindmost ones are longer than those in the middle, and ash-coloured: the greater coverts are white on the margins of the upper side; the rest are ash-coloured: the eleven *tail-feathers* go tapering, have white borders, and are grey at the bottom: the *bill* is of a blackish grey, and soft: the *upper mandible* covers the lower: the *teeth* in the margin of the lower *mandible* are lamellated: the *head* is brown like the chin: a white line passes below the eyes: all about the eyes is green: the *neck* and the fore part of the *back* are covered with white feathers, spotted with black: the hindmost part of the *back* and the *uropygium* are ash-coloured: the *feathers* which cover the upper part of the *neck* are white, with black spots: the black feathers covering the *uropygium* have white borders: the *breast* and the *belly* are white, and spotted with black backwards: the *feet* and *legs* are ash-coloured: the three *fore-toes* are joined; the *hind-toe* is free: the *membranes* have crenated edges: the *female* is covered at the top with black feathers, but at the extremities with reddish white ones; it

is

CHINA. 1751. 35

is white below, with black spots: the *chin* is white: the *head* and all about the eyes is of a whitish grey: the *quill* and *tail-feathers* are almost the same as in the male. The *Chinese* call this sort of ducks *Hina-a*. There is another sort of ducks to be met with at *Canton*, which is called *Kong-ao*, but this I have not seen.

The bird which the *Chinese* make use of for fishing is represented in several voyages, and is here called *Lou-foo*[a]; but no author has given a full description of it: I offered a reasonable reward to any one who would procure me such a bird for a short time; but in vain, though this way of fishing is said to be used in *Macao*. According to the representations of this bird in the books of travellers, it must be very like the *Man of War* (*Pelecanus aquilus*). They describe the fishery to be performed in the following manner: the fisherman fastens an iron ring about the bird's neck, so that it may not swallow any fishes: on the ring is a rope with which the bird is held: As soon as a fish is observed about the boat, the fisherman tosses the bird into the water, who imme-

[a] In the Ambassade de la C. O. des Provinces unies, p. 172. t. 173. it is called *Leuva*.

D 2   diately

diately does its duty, and then is pulled up with the fish in its bill. This method of fishing is very expensive. Its price is settled, and is said to amount very often to fifty *tale*. Besides this, the fisherman pays a certain sum of money as an annual contribution.

1752.

The 1st of *January*.

HAVING taken in our cargoe in porcellane, tea, silk, &c. according to the following account, and provided ourselves with water for our return as far as *Java*, we yet took in this day some *Chinese* potatoes, turneps, yams, carrots, leeks, cabbages, and other garden stuff.

Bill of Lading.

Teas.

1,030,642 pounds of *Bohea-tea*, in 2885 chests.

96,589 lb. *Congo-tea*, in 1071 large, and 288 lesser chests.

67,388

67,388 lb. *Soatchoun-tea*, in 573 large and 1367 lesser chests.
17,205 lb. *Pecko-tea*, in 323 chests.
6,670 lb. *Bing-tea*, in 119 chests.
7,930 lb. of *Hyson-Skinn-tea*, in 140 chests.
2,206 lb. of *Hyson-tea*, in 31 tubs.
3,557 lb. of several sorts of tea, in 1720 canisters.

Silk Stuffs.

961 Pieces of poisies damask.
 67 Pieces of ditto, of two colours.
143 Pieces of damask for furniture.
673 Pieces of sattin.
 15 Pieces of sattin, of two colours.
 16 Pieces of ditto, coloured flowers.
681 Pieces of paduasoy.
192 Pieces of gorgoron.
1,291 Pieces of taffety.
 16 Pieces of lampasses.
5,319 Pieces of yellow cotton *Nankin* stuffs.
5,047 lb. of raw silk, in 33 chests.

Sundries.

35,314 lb. of *Galanga* roots.
 6,359 lb. of *China* roots.
 2,165 lb. of mother of pearl.

6,325

6,325 lb. of thin canes for hoops.
10,709 lb. of fagoe.
4,171 lb. of rhubarb, in 24 chests.
9,314 lb. of painted paper.
1,250 Pieces of flowers, &c.
3,400 round jettoons of mother of pearl, 140 in each set.
62 ditto, 10 in each set.
108 japaned play-boxes, with mother of pearl jettoons.
18 japaned tablets, or boxes for a toilet.
10 japaned tablets.
6 tons of arrack.

Porcellane.

222 chests, 70 tubs, 52 lesser chests, and 919 packs.

THE ship was twenty-one feet ten inches behind, and twenty feet five inches before, in the water.

The 4th of *January*.

AFTER a stay of four months and ten days in *China*, our ship and the other *Swedish* ship began

began their voyage home. Every one leaped for joy, and my *Tea-ſhrub*, which ſtood in a pot, fell upon the deck during the firing of the canons, and was thrown over-board without my knowledge, after I had nurſed and taken care of it a long while on board the ſhip. Thus I ſaw my hopes of bringing a growing tea-tree to my countrymen at an end; a pleaſure which no one in *Europe* has been able as yet to feel, notwithſtanding all poſſible care and expences. Some have brought tea-nuts as they get them from the *Chineſe*; but in caſe they could get them freſh (which I very much doubt), they are ſpoiled on the voyage: others have bought tea-ſhrubs in pots, which they commonly get in flower juſt before their departure from *China*, but they withered about the *Cape of Good Hope*.

If the *Europeans* were themſelves allowed to go into the tea-woods, and to gather there ſuch ſeeds as are neither too dry nor unripe, nor boiled, they might be kept in any thing; but without this they can only get ſhrubs (in the factories) in little flower pots, with too little earth, or with ſuch as is not fit for their tender roots. The tea-ſhrub would doubtleſs habituate itſelf to our climate; but if we want to receive the benefit of it, we should first learn to prepare tea, which may turn out more difficult than we have hitherto imagined; for some prepare tea so ill even in *China*, that it does not taste so well as one of our *Swedish* teas. But, supposing we knew the best method of drying it, we could never sell a pound of home-made tea so cheap as the *Chinese* tea, while *Sweden* has not proportionably the same number of industrious inhabitants as *China* [b].

After we had sailed a good way, we saw a great mouth of the river opening into the sea on the right; but we sailed to *Bocca Tiger*, whose castles were situated on the naked hills of two islands, about which only some trees were planted. They were exactly opposite to each other. That which is nearest to the continent is the highest.

In the evening we cast our anchor along with a *French* ship bound for *Macao*.

[b] Dr. *Linnæus* has had since (the 3d of *October*, 1763,) a fine tea-shrub brought him from *China*, by Captain *Carl. Gustav. Eckeberg*, which is, as far as we know, the only one in *Europe*. F.

The

The 5th of *January*.

In the morning we weighed our anchor, and soon after passed the sands at *Bocca Tiger*, where we found ground at four fathoms depth, in high water.

The 6th of *January*.

Cloudy sky. Fresh gale.

The pilot left us. We directed our course from the great *Ladrone Island*, to the *English Sand*, and afterwards to the island of *Zapata*, which the *Portugueze* call a *Last* on account of its form.

The *Monsoons* are constant winds which blow for half a year together in the *East Indian* sea, and they were now N. E. and sometimes varied a degree or so on either side. They continue N. E. all *November, December, January, February,* and *March,* with dry weather. In *April* and *September* they turn about, and at that time the most frightful storms blow from all sides. The worst of all is that which the

Chinese

Chinese call *Taifun*; for (as I have been told by a *Swede* who had been in the *East Indies*) it continues often for twenty-four hours together with such violence, that nobody is able to walk up and down, but is as it were confined to his place. At least it is always reckoned the worst hurricane which can possibly happen on a voyage to the *East Indies*. In *May*, *June*, *July*, and *August*, the wind is always southern hereabouts, and generally attended with rain.

The 8th of *January*, 15°. 45'. N. L.

The *English Sand* had thirty-six fathoms of water. The ground was red sand, mixed with corals.

The 10th of *January*, 10°. 38'. N. L.

Changeable weather, sometimes clear, sometimes cloudy. The wind blew hard, and the sea was very boisterous. About four o'clock in the afternoon we had the island of *Zapata* west.

Sterna *nigra, fronte albicante, caudâ cuneiformi,* (*Chin. Lagerstr.* 9.) was here caught. It had

had twenty-feven quill-feathers and eleven tail-feathers, and was of the fize of a jack-daw.

The 11th of *January*, 8°. 11'. N. L.

GENERALLY clear fky. Frefh gale.

WE thought we paffed *Polo Candor* in the morning dawn, at leaft we did not fee it this time. (*Polo* is the *Indian* name of an ifland.)

The 15th of *January*.

CLOUDY, changeable, rainy weather, which was looked upon as very uncommon in this latitude.

THE *Ifle of Lingen* (which is exactly under the equator) we paffed the night before. Though this place is very hot, yet it is not fufficient to produce men without parents, as a *Pagan* writer from the ifland of *Wack-wack* relates. See *Bayeri Comment. de Orig. Sin.* 278. *Polo Toya* was on our right in the forenoon. At noon we had the feven iflands on our left, two of which are higher than the reft. Near the firft high ifland there feemed to be another small one: but perhaps it is not separated from the other.

The 16th of *January*.

GENERALLY rainy and inconstant weather.

THE last night we anchored in the *Straits of Banka*, near the shores of *Sumatra*, where the river *Palimbanka* discharges itself in the sea, after we had, the night before, passed by *Monopin*, or the last high mountain on the island of *Banka*, opposite *Sumatra*.

FREDERICK-*Henry*, a rock hidden under the water, (which has formerly been the ruin of many ships) was passed very happily.

ABOUT noon we saw the third (but counting from *Canton* the first) *Cape on Sumatra*, covered with the finest and scarcest trees, so that it looked as if the whole country consisted of a cut garden-hedge. The most outward were probably *Indian* canes, and the rest some kinds of *Palm* trees. The country appeared finer at this distance than I am able to describe. The people were described to me as assassins;
and

and it was believed that in every bufh were crocodiles and other hurtful animals: but if I fhould have met lions and tigers, I muft neverthelefs have wifhed myfelf on fhore, had it been but for an hour. But we fteered towards *Salari*, a mountain on *Banka*. And after we had likewife paffed the fecond neck of land, we caft anchors at night.

The 17th of *January*.

TO-DAY, excepting the morning, we had fine clear weather, but little wind. We began to fail very early, as did the other fhips, which we left near *China*, but joined here again. At noon we paffed the ifle of *Lucipara*: the paffage for great fhips between *Sumatra* and this ifland is very inconvenient, becaufe there is but three and a half fathom of water on the fand bank; but as foon as you are got by, and have *Lucipara* (I fpeak as coming from *China*) N. E. you are then out of danger.

The 18th of *January*.

AFTER eight o'clock in the morning we had the *Two Brothers* on the left, quite near us. This

This is the name of two iflands covered with trees, between which the water is faid to be fo low, that not even a little boat can pafs.

We here obferved confiderable breakers.

About four o'clock in the afternoon we had *Toppers Hat* and the high woody fhore of *Bantam* on the left; but fomewhat farther on, about fix o'clock, we had the *Hat of Brabant*, a little woody rock, on the fame hand: and directly oppofite to it, on our right, a long, narrow ifland, which is called *Acrofs the Way*.

The 19th of *January*.

After a fortnight's voyage from the *Ladrones*, we anchored about noon in the *New-Bay*, the ufual harbour; and we took as much water from *Java* as would fuffice for the whole voyage. In the afternoon I went in a boat on fhore near the place whence we took in water. It is difficult to reach the fhore, becaufe the ground is fo full of corals (*Millepora Javanenfis*), that we were obliged to leave the boat a good way behind us, and the people got out and waded up to their breafts in water, and with difficulty carried me to the fhore on

their

their shoulders. The country here is very high, and the water which comes hither from the fens in the wood runs roaring into the sea. The sailors fix a leathern spout which reaches to the boat, and thus fill their tubs. The water itself was pretty good, and in my opinion the best I ever drank on my voyage. The soil on the shore consists of a fine whitish grey sand, in which all sorts of corals, such as *Madrepora organum*, and *Star-stones* (*Millepora*), and likewise *Cowries* (*Cyprœa*) and other shells, were to be met with. But I left all these and went into the forest with the carpenter, who looked for some timber for his purposes. We kept close together, because we were in danger of not meeting again in case we had separated. The forest was so close, that we passed through with great difficulty; and the cries of birds, and lizards, and other noises, would not permit us to call to each other. In some places it was so wet, that I followed my companion with reluctance, for it rained about this time every night and forenoon, and sometimes even all the day long. The excessive high but slender trees make the forest dark; and a quantity of *Palm* trees of six yards high, whose leaves were prickly, tore our cloaths, nay even the

skin

skin off our hands and faces. This little *Palm* tree is

Caryota (urens Linn. [c]) *frondibus bipinnatis, aculeatis, foliolis cuneiformibus, rotundato præmorsis.* I did not see the parts of fructification, and therefore am not quite certain of the genus. The *frondes* are, as in the *Caryota*, bipinnated and whitish below: the *leaves* are opposite, almost oval, plicated; the upper margin as it were lacerated: the *petioli* are covered with many opposite, hamated spines, not only at the beginning of the *foliola*, but even at the second and third pair of them.

ANOTHER sort of little *Palm* trees[d] (*Calamus Rotang* Linn.) was likewise in our road. The *stem* was without branches, had a crown at top, and was every where beset with straight spines. This is the true *Indian* cane, which was not visible on the outside; but the bark being taken off, discovered the smooth stick, which has no marks of spines on the bark, and is exactly like those which the *Dutch* sell to us, keeping this matter very secret, left travellers going by should take as many canes as they want out of these woods. *Sumatra* is said to be the place where most of these sticks

[c] *Javanica.* Osbeck.   [d] *Palma Baculus.* Osbeck.

grow.

grow. I took two to try them, but left them behind during my voyage. Such plants ought to be chofen as are of a proper growth between two joints, fuitable to the fafhionable length of canes as they are then worn: but fuch are fcarce. I do not know that any one before has given an account of the *Indian* canes while they are growing.

AFTER we had got a good way in this foreft, which is reckoned fo dangerous on account of tigers and other beafts of prey, my honeft carpenter, having tried feveral forts of wood, at laft met with a long naked ftem, which he felled. The timber of the tree was of a fine yellow colour, at leaft while it was newly cut. I looked for the parts of fructification in this felled tree; but thefe not appearing, I could not afcertain it. On its bark grew,

Hypnum Javanenfe.

Lichen pulverulentus viridis et albus, and

Afplenium Nidus; this formed a fort of cup in the angles between the branches, in which the birds made their nefts.

CALAMUS *Rotang (varietas)* is a little flender tree without branches or twigs, winding about the high trees near it, even to their tops, and tying them as it were together. I saw here a tree with eight branches, each of which (being of the thickness of a finger) bent down and formed roots, by a natural direction, unassisted by art. These branches were beset with eniform leaves; but I found neither flower nor fruit on the tree.

The *Sio-lock-tao* of the *Chinese* was twisted round the trees. On an unknown tree, which had no flowers at that time, I saw a fruit both in colour and shape like *Hips*.

Little *Palm* trees, whose fruit was like the *Nux vomica*, with green or brown shells, grew not far from the shore. In the same place I found a plant resembling the *Alpinia racemosa*, together with many other uncommon trees and herbs, which I could not ascertain, because I could find no parts of fructification.

Epidendrum *amabile* grew on the branches of trees on the shore. This plant hath great white odoriferous flowers, such as I never observed before. I had this plant lying in my room for some days together; but the flowers
did

did not wither, and filled it with the most agreeable smell. On the *Isle of Ternate* none but princesses are allowed to wear this precious flower, which is but too scarce [a]. The shape of it is as follows:

The *corolla* is pentapetalous: the three exterior *petals* are oblong: the two interior ones are roundish oval, expanded; the upper lip of the *nectarium* is shorter and inflected; the lower is pinnatifid and inflected; it has four *laciniæ*, of which the two greater ones are obtuse at the bottom, but the two others are very small and sharp: the gland at the bottom of the *nectarium* is bifid, yellow, with little red dots: the point of the *lower-lip* has two filiform appendages: the *roots* are numerous, soft, flat, and stick to the barks of trees. It has only three *leaves*, which stand at the root, are undivided, and without nerves, almost falcated: the *stalk* is undivided: the *flowers* are alternate at the top.

PAVETTA *Indica*, a little tree, which was not far off the watering-place.

JASMINUM *azoricum* grew below the high trees.

[a] *Rumph.* Herb. Amb. Angræcum alb. majus.

HIBISCUS *populneus*, a tree with fine great flowers, stood below the aforementioned plant. Its *leaves* were somewhat soft beneath, and had *stalks* which were reflected: the *bracteæ* are round: the outward *calyx* is short, divided into eleven parts; the inner is quinquefid, six times longer than the outer: its *leaves* are lanceolated.

THE shore was almost every where covered with corals, especially *Madrepores* and *Coral-organs*; besides these, petrified spunges (without stalks) and shells were to be met with. But the trees (which in most places hung over the water) did not afford us a free passage.

THE *Hermit crab*, or *Cancer Eremita Javanica*, was found in a shell. Its *left claw* was larger than the right, but it is however a different species from our common *Cancer bernhardus*.

LICHEN *marinus*, *Cluf.* Hist. p. ccl. was in plenty on the shore.

NIGHT obliged me to break off this agreeable employment sooner than I could have wished:

wifhed: and having feen the trees with many branches, from which a number of roots hung down perpendicularly, near the wateringplace, I was forced to go on board again with the boat. Here I found two fcarce fifhes, which a friend of mine had got for me, that I might put them into fpirits. They were:

Chætodon faxatilis? a yellowifh flounderlike fifh, with broad black tranfverfal *fafciæ*: the fingle *dorfal-fin* is low, and reaches to the tail: its thirteen *foremoft rays* are prickly, the remaining twenty-fix are longer, have a black ftripe below, and likewife black tops: the *pectoral-fins* have fixteen rays: the *ventralfins* have fix rays: the three firft rays of the *anal-fin* are prickly, but the other twenty have black fpots, which taken together make a narrow ftripe: the *tail* is entire, and has twenty rays: the *body* is broad and compreffed, with quadrangular fcales: the *opercula branchioft.* are fcaly.

Sparus Spinus was like a fort of dried fifh which we bought at *Canton* for our voyage. The *dorfal-fin* reaches from the head to the tail, and has twenty-four rays, of which the thirteen foremoft are prickly and fhorter: the *pectoral-fins* have fifteen rays: the *ventral-fins* have five rays, of which the two extreme ones are prickly: the *anal-fin* begins at the middle of the fish, and goes to the tail, and has fifteen rays, of which the first seven are prickly: the *tail* is bifid, and has eighteen rays: the *sides* are grey, except towards the belly, and have a bent lateral line: the *belly* is white: the *lips* are soft: the length of the *body* is a span.

The *Javanese* brought the following things to sell on board our ship: apes, shells, *Turkish* corn, and

Java *deer (Cervus Javanicus).* The *upper primary teeth* are wanting: of the inferior eight lower the two middle ones are three times broader at the ends than the rest: the three *cutting teeth* on the sides are pointed: the *upper-jaw* has a sharp canine tooth on each side, which is of the length of the cutting teeth; therefore this animal is not *Capra perpusilla*, Muf. Reg. Suec. p. 12. I have seen the buck and the doe, neither of which had horns, though our sailors assured me they have seen them with horns. Of the nine grinders the six inner ones are double, and the three exterior ones are laciniated (*lobati* [b]). This

---

[b] The feet of this species of deer are sometimes set in silver, and used as tobacco-stoppers.

species of deer equals a new-born lamb in size. The colour is a reddish brown. The buck (whose head I have now been describing) is larger than the doe, and has white stripes on his sides which run longitudinally. They lived upon fresh blades of rice, which we sowed in pots for that purpose.

It has been said that *Parrot fishes* were to be found hereabouts, but I never was so happy as to get one.

The 20th of *January*.

A HEAVY rain kept me from going on shore in the forenoon; but in the afternoon I went to the little uninhabited island called *New Island*, (see vol. i. p. 131.) which was a good way off our ship, and near *Java*. We landed at a little brook, in which our people washed their linen. Formerly, as the ship *Ritterhouse* was on her voyage to *China* she came too late to *Java*, and the contrary monsoon being already set in, she was obliged to stay here till the wind changed. During that time the sailors built huts on this island, and cut the year of our LORD 1743 on a good many trees, as we

observed

observed in several places. The bottom of the sea, which was at the depth of two fathoms, more or less, was full of sharp ramose corals. On the shore were to be met with *coral-stones, coral-organs, hippuris saxea,* and several shells, most of which were spoiled and worn away by the water. Among the shells were principally *cypræas, harpago 5 cornibus,* (*Strombus Chiragra* Linn.) and others.

I ADVANCED somewhat further on the island, and saw the *Plantain-tree* (*Musa Paradisiaca*) growing spontaneously, and the monkeys jumping from one tree to another, as squirrels do in our country. The continual cracking noise which I heard was, as our people said, made by a sort of lizards, of which I could not procure one specimen.

SEVERAL butterflies flew about me; but my eyes were fixed upon the *Flora.* I went along the shore because the woods appeared too crouded for me, and observed the following scarce trees:

Sophora alopecuroides, a little tree with a soft stem.

Morinda citrifolia.

Guettarda

Guettarda speciosa, a ramose tree with odoriferous flowers. The *calyx* is cylindrical, with an almost entire margin: the *corolla* is monopetalous: the *tube* cylindrical, longer than the calyx: the *limbus* is divided into seven oblong *laciniæ*: seven short *filaments*: the *antheræ* are longer than the filaments, and of equal thickness: the *germen* is almost round: the *stylus* is filiform, longer than the *stamina*: the *stigma* is shaped almost like an egg. The *fruit* is nearly round, and contains many nuts: the *branches* of the tree are quadrangular, with dots, and horse-shoe-like spots.

Lobelia Plumierii is a little tree which stood on the shore, and had the following characters: the *calyx* is very short, quinquefid: the *segments* of equal breadth, and equidistant from each other: the *corolla* is monopetalous, on one side split open down to the bottom, four times longer than the calyx: the *tube* is cylindrical, hairy in the inside, longer than the limbus, hiant on one side: the *limbus* is quinquefid, hairy, with lanceolated *laciniæ*, which are curled up on the margin; the middlemost is the thickest: the five *filaments* are filiform, fastened to the *receptaculum*, and of the length of the *pistillum*: the *antheræ* are oblong,

long, narrow, and furround the *ftigma*: the *germen* is egg-fhaped, pentagonal, compreffed, and below the flower: the *ftylus* cylindrical, of the length of the filaments, bent fo as to incline through the incifions of the *corolla*: the *ftigma* is fcyphiform, and hairy: the *nut* is almoft round, and of the fize of a pea: the *tree* has wrinkled and hanging branches, and grows on the fea-fhore. The *leaves* are inverted-oval, mucronated, fmooth, without incifions, almoft without nerves, petiolated: the *ftalks* of the leaves are of equal thicknefs all the way: the *flowers* are white, and axillar.

Crinum Afiaticum with its glorious white flowers, enriched the fandy fhore. I brought both the *plant* itfelf in a flower pot, and the *bulbs* or roots of it preferved in fand, to Sweden.

Corypha umbraculifera was likewife growing here. Of this the great round fans are made, with which the mufquitoes or gnats are expelled in *China*.

Cordia Myxa flowered on the fhore: the *leaves* are oval, petiolated, without incifions, alternate: the *tree* is very ramofe: the *branches*
are

are wrinkled, round: the *flowers* are yellow, and ſtand in *corymbi* at the top.

Phytolocca Javanica, a large tree on the ſhore, whoſe leaves are ſmooth, but its branches villoſe: the *calyx* is wanting: the *corolla* is monopetalous, quinquefid: the *ſegments* are oval, very ſmall: the ten *filaments* are bent at the top, faſtened to the receptacle, and longer than the *corolla:* the *antheræ* are almoſt round: the *tree* is very ramoſe: the *branches* and *leaf-ſtalks* are woolly: the *leaves* are broad, lanceolated, petiolated, without inciſions, ſmooth, and have ſeven nerves: the *flowers* are corymboſe and ſmall.

Flagellaria Indica. Its *boughs* twine about other trees, as the ſtem is no thicker than a tobacco-pipe, but generally ſome fathoms long: the *calyx* is monopetalous, bidentated, very ſhort, on the outſide of the flower: the *corolla* is monopetalous, oval, globoſe, and cloſed up: the *filaments* are ſhort, filiform, faſtened to the receptacle, the *antheræ* are oblong, erect, and longer than the filaments: the *ſtylus* is ſingle: the *ſtigma* obtuſe: the *flowers* grow at the extremities in bunches like grapes (*Corymbi*): the *ſtalk* is round, ramoſe:
the

the *leaves* are alternate, arundinaceous, scarce visibly petiolated, and end in tendrils.

Convolvulus pes capræ grew in the sand by the water side.

Chiton marginibus dorsi spinosis was found in the sea by a sailor.

WE weighed anchor; but were forced by the contrary wind to cast again not far from the first place, namely near

Prince Island, which is larger than *New Island*. It has been said, that a petty prince, master of this island, lives on it, and that he formerly used to visit the ships, and was satisfied with trifling presents. In the afternoon we went on shore near a little river, where we could take in water, which however is not so good as that in *Java*. I did not observe any mountains here, nor on *New Island*. On the river we found a little hut, which our people believed to be built by some *Englishmen*. We pressed into the woods, but were forced to turn back to the shore, where the great trees (which hung quite over the water) likewise greatly opposed my passage. On those trees I found two species of ferns, one of which

was

was *Polypodium Parafiticum.* But I loft both while I was carried back over the river. On the trees grew:

Lichen pulverulentus viridis et albus, and under it,

Boletus caulefcens, coriaceus, pileo cinereo et rubro.

Calla Javanica foliis lanceolatis, and

Amomum Zerumbet, or wild ginger; of which I made the following defcription: the *calyx* is wanting, inftead of it are two egg-fhaped *bractea*: the *corolla* is dipetalous: the two *filaments* are fhort, filiform: the *antheræ* are long, of equal breadth, and faftened to the fide of the *corolla*: the *germen* is cylindrical and fhort: the *ftylus* filiform, longer than the *ftamina*: the *ftigma* is oblong: the *capfula* is egg-fhaped, oblong, flat on the inner fide, obtufe on the outer, triangular, multilocular, full of juice, white: the *feeds* are egg-fhaped, narrow, red, covered, and about fix in number: the *plant* grows on fhady fhores: the *root* is like that of ginger, and has long fibres: the *ftalk* is round with obtufe *bractea*, which ftick very clofe to it: the *flowers* and *fruit* make an oval catkin (*amentum*): the radical
leaf

leaf is pinnated, with lanceolated, entire *foliola*.

MAMMEA *Asiatica*, a great tree, generally stands on the shore and hangs over the water. Almost every tree, particularly this, was full of great black ants, for which reason I could not easily mount the branches; however I was forced to do so, before I could make the following description:

The *calyx* is biphyllous, with great, oval, concave, persistent leaves, which include the *corolla*; this consists of four oval, closed petals, which are deciduous at the same time with the filaments, and are like them longer than the *calyx:* the *filaments* are numerous, filiform, bent, shorter than the *stylus*, but longer than the *corolla* and the *calyx*, and at the bottom joined with the petals: the *antheræ* are almost round and small: the *germen* is below the *corolla*; it is obovated: the *stylus* is very long: the *stigma* pointed: the *tree* is very ramose, and bends down with its top: the little *branches* are round: the *leaves* grow in bunches at the extremity of the little branches; they are entire, without stalks, smooth, carnose or pulpy, somewhat crenated

at

at the top, and have alternate tranſverſal nerves.

HERNANDIA *ſonora*. Of this great remarkable tree I only ſaw two on the ſhore. It affords a ſure antidote againſt poiſon, if you either put its ſmall roots on the wounds, or eat them; as was diſcovered to *Rumphius* by a captive woman in the war between the People of *Macaſar* and the *Dutch* in the year 1667. The ſoldiers of the former always carry this root about them, as a remedy againſt wounds with poiſonous arrows. The *leaves* of this tree are thick and ſmooth. Another tree like this, which likewiſe grew here, had not ſuch thick and ſmooth leaves.

MELIA *Paraſitica*, a little plant of ſcarce a finger's length, grew on the ſtems of the trees. It is ſo ſcarce, that, as far as I know, it has never been noticed before. The *calyx* is monophyllous, tridentated, cylindrical, and is half the length of the *corolla*: the *corolla* is monopetalous, cylindrical, quinquefid, with oblong *laciniæ*: the *nectarium* is bell-ſhaped, obtuſe on the margin: on the inner ſide of the margin ten extremely ſmall filaments are ſituated: the *antheræ* are almoſt quadrangular:

the

the *germen* is cylindrical, pentagonal: the *stylus* is pointed below, and villose: the *stigma* elevated: the *flowers* grow in the form of a bunch of grapes. The plant had little leaves.

After so short a visit on this excellent isle, I was forced to go on board again, to wait for a fair wind that might forward us on our voyage.

The 22d of *January*, 8°. 34′. S. L.

Rain.

Early in the morning we sailed from *Prince Island*, and in the afternoon left *Java* out of sight.

The 26th of *January*.

Very rainy weather. Almost calm. We caught two *bonets* (*Scomber Pelamis*). Its two *pectoral-fins* were put upon a fishing-hook, to represent a likeness of a flying-fish, which the *bonet* often pursues with all its might, and frequently jumps up very high above the water.

The

The 27th of *January*, 10°. 38'. S. L.

CLOUDY and rainy weather.

CAMELLIA, which I had in a pot, began to open its flower buds. *Obf. Gemmæ axillares, conico-imbricatæ, foliola gemmæ ovata, obtufa alterna, imbricata. Foliatio equitans.*

The 28th of *January*, 12°. 35'. S. L.

ALMOST all the day fine weather; and contrary wind.

FOUR *dolphins* (*Coryphæna Hippurus*) appeared near the ship. This fish looks like the falmon, but has a colour which changes from blue to green in the water. It was thought to be the beft fish that we had caught during the voyage.

The 29th of *January*, 13°. S. L.

CLEAR weather. The trade-wind was juft now beginning.

We discovered a whale in our neighbourhood, by its throwing up the water.

The 3d of *February*, 15°. 44'. S. L.

Larva *feneſtrata*, which I found the 13th of *September* of the paſt year on the *Croton ſebiferum*, and which changed a ſecond time the next following night, now got out of its grave, where it had been near five months, and became *Phalæna Atlas* Linn. as far as I could ſee, though it was very ill ſhaped.

Dermestes *ſubrotunda atra* was buſy in eating the *Deontſai-feed* which I bought in *China*. As ſoon as it had eaten the kernel, the empty huſk juſt fitted it: and accordingly I found ſome time after each of them dead in its huſk.

The 6th of *February*, 18°. 50'. S. L.

Clear weather. Freſh gale.

I had no thermometer; but the leaves of *Camellia* and of the *Batatas* ſhewed that it was colder

colder here than in *China*. The accounts of seamen of a greater degree of cold at the south pole are pretty probable.

The 8th of *February*, 20°. 47'. S. L.

A FLYING fish was now and then observed in these parts.

The 11th of *February*, 22°. 54'. S. L.

CLEAR weather. Temperate wind.

A LIZARD had acccompanied us from *Canton*, and was now found in a cabbin. It was *Lacerta (Chinensis) cinerea, caudâ ancipiti, corpore paulo longiore, pedibus pentadactylis omnibus unguiculatis.* The *head* is flat, shallow, oblong, even: the *eyes* are covered with a skin, which at its transversal opening has in the middle three gold coloured points opposite to each other: the *nostrils* are round, largest near the snout, one on each side: higher up are three less ones on each side; and besides these are a good many less holes near the eyes: the *teeth* are numerous, small: the *tongue* is flat, obtuse, crenated in the middle; the *body* is broad,

broad, flat, with compreſſed ſides: the *back* is covered with blackiſh and whitiſh elevations: the *anus* is tranſverſal: the *tail* is a little longer than the body, has two ſides, is compreſſed, and has yellowiſh ſcales, which are here and there on the ſides: the *fore* and *hind feet* have five toes, are divided, and all the toes have hamated nails: the *fifth toe* is the ſhorteſt; all the toes are webbed below, and the webs ſit croſs-ways: the upper ſide of the body is aſh coloured: the *tail* has eleven black ſpots: the *belly* is white.

The 13th of *February*, 24°. 7'. S. L.

Cloudy ſky, rainy, inconſtant weather; and afterwards a uniform wind.

The water which we had taken with us from *Java* was now full of ſea *Millepedes* (*Oniſci*), which ſkipped about in it like young frogs.

The bulbs of the *Crinum Aſiaticum*, which I had put into a flower-pot at *Java*, now began to ſhoot leaves.

The 17th of *February*, 27°. 20'. S. L.

THE trade-wind ceafed to-day.

The 19th of *February*, 27°. 59'. S. L.

CLEAR, calm, fultry weather.

WE faw a whale; and a great dog-fifh paffed us, accompanied by four of the fifhes called pilots. We put half a chicken on our fifhing-hook to catch the dog-fifh, but he was not hungry. In the dawn we faw fome porpoiffes.

The 20th of *February*, 28°. 32'. S. L.

RAIN, but afterwards clear weather. Frefh wind.

The 22d of *February*, 29°. 49'. S. L.

CLEAR weather, calm fea, moderate wind. We were now almoft directly oppofite *Madagafcar*.

The 23d of *February*, 30°. 2'. S. L.

CLEAR and calm, toward the evening middling wind.

WE faw a dolphin near the ſhip. The water flowered, as it is uſually ſaid.

The 26th of *February*, 29°. 52'. S. L.

CLEAR weather. Contrary wind. It was cold in the morning.

A PIECE of wood with ſome ſea-graſs ſwam by us.

DOLPHINS and porpoiſſes gathered about the ſhip.

The 5th of *March*, 34°. 23'. S. L.

TOWARDS evening we had thunder, lightning, and a great deal of rain.

THE flames, which have been mentioned before, ſhewed themſelves now on all the three

three tops, at seven o'clock at night, when it was quite dark after the storm.

The 7th of *March*, 35°. 41'. S. L.

GOOD weather and wind, almost calm in the afternoon.

GANNETS (*Pelecanus Baffanas* Linn.) a sort of great white birds with long necks, and black tops of the wings, flew very high in the air. They are said to be a sure mark of the sand at the *Cape*. About noon therefore we heaved the lead, but could not find ground. Some thought we were half a degree more to the south than appeared from the ship's reckoning.

THE next night about twelve we missed a second mate, by calling the watch, whom we never saw again. It was thought that in his sleep he fell into the sea through a port-hole.

The 8th of *March*, 35°. 36'. S. L.

CLEAR and almost calm weather. Wind towards night.

The porpoisses were observed here tumbling about in great numbers.

The sailors affirmed to me that the water flowered; when drawn up, some-what in it looked like the roe of a fish. I put some of it by in a glass, which at night gave a pale blue light, as if a million of little pearls lay close together, but the next day the light was gone. This matter swam every where on the sea water, with which it was mixed. By day-light or candle-light it looked like a red, brown, thick, *sago* soup; and when it was put on paper, it looked like little water-coloured *sago* grains, or fish-roe; but I observed no motion in them. The next morning every thing was sunk to the bottom, and was curdled in the glass; the water above it was quite clear, tho' somewhat reddish. I again put some of it on paper, and found the grains water-coloured, but the paper was stained with red spots from the water.

The next night we found ground with the lead at ninety fathoms. We had now been sixty-three days on our voyage from *China*.

The 10th of *March*, 33°. 13'. S. L.

A species of sea-weed swam by our ship several times this afternoon, and was called *Trumpet-weed* by our sailors [a]. It was above a yard and a half long, as thick as an *Indian* cane, and commonly some stalks were joined together: it formed as it were fly-flaps at the tops. My company on the ship thought it came from the islands west of the *Cape of Good Hope*. When the sailors see *Trumpet-weed* on their voyage, they are pretty certain that the *Cape* is not above ten *Swedish* miles off.

The 17th of *March*, 28°. 34'. S. L.

Clear and calm weather.

Besanties swam on the water, and seemed to have a little bow-shaped expanded sail on their backs. These little animals change

---

[a] Fucus (Maximus) caule tereti, fistuloso, simplici, flabello quasi terminato. An Fucus pavonicus? confer Trombas. G. M. A. V. V. L. Descriptio itin. navalis in Ind. p. 51. fig. mala. The leaves stand at the top in bunches in two rows (*disticha*), and decrease in size by little and little. The stalk had no leaves.

their colours. We caught a *Befantie*, but it was small and like the air-bladder of a fish. I had scarce had it one day in sea-water, when it died, as might be observed by the *tentacula*, which were dissolved into a slime; and it became as distorted as those which are sometimes brought to *Europe* in *Spanish* brandy. The description was made as soon as the animal was got out of the water, and is as follows:

Holothuria Physalis. Befanties. Rumph. Amboin. p. 49. The *body* is blown up, egg-shaped, transparent, with a yellowish green tail: the *back* is dark green, sharp; seven or more veins came out of it, which are yellowish red before: the *bill* is spiral, and of a yellowish-red colour: the *tentacula* are numerous, the shortest are round, the middlemost are the tenderest, transparent, and globose at the top: the remaining *tentacula* are petiolated, and are longer than the rest; the one in the middle is thicker and much longer than the others, and dark blue: opposite to these is a compounded blue elevation on the other side, which is perhaps the sail which the animal expands in the sea.

The 25th of *March*, 12°. 10'. S. L.

CLOUDY, and afterwards clear weather.

BONETS (*Scomber Pelamis*) and *Tunnys* (*Scomber Thynnus*) were now caught again. We used the *Cuttle-fish* (*Sepia Loligo*) when we could get it, for a bait.

THE *Camellia*, which I brought with me from *China*, now began to wither. The tea-shrub, birds, and whatever is taken alive from *China*, commonly die in the latitude of the *Cape of Good Hope*, though it is the same latitude as *Spain*, or rather nearer the æquator. I do not remember to have seen an entirely clear horizon on the south side of the line.

The 30th of *March*, 16°. 63'. S. L.

ALMOST clear; afterwards cloudy. Favourable wind.

A TROPICK bird flew very high as usual hereabouts (*Phaëton æthereus*).

FLYING

FLYING *fishes* and *bonets* were here in great numbers.

ST. HELENA, an island belonging to the *English*, came in sight of us. This island, according to the accounts we have, is said to be near three *Swedish* miles in circumference, and two in breadth. It is situated in 15°. 56'. S. L. in the open sea, nearer to *Africa* than to *America*, about 200 *Swedish* miles from the nearest continent, and 600 leagues from the *Cape of Good Hope*. This island, which is said to be very agreeable, and to produce many *Indian* fruits, is very high, and mountainous on the sea-side, for which reason it can be seen at the distance of twenty leagues. It first got its name from the *Portugueze*, who discovered it in the year 1501, on *St. Helen's* day. In the year 1600 the *English East India* company conquered it; and in the year 1672 the *Dutch* took it; but the *English* have since, 1673, inhabited and fortified it; in 1701, two hundred families, mostly *English*, were settled on it.

YAMS (*Dioscorea alata*) are here, as I am told, planted and eaten instead of bread by the poor.

THE

ASCENSION ISLAND. 1752.

THE navigators who will land at *St. Helena*, muft take care not to take their courfe too high, elfe they cannot reach the fhore. The *Swedifh* fhips generally ftop here to take in refrefhments, but we fteered ftrait on to the *Ifle of Afcenfion*.

The 3d of *April*, 8°. 50'. S. L.

CLEAR weather, middling wind.

TO-DAY and the day before we faw *flying fifhes*.

The 4th of *April*.

GENERALLY clear weather, and middling wind.

WE fteered from W. by N. to get the longitude of *Afcenfion Ifland*, near which we failed in the forenoon; and at laft caft anchor in the *Crofs-bay* on the fame ifland, with twenty-four fathoms ground.

The 5th of *April*.

Thirty-one *tortoises* were caught last night.

In the morning we went on shore on the right side of the *Cross-bay*.

Ascension is an island which is situated under the 8th degree of latitude south of the æquator, and 8°. 24′. from *St. Helena* in the great *Ethiopic Ocean*, at a great distance from the continent. Its length is reckoned above a *Swedish* mile, and its breadth about half a *Swedish* mile. The *Portugueze* gave it this name because they discovered it on *Ascension-day*. It is entirely uninhabited, and without woods. The largest turtles, or sea-tortoises, have their residence on it, and are sometimes caught by hundreds in one night. The *European* ships on their return from the *East Indies* seldom sail by this island without going on shore to catch as many turtles as they want; but they never come in sight of it on their going to those parts.

The breakers on the shore are very violent, and would astonish those who have never seen

the

the like before. A boat may be thrown a good way on the shore by them, as happened to the *Swedish East India* man the *Gothic Lion*, whose sloop, with some men, was lost by this accident. The best times to go on shore here are the first months in the year, and as early in the morning as possible. The shore for the greatest part is covered with a species of sand, which consists of little else than broken shells, which form roundish grains, larger or smaller, shining like pearls. This sand deserves to be called *Shell-sand*.

THE tortoises creep out of the water upon the shell-sand which is loose, and occupy some fathoms in breadth upon the shore, and often lie so high that it is inconceivable how they can get up, since it is troublesome even for men to get along, because the sand slips under their feet, as if they walked upon pease. As soon as a tortoise is got a little way from the water, she makes a round hole in the sand, in which she lays her eggs, and covers them over again with sand so neatly that no one can find out where she has been. She afterwards gets into the water again, and is quite unconcerned about her young ones, which are hatched by the sun, and find the way to the sea as well as their mother, as foon as they have broken the fhell.

The failors lurk at night on the fhore; and when a tortoife is crept up they turn it upon its back, with hooks (or, if they can, with their hands alone). In the latter cafe, they muft take care of the animal's mouth, for it bites off a finger with eafe; a misfortune which one of our failors experienced this time.

The *tortoifes* (*Teftudo Mydas*) are principally caught in two well-known bays; namely, in the *Englifh-bay*, where the taking them is faid to be attended with difficulties, and in the *Crofs bay*, on the right hand of which our captain had pitched his tent, on the fide of a mountain. In this mountain were two grottoes, or natural caves, at a little diftance from each other. In that which was next the fhore were feveral *French* and *Englifh* letters, of laft year, as advices to new-comers: the upper one is faid to have been the habitation of an *Englifh* fupercargo, who fome years ago was left here as a punifhment for a deteftable crime, with fome victuals, and an ax, to kill tortoifes, which he was forced to roaft by the heat of the fun on the mountains. It is likewife related

lated that another nation afterwards helped him away.

I NEVER faw a more difagreeable place in all the world than this ifland. The climate in itfelf is hot, being fo near the line; but it would be tolerable if there were only fome trees under whofe fhade one could take fhelter. The ifland has formerly had woods, as appears from feveral perfect petrefactions of branches of trees, and pieces of wood; but in particular from a large petrified ftump. The ifland is every where covered with ftones; they are not pebbles, but angulated pumiceftones, containing more or lefs iron. When you meet with a plain, it is covered between the ftones with a coarfe earth which looks like foot, and under it you meet with a reddifh fine fand. Here and there, efpecially on the fhore, are fome rocks. On the low places, where the water gathers during the rainy feafon, the earth was covered with a brown cruft, which would break like thin ice under one's feet. Here and there fome pieces of glimmer were found. A mineralogift might have collected many forts of ftones here, which are not to be met with in other places. The heat is intolerable, and difables one from carrying any

any thing, it being difficult to support even the cloaths upon one's back, especially as walking is so difficult. He who chooses to walk here must wear shoes with thick soles; and must notwithstanding expect to bring aching feet home at night. If the stony *Arabia* is like this place, I pity those who are forced to wander through it.

There are several great hills on this island, which consist of the abovementioned earth and coarse blackish brown sand: in the latter lie larger or smaller pumice-stones[b], which are dangerous to walk on, as by their rolling down one may break one's limbs.

As soon as we got on shore I went to a conic mountain a good way off the place where we landed. It was steep, and of difficult access, because with each step the sand and stones rolled down: the heat increased, and I was forced to rest several times. In my opinion, this mountain was quite as large as our *Kinnekulle*. Neither on the sides, nor at the top, did I meet with one single plant; on the summit, where the air was very cool, stood a pole

Pumex cupri. Mus. Teff. 79. 2.

three

ASCENSION ISLAND. 1752.

three fathoms long, which was provided with the neceffary ropes for hoifting a flag. From the pole hung two croffes, the lower of which was wooden, and had the letters I. N. R. I. carved on it. Scarce a fathom above the wooden crofs was a brazen one, at the bottom of which we could fee 1748, the 15th of *November*; and higher up a *French* Infcription, which could not be read, it being too high. On the pole and the wooden crofs feveral dates of years, and feveral names, were carved.

THE country hereabouts looks like the rocks about our mines. The birds refted here and there without being frightened, after they had filled themfelves with fifhes in the fea. In fome places they had ftained with their dung the heaps of ftones quite white, which then looked like ruined towns, of which nothing but fome white-wafhed chimneys remained.

THE affiftant *Thollander*, a friend and promoter of fcience, parted from me a little while, and found in the mean time the fcarce *Ariftida Adfcenfionis*. It is faid there is a fpring, or rather a cave, where the rain water gathers, on the fame mountain: but it was dried up at this time.

The goats, which the *French* brought upon this ifland, were by this means forced to live without water; for, befides fea-water, none is to be met with. But they eat the juicy wild *Purflane* (*Portulaca oleracea*), which grew in feveral places between the ftones, was very young at this time, and had but two or three leaves.

The *French* had buried fome of their dead this year in one part of the ifland, and in remembrance of them had put upon the graves croffes and white banners.

The following are the natural curiofities which I found on the ifland, befides the abovementioned ftones:

Rats abound here, being brought by *Dampier's* fhip, which was forced to put in at the ifland after it had fprung a leak, and to ftay here till another fhip came and took the crew away. Sailors that have been here before relate, that though they hung up their bags of meat on upright poles, they were by no means fafe from thefe vermin; nay, that when the people fat down to meals, they came

out

out as if they demanded a fhare of the victuals with them.

The goats have increafed pretty well. I faw a flock or two which were very fhy, yet they might be caught by any one on foot, for they do not run very faft. One of them was taken and brought to our fhip. It was of the leaft fort, and very lean. We obferved immediately that it was not ufed to water; for tho' it drank fome, it immediately ran through it, as if the water had been poured through an inclined tube. It was killed, but its flefh was liked but by few.

Sea birds are numerous here, and, what is remarkable, they were fo bold, that they would let any one come up and take them with his hands.

The birds which appeared at this time were:

Tropick birds (*Phaëton æthereus*) Grew's *Muf.* p. 74. *Avis Tropicorum.* Willoughby. This bird is of the fize of a duck: the feathers on the under fide of the neck, breaft, and belly, and below the tail, together with fome of the moft outward coverts of the wings, are quite white:

white: the feathers which cover the head, the upper part of the neck, the wings, and the whole back, are all marked with black tranfverfal ftripes of the breadth of a pack-thread. But the *vent-feathers* are fomewhat blacker: the feven *quill-feathers* have black edges at the extremities, and are white towards the infide; but the fecondary ones are black in the middle, with white tops: the *coverts* below the wings are quite white: the *wings* are fhort: the *bill* is above two inches long, fharp, very narrow, fomewhat inflected on the fides, and entirely red: the *jaws* are almoft equal, though the upper feems to be rather fhorter: the *margins* are ferrated towards the infide, for the advantage of holding their prey: the *noftrils*, which are almoft in the middle, between the point of the bill and the eyes, are narrow, and end in a little furrow towards the point of the bill: the feathers hang down about the eyes: a black ftripe runs down to the head from the eyes: the *feet* are half naked and footy: the *back-toes* are very fmall: two of the *tail-feathers* are longer than the whole bird; and, like all the other *tail-feathers*, white, with black fhafts. We faw thefe birds in feveral places within the *Tropics* at an exceffive height, often far from land; and generally hovering

over

over the fame place : from whence fome failors have concluded that they continually remained in the air at that height.

THE *Pelican* (*Pelecanus Onocratalus*[c]), with the red bag under its neck, flew up and down, but would never fettle. It is the fame which in hieroglyphical defcriptions is ufed as the emblem of great tendernefs towards its young. It lives generally in the great *African* fandy defarts, where no water is to be met with; but it brings it for many miles in the bag below its throat, and fills the neft of its young ones; whither camels and other animals likewife refort to affuage their thirft. People who have feen it emptying its red water bag, have thought that it ripped up its breaft and gave its young ones blood for want of water; but they were miftaken.

PELECANUS *Aquilus:* its *bill* is more than a hand's breadth long, and is narrow: the *upper-jaw* is fomewhat the longeft, with a hook-fhaped point: the *cere*, which is blue, covers the bill from the eyes to the hook-fhaped point: the *mandibles* have no fuch ferrated incifions (fupplying the place of teeth) as are ufually found in fea birds: the *head* is covered

[c] *Orientalis.*

with short feathers as far as the eyes, which are pretty large: the *tongue* is large, almost trifid at the top; the corner at its bottom is split: the *temples* are naked: the *wings* consist of three parts, and are very long; of the twenty-two *quill-feathers*, the first ten are of a considerable length; the two inner joints contain, besides the coverts, twenty-two secondary feathers: the outward of the twelve *tail-feathers* are much longer than the middle ones, which make the tail look like a pair of scissars. The bird is about the size of a goose, and is a yard long: the colour of the whole *body*, and of the *toes*, is black: but the *head*, *breast*, *belly*, and fore part of the *neck*, are of a fine white. Its food is fishes, which it takes from others, because it is not formed to catch them itself: the *English*, for this reason, call it Man of War (Q. an *Fregata Barere?*) [d]

On our arrival at the isle of *Ascension* these birds met us, and generally kept hovering about the streamers as if astonished at them. They fly slowly like kites (*Falco Milvus*).

[d] The *Fregata of Barrere* is, with Dr. *Linnæus*, *Procellaria Fregata*. F.

DIOMEDEA

DIOMEDEA *Adfcenfionis* was caught here. It was entirely white, not even the thirteen feathers in the tail excepted; had red feet, formed chiefly for fwimming; and only black tips to its wings: for the reft, it is like the *Diomedea pifcatoria* (*Pelecanus Pifcator*), which is likewife to be met with here. We alfo faw a fpecies of little black fea birds, but only upon the wing.

TORTOISES (*Teftudo Mydas*)[e]. They are afh-coloured at top, and pale yellow below: the *fore-feet* are longer than the hind-feet; the firft are two feet, and the latter about fix inches, long: the *neck* is two feet in circumference: on the middle of the *back*, longitudinally, are five fcales, and next to thefe, on each fide, four pair of fcales, of which the two next are oblong, and very large; but the other two pair are unequal: all about the fides are twenty-five fcales: the *breaft* is longitudinally covered with thirteen fcales, which have four pair of larger ones on each fide: befides thefe, there are feven or more pair of lefs ones about the jaws, one at the tail, and

---

[e] *Teftudo atra. Muf. Regis.* p. 50. *Amœn. Acad.* I. p. 84. Vulg. *Turtles.*

likewise some scales on the sides: the *eyes* are large, and on one of their sides the raw flesh appeared; the skin of the eyes is as it were covered with several red points or scales: on the *fore-foot*, quite at the paw, is a round scale like a coin: the *shield* which covers the back is frequently above four feet long, and of a proportionable breadth. These tortoises weigh from 500 to 700 pounds of *Swedish* grocery weight. Their flesh being boiled swells exceedingly, and for this reason a tortoise from *Ascension Island* is reckoned equal to an ox, and sufficient to make a meal for 130 men. The catching of tortoises is a great saving to the company, as they can keep them alive without food for five or six weeks together [f], if they are only watered with sea-water four or five times every day, sometimes laid on the back, and sometimes on the belly (in which latter case something is put under their neck), and if guarded from rain and heat. When they are to be killed, the head is first severed from the body, and the shell is next cut off. The flesh is grey, and the blacker it is, the fatter it is reckoned. When

[f] In 1755 a great tortoise was brought alive to *Gottenburgh*, but was killed there soon after its arrival.

the

the fat is boiled, it grows green, and taftes like marrow; the reft of the flefh is moftly white, and taftes like beef. The flefh is boiled in a broth prepared with tortoife eggs, and is eaten with vinegar. It is an excellent remedy againft fcurvy, coftivenefs, and other difeafes. The breaft is roafted, with fhell and flefh, by the name of *callopée*, and eats exceedingly well, efpecially while the animal is yet fat; but after it has been without food for fome weeks, it is no wonder that the flefh fhould become lean and unpalatable. The bowels and liver are likewife eaten. A tortoife has frequently 500, or 600, and as I have been told, fometimes 1500 eggs: they are quite round, have no white, and are furrounded with a foft fkin: they are never eaten by themfelves, but either in foups or pancakes; but the fifhy tafte prevails, however they are dreffed.

SQUALUS *Adfcenfionis*, is a fifh whofe body is blueifh at top, and white below: the *head* is very flat: the *eyes* are on the fides, and not at the top: the *anal-fin* is near the tail: its *length* is above two feet: the *membrana branchioftega* are below the *fpiracles*, and have fix rays.

BALISTES

BALISTES *vetula*, which is called the *Old Wife fish* by the mariners: the first *dorsal-fin* has three, the second thirty, the *pectoral-fin* fourteen, the *ventral-fin* twelve, the *anal-fin* twenty-eight, and the *tail* twelve, rays. In size and figure it is like the *Cyprinus Ballerus*. It is of ash colour, approaching towards yellow: the *skin* is rough, thick, and covered with rhomboidal scales. When the fish is caught, it mutters, whence it has got the name of *Old Wife*. The first *dorsal-fin* is triangular, with excavated semi-circles: it has three rays, of which the first is the strongest, and has a sharp edge on the foremost side, with a great many very short teeth; this fin can be folded into the furrow on the back of the fish, so that it will scarce be visible: the second *dorsal-fin* is not armed, but crenated on the upper margin; it has the figure of a parallelogram, is opposite the anus, and has thirty rays, which (except the second, which is very long) are all equal in length: the *pectoral-fins* are oval, opposite the first dorsal-fin, and have fourteen rays: the *ventral-fin* is single, on the middle of the belly, and reaches to the anus; the first ray of it is strong, sharp edged on the out side: the twelve lower rays have

have twelve teeth in three rows at the bottom, which accordingly make thirty-fix: the *anal-fin* reaches from the *anus* almoſt to the tail, is like the ſecond dorſal-fin, and has twenty-eight rays: the *tail* is falcated, and has twelve rays, of which the outermoſt are the longeſt: the *length* of the whole fiſh is ſcarce a foot: the *teeth* are broad, and eight in each jaw: the *lips* are thick, moveable, and marked with a blue line on the inſide: on each ſide run two blue lines, and above theſe a green one, from the mouth to the pectoral-fins: from each *eye* ariſe nine crooked green rays on each ſide: the *eyes* are in the upper part of the head, near the firſt dorſal-fin; towards the pectoral-fins they are large, have a green circle, and are marked with ſix oblong blue points at the top: the *anal-fin* and laſt *dorſal-fin* are blue, and this colour is likewiſe at the bottom and margin of the tail: the ſides are ſhaded green below the ſecond dorſal-fin: the *belly* is white, oblong, thick. The fiſh eats oyſters and ſnails, and is generally caught at the bottom of the ſea.

BALISTES *ringens* Linn. *Nigra* Oſbeck. This fiſh may frequently be caught with the hands, namely, when the water throws its waves a great way on the land, and

you

you throw some bread to the fish; for here both birds and fishes are as it were tame. The first *dorsal-fin* has two, and the second thirty-four rays: the *pectoral-fins* have sixteen rays: instead of the ventral-fins, there is only one single ray: the *anal-fin* has thirty-one rays: the *tail* is falcated, and has thirteen rays; eight lines run towards the tail: the *scales* are rough and rhomboidal: the *teeth* are like mens teeth, but double: the *anal-fin* and second *dorsal-fin* have a blue stripe at the bottom: the rest of the body is black. The fish is like the preceding (*Balistes Vetula*), but generally larger.

SEA *Blewling, Scomber* (*glaucus* [g]) *eminentiis lateralibus caudæ aculeatis*. The first *dorsal-fin* has seven, the second twenty-five, the *pectoral-fins* twenty, the *ventral* five, and the *anal-fin* twenty-five, rays: the seven rays of the first *dorsal-fin* are somewhat prickly: the first seven rays of the second *dorsal-fin* are the longest, and begin before the *anus:* all the other rays are shorter, round, and do not prickle: the space between both is very small: the *pectoral-fins* are bent, and have twenty rays, of which the most outward ones are four inches long: the *ventral-fins* are but half the length of the

[g] *Adscensionis*. Osbeck.

pectoral-fins, and have five rays: the *anal-fin* is higher forwards: the *body* is narrow, grey at the top, white below, above a foot long, and covered with a skin: the prominences on the sides of the tail consist of many close spines, (27, 49) which form the hind part of the lateral line: its fore-part is bent and unarmed: the *head* is obtuse: the *mouth* oblong: the *teeth* small: the *lower jaw* is the longest: the *opercula branchiostega* have no incisions.

PERCA *Adscensionis*: the *membrana branchiostega* has eight, the *dorsal-fin* twenty-seven, the *pectoral-fins* sixteen, the *ventral-fin* eight, the *anal-fin* fourteen, and the furcated *tail* twenty-six, rays: the *dorsal-fin* is towards the middle of the fish: its first eleven rays are pungent, the sixteen following (of which the two first are the highest) are not armed: the *opercula branchiostega* consist of two plates, which are dentated; two of these teeth are large, the others small and numerous: the *jaws* are dentated above the nostrils: the first ray of the *dorsal-fin* is the shortest; the second is the strongest, sharp pointed, and striated backwards; the third is somewhat shorter and thinner; the rest are not armed: the *body* is narrow, reddish at the top, and whitish below: the

the *scales* lie transversally, are oblong, and dentated before.

TRACHINUS *Adscensionis.* This fish tastes exceedingly well, and is distinguished from others by the following marks: the *dorsal-fin* has twenty-eight rays, the *pectoral-fins* eighteen, the *ventral-fins* five, the *anal-fin* eleven, the *tail* sixteen, and the *membrana branchiostega* six rays; the latter is white with brown spots: the single *dorsal-fin* is every where of equal breadth, and runs from the head to the tail: its first eleven rays are sharp pointed: the *pectoral-fins* are obovated; and so are the *ventral-fins*; and their first ray is prickly: the three first rays of the *anal-fin*, which is likewise obovated, are prickly: the *tail* is wedge-shaped, with short rays: the *body* is somewhat compressed, and not quite round, covered with a white skin, on which the brown spots run into one another: the *head* is somewhat compressed: the *opercula branchiostega* consist of three scales, of which the middlemost ends in two teeth; one of them is long and pointed: the *eyes* are near each other, in the upper part of the head, and are large: the *nostrils* are round; besides them are two greater holes in the forehead: the *teeth* are fixed in the gums

gums and throat in several rows; they are numerous, long, and very sharp; five of them are longer, namely, three in the upper-jaw, and two in the lower: the *jaws* are equal in length.

Of insects I found:

Dermestes elytris hirsutis cinereis, in the sand.

Hippobosca nigra, on the *Pelecanus Aquilo.*

Musca vulgatissima.

Musca nivea.

Cancer Adscensionis. A sort of crabs with white points on the feet. They run on the sea-shore between the stones, and are difficult to be caught; for as soon as they are pursued, they jump very nimbly between the stones.

Asterias. Of this Mr. *Torcen* said he had found one petrified on the shore. Several shells lay on the shore, but were generally broken by the waves.

VERY small oysters (*Ostrea Adscensionis*) lay on the rocks on the shore.

Of plants I found only the following:

Ariftida Adfcenfionis, on a mountain.

Sherardia fruticofa, a fingle plant on a plain.

Convolvulus pes capræ, on the fhore.

Euphorbia origanoides, between the ftones, the food of the goats.

Portulaca oleracea, among the ftones; tho' as yet very tender. This plant was the moft common. Such a poor *Flora* is feldom to be met with on fo great an ifland. Where the foil was not covered with ftones, it looked like a diftrict where a foreft had been burnt down. And fome of the aforementioned plants grew here and there. However, on the ftones grows yet

Lichen foliaceus albus, and *farinaceus,* namely, green and yellow, but I was not able to carry any ftones on account of the great heat: Yet I took a couple of pieces of perfect petrified wood with me. One of thefe petrefactions was half a branch of a tree, in which the bark, wood, and grain, were all diftinguifhable. The other was a branch which was fo
similar

similar to wood, that without a knife it was impossible to distinguish whether it was stone or wood. After we had been quite spent with the unspeakable heat, such as I had never experienced before, we reached, with some difficulty, the place where we had landed, and regaled our parched bodies. Afterwards, I found on the mountains along the shore:

Fucus lendigerus,
Fucus muscoides, } which the water sometimes washed up.
Ulva lactuca,

At last we went about the *Crofs-bay*, over several mountains, to a little creek, where our sloop waited for us. As I was just going upon this dangerous road, over a heap of stones which by little and little had rolled down the hill, a huge stone rolled down, and was within an hair's breadth of making an end of me; but I happily escaped, although in the greatest consternation. In this bay boats can land very securely, and lie very quietly; for it is surrounded with rocks on both sides, which hinders the water from beating against the shore with such violence. Though here is but little sand, yet a ship is said to have caught eighteen tortoises in one night.

night. We caught most of ours in the *Cross-bay*, because it was nearer to our ship than the *English bay*: though in the latter more tortoises come on shore than in the former; but it would be too difficult, if not impossible, to bring them over by land from one bay to another; and for this reason the boats ought to land where the tortoises are to be had.

The 8th of *April*.

CLEAR weather. Little wind.

AFTER we had got all our men on board again, and 41 tortoises on the deck, we weighed anchor. With the cable we pulled up a piece of coral, on which a red shell (*Pecten Adscensionis*) was growing, which on its valves represented many branches. We took it with us, and at present it is preserved in one of the greatest cabinets of natural curiosities in *Sweden*. In the forenoon we set sail towards *Fayal*, in company with the *Gothic Lion*.

ASCENSION ISLAND. 1752.

The 15th of *April*, 1°. 34'. S. L.

AFTER a calm for three days together, we got a little wind.

WE met a *Dutch* ship, which had sailed two months from *Capon*, an *African* province exactly under the æquator. Her cargo consisted of gold-dust and ivory from the *Guinea* coast; but she was in great distress. The captain and the greatest part of the crew were sick, so that this ship, notwithstanding her rich lading, was in a very deplorable condition. We assisted her with some victuals from our ship *gratis*.

WE caught two bonets.

The 16th of *April*, 15'. S. L.

CLEAR weather. Little wind; but excessive heat.

IN the bonets which we caught to-day were little worms surrounded with wrinkles or circles, having a proboscis on the side of the opening at the head, and a globose tail.

We likewise caught a species of small fishes, which in size were equal to sticklebacks. It was

Gobius tropicus. The *membrana branchiostega* has three or four rays: the *dorsal-fin*, from the head almost to the tail, has twelve and more rays: the *pectoral fins* have fifteen, the *ventral-fins* have eight, and the *anal-fin* has twelve, rays: the *tail* is round: the *body* likewise, and thin towards the tail: the *scales* are sharp: the *head* is great, wrinkly: the *opercula branchiostega* consist of two long, linear, dentated *orbiculi:* the *mouth* is great, almost round, and covered with the skin of the head: the *eyes* are large, and stand on the sides.

We again saw a grampus, which spouted up the water with great force.

The 20th of *April*, 3°. 4′. N. L.

The sea was entirely calm. We caught bonets and tunnies both to-day and yesterday, and the day before.

The

The 22d of *April*, 3°. 23'. N. L.

LITTLE wind. Thick air.

IN the tunnies (*Scomber Thynnus*), we found two forts of fifhes, befides the *Sepia Loligo*, or cuttle-fifh. The one was very like a *Crufian*. It was

Clupea Tropica. The *membrana branchioftega* has feven rays: the fingle *dorfal-fin* runs from the middle of the back to the tail, and has twenty-fix rays: the *pectoral-fins* have feventeen rays: the *ventral-fins* fix, and the *anal-fin*, which is the length of the dorfal, twenty-fix rays: the *body* is fharp, deep, with white fcales: the *lateral-line* is ftrait, and runs away near the back: the *belly* is ferrated: the *head* is obtufe: the *lower-jaw* is longer than the upper: the *mouth* oblong, great: the *teeth* are in one row in the jaws; they are numerous, fmall, and fharp: the *eyes* are near the mouth: the *opercula branchioftega* confift of two *orbiculi*, which are both covered with fcales: the *tail* forms a wedge, and has twenty rays. This is a new fpecies.

The other species of fish was reckoned a *Flying-fish*, but its *pectoral-fins* were very short.

The 23d of *April*, 3°. 25'. N. L.

In the forenoon heavy rain.

The 24th of *April*, 3°. 36'. N. L.

Rainy weather, and good wind.

Some *tunnies* were caught.

The 25th of *April*, 5°. N. L.

Dark sky. About noon heavy rain.

A Dog-fish was caught as usual with a hook baited with an *Old Wife* fish (*Balistes Vetula.*)

The two next days were calm, and we likewise caught dog-fishes.

The 28th of *April*, 6°. 2'. N. L.

The N. E. wind now began to blow, and in the space of a fortnight helped us over the tropic of *Cancer*.

This wind is constant here all the year long, though it varies sometimes to one and sometimes to the other side. The ships, both on their going and return, are obliged to avail themselves of the same trade wind. They are therefore obliged to get on against the wind, and sail with a considerable bend till they at last gain the right course with western winds, and are enabled to get out of this calm sea.

Bonets and *tunnies* were caught, and in their bellies we found *Cuttle-fish* and little *crabs*.

We saw a ship to the leeward, which we thought was an *East Indiaman* on her voyage to *India*.

In the next twenty-four hours we caught sixty-eight *tunnies* and *bonets*.

The 1st of *May*, 8°. 57'. N. L.

CLEAR weather. Fresh trade wind.

FLYING-FISH (*Exocœtus volitans*), which were three or four inches long, and somewhat different from the *Exocœtus* of *Artedi*, were caught here. The *membrana branchiostega* has eight, the *dorsal-fin* four, the *pectoral-fins* twelve or fifteen, the *ventral-fins*, which are in the middle between the pectoral and the anal-fins, have six, the *anal-fin* nine, and the *tail* nineteen, rays; those of the tail are very small.

SOME *tunnies* were caught, whose bellies were quite empty.

The 2d of *May*, 10°. 6'. N. L.

CLEAR weather. Fresh trade wind.

BONETS, *tunnies*, and *flying-fishes* were seen in great numbers. In a *tunny* we found a narrow, white fish, seven inches and a half long, which the sailors call the *Chinese Garter*.

It

It is *Syngnathus argenteus*. The *membrana branchiostega* has one ray: the *dorsal-fin*, which extends from the head to the tail, has forty-six rays: the *pectoral-fins* are near the head, and have fourteen rays: the *ventral-fin* consists of a single very small ossicle or ray, which stands under the belly very near the breast: the *anal-fin* is an inch and a half before the end of the tail, and has twelve rays: the *tail* is entire, and has twenty-four rays: the *head* is pointed, and is somewhat above an inch long: the *lower-jaw* is the longest: the *teeth* are sharp-pointed, stand in one row; thirty-one of the largest stand before in the upper-jaw: the *eyes* are great: the *body* is narrow, of the thickness of a finger: the *scales* are small.

Some of our sailors said, that when they were at *Aynom* in the ship called *The Queen*, they had eaten a species of dried fishes which were very like this; that if they were eaten fresh they would do no hurt, but would be more unwholesome if dried.

An eclipse of the sun, which could not be observed in our country, was very considerable here. The clouds hid the sun from us before
the

the beginning of the eclipse, which hindered our observations till three quarters past five o'clock, when the moon covered two thirds of the sun, after which the sky presently became cloudy.

The 9th of *May*, 19°. 20'. N. L.

In the night we were past the sun (for so the sailors call the sun's passing through the *Zenith*) for which reason we could make no observations to-day, though it was fair. In the afternoon the wind grew changeable and calm. *Tunnies*, *bonets*, and *flying-fishes* were still caught as in the last week. The sea-weed which swam by us, and had been observed yesterday, was a fore-runner of the so much wished for *Grass-sea*.

Some of our people suffered a great deal from head-aches: some of them thought that the complaint arose from the smoaked *tunnies* and *bonets*; and remembered that when they were on board *The Queen*, where they had the same food, they suffered by the same disorder.

We now again observed a *Tropick-bird*.

The

THE GRASS-SEA. 1752. 109

The 10th of *May*, 22°. N. L.

CLEAR weather. Weak trade wind.

THE *Grafs-fea* is that part of the ocean in which the *Eaft India* failors meet with feaweed (*Fucus natans*) fwimming in greater or lefs quantities; though all forts of *Fucus* are called fea-weeds. We entered the *Grafs-fea* in our return on the 7th of *May*, in feventeen degrees and a half north latitude, and twenty-two degrees and a half of weft longitude, from *Afcenfion Ifland*, and 37°. 21'. weft longitude from *London*. The weed in the firft days came but ever now and then, in fmall quantities; but in 26°. latitude in great heaps, fometimes feveral fathoms long. This appearance continued to the 25th of this month; when a frefh foutherly wind at twenty-four degrees and a half latitude, twenty-four degrees and a half weft from *Afcenfion Ifland*, and 39°. 9'. weft from *London*, brought us out of the *Grafs-fea*, on which we had fufficient time to make obfervations, by the calms and very gentle winds which then prevailed.

IT

It seemed at first as if this wandering sea-plant (*Fucus natans*), which met us with a northern wind, came from the *African* coast, or the isles on that side. But in that case, it is plain we should have met it on our going out; because in this very latitude we sailed much nearer to that continent, but yet never saw any such sea-weed there. The northern trade wind, which pushed us onward from the sixth degree of latitude on this side the æquator, makes the *East Indiamen* on their return take their course more to the west than would else be necessary; and then they meet with more or less sea-weed in proportion as they approach more or less to the *American* continent. From whence we may conclude, that this plant comes from *America*, since it likewise appears from the accounts we have, that it is to be met with in great quantities in the *Gulf of Florida,* whence a great storm drives it into the open sea; and the westerly winds carry it so far, that even those who come from the *East Indies* get a sight of some of the produce of the *West Indies:* but other winds keep it from coming quite to *Africa*, and keep it floating about the ocean. From this, *bonets, tunnies,* and other fishes get their subsistence; they

they search this weed well, and take what they like out of it: not to mention that one sort of little fishes or insects which inhabit this sea-weed, serves as food to others.

THE stalk of this ramose plant, which however is scarce distinguishable in thickness from the branches, was not above a foot long, and without all appearances of roots; yet it was able to push out new leaves for further encrease: the globose parts of fructification were (like some of the leaves, stalks, and branches) harder than usual; occasioned, as it seemed, by the slime which sometimes fastens itself on the leaves, branches, or other parts: in this some very small blackish grains, or rather eggs of crabs, and insects, are inclosed: when these insects afterwards forsake their habitations, they leave marks in the hardened slime behind them. Sometimes a slime exceedingly like the whites of eggs sticks to the leaves, in which an innumerable quantity of snail's eggs joined together make a white or yellow chain, like a *Tænia*, so wound backwards and forwards that one can neither find its beginning or its end. I could neither in these nor in the preceding ones, observe any sort of shape or life, with the microscope. After they had been

been put into water, for some hours every part was put into disorder and dissolved. If this and the preceding matter is not *Dampier's* fish-roe, which is said to swim in the *Sargazo*, I have not met with it. In stormy weather the *Sargazo* does not sink, but keeps on the surface of the water, except when the force of the waves or the course of the water (when it approaches the ship) suppress it; in this case it sinks lower, and gives a green light, though its colour is yellow. If it is again thrown into the water, it makes the latter to foam violently. In wet weather it exsudes a saltish substance, tho' it was well dried before. If it is prepared with vinegar, it is reckoned as good as *samphire* (*Crithmum*), which in *Spain* and *England* relishes so well with roasted meat. Why may not some of our species of sea-weed serve the same purpose? In this case we should have a sufficient quantity both for inland use and for exportation. In this migratory sea-weed were the following animals:

THE *American frog-fish*, Lophius Histrio Linn. *Syst. Nat.* or *Lophius tumidus Mus. Reg.* p. 56, and Dr. Linnæus's *Westgothic Journey*, tab. iii. fig. 3. Its *cirrus* and first *dorsal-fin* are bristly at the top, and those bristles are soft.

The

THE GRASS-SEA. 1752.

The whole body is covered with a flimy fkin, and little *foliaceous fulcra*, which are fcarce obfervable while the fifh is in the water, becaufe they fit fo clofe to the body. The *mouth* and *belly* are large, in order to receive many fpecies of crabs or young fhell-fifh. Perhaps Providence has clothed this fifh with *fulcra* refembling leaves, that the fifhes of prey might miftake it for fea-weed, and not entirely deftroy the breed.

Cyprinus pelagicus. The *dorfal-fin* reaches from the head to the tail, is lower in the middle, and has thirty-fix rays: the *pectoral-fins* have fifteen, the *ventral-fins* fix, the *anal-fin* twenty-eight, and the furcated *tail* twenty-two rays: the *irides* of the eyes are yellow like gold: the *mouth* is oblong: the *body* is very narrow, whitifh, and every where covered with very fmall fcales.

Syngnathus pelagicus, corpore medio heptagono pinnâ dorfi anum verfus. The *dorfal-fin* has thirty-one, the *pectoral-fins* have fourteen, rays: the *ventral* and *anal-fins* are wanting: the flabelliform *tail* has ten rays: the whole *length* of the fifh is about a fpan: it is as *thick* as a goofe-quill. From the head to the *anus*, or nearly to the middle, it is heptagonal, and has eighteen rings; but lower down it is quadrangular to the tail, and has thirty-two rings. The *female* (according to *Artedi's Syn.* iii. p. 3.) has the ovary near the *anus*, where he likewise says, that the *body* is polygonal, and broader below: the *beak* is long, cylindrical, and narrow.

Scyllæa pelagica, or the *Sea-hare*. Seba took them for the young ones of the *Lophius tumidus, Muf. Reg.*: but it is difficult to persuade one's self of the truth of this; unless somebody would keep them, and observe their changes. The following is their description: the *body* is like a jelly, oblong, narrow, of a yellow-grey colour, and has a longitudinal fissure below, by means of which it can surround the sea-weed (*Fucus*) both lengthways and crofs-ways with the fore-part or hind-part: it is two inches long, and scarce one inch broad: the *sides* are flat, with little carnose, cone-shaped, whitish prominences: the *back* (which by some has been mistaken for the lower-part) is almost flat, with very short, dark bristles, and sharp-pointed margins, to which some appendages (*Fulcra*) or *arms* and *fins* are fastened: the *head* is compressed, preffed, fomewhat pointed, and difficult to be diftinguifhed when dead: the *antennæ* are fhorter than the head: the *mouth* has no teeth, and has a pilofe margin below the beak: the *throat* is fmall, almoft round: the *tentacula* are upwards, not far from the top of the beak; they are oblong, foliaceous, fhorter than the fins, fomewhat broader before, with a deflected hairy margin, and a carnofe cone in the middle; they likewife ferve to grafp the fea-weed. The animal has on each fide two fins at equal diftances; they are foliaceous, oblong, fomewhat broader before, curled, with briftly or lacerated edges, and are placed on the rough margin of the back: the *belly* is in the middle of the body, narrow, oblong. The parts of fructification of the fea-weed, which it eats, were vifible in it. The *tail* is perpendicular, foliaceous, almoft round, broader, but fhorter than the appendages, and ciliated. This animal moves very flowly in the water[a], by bending its extremities.

Cancer pelagicus, brachiperus, manuum articulis omnibus dentatis, extimo heptagono. The *pinchers* of the *chely* bend out very little, are

[a] I fhould perhaps have called the tentacula, *hands*, and the fins, four *feet*.

ſtreaked, dentated, and of equal length: the the other *feet* have but one toe: the ſides of the *thorax* are ſerrated, the hind-part is long, ſtrong, ſharp-pointed: the *colour* is a browniſh yellow, with whitiſh unequal ſpots: the *tail* of the *female* is much broader, round (with a ſhort point), and conſiſts of ſeven articulations: the *tail* of the *male* is almoſt triangular, and has four articulations: on each ſide of the tail is a ſingle, long, bent briſtle, which is thicker below, and bears a great reſemblance to the lateral rays of a fin.

Cancer minutus is the moſt numerous of all inſects here, and feeds upon *ſepias* and little crabs. It ſkipped about on the ſurface of the water with exceeding great agility, from one heap of ſea-weed to another, which is ſometimes ſeveral fathoms diſtant, and when it caught a worm, it tore it with its *chely*, and crammed it into its mouth bit by bit.

The 12th of *May*, 24°. 15′. N. L.

YESTERDAY and to-day we had generally a calm.

THE *dolphin*, or *Coryphæna hippurus*, had the following characters: the *membrana branchiostega* has seven rays: the *body* is greenish dotted with blue, two feet long, narrow, sharp-pointed: the *head* is obtuse, short: the *lower-jaw* is the longest: the *eyes* are globose: the *irides* are gold-coloured: the *teeth*, which are short and numerous, stand in the jaws and gums: the *back* and *belly* are sharp: the *tail* is furcated: the single *dorsal-fin* begins on the middle of the head, and goes to the tail; towards the head it is the broadest; it has sixty rays: the *pectoral-fins* have nineteen, the *ventral fins* six, and the *anal-fin*, which extends from the *anus*, or from the middle of the fish to the tail, has twenty-six rays: the *tail* is bifid, and each of its parts has twenty rays. The fish is exceedingly quick in its motions, and in the water seems shaded with black and green: the *ovary* is oblong, double, and large: the *lateral-line* is bent, runs directly by the back, and is scarce distinguishable between the head and the *anus*. This fish is very seldom met with, except in such places where the winds are changeable, that is, only within the *Tropics*.

BONETS and *tunnies* were more scarce at present; but appeared in shoals the next day towards evening. To-day, as well as the following days, the afore-mentioned natural curiosities were caught in the *Grass-sea*, and put into spirits, to be brought home.

The 20th of *May*, 28°. 34'. N. L.

AMONG other fish we met with the *Dorado*, which is about a yard long, and very like the *dolphin*, for which reason *Artedi* makes it the same species of *Coryphæna*. But that which we caught at this time was different in the following particulars:

Coryphæna Equiselis. The *dorsal-fin*, which extends from the middle of the head to the tail, has fifty-three, the *pectoral-fins* have nineteen, the *ventral-fins* have six, the *anal-fin* has twenty-three, the *membrana branchiostega* six, and the *tail* has twenty, rays. This *Dorado* is in general much more scarce than all the rest, so that many people have often been in the *East Indies*, without ever having seen it.

THE GRASS-SEA. 1752. 119

The 22d of *May*, 30°. 45'. N. L.

A VESSEL which we had seen for some days together, now came near us. The name of the ship was *Duc de Parme*; it was commanded by Chevalier *d'Arquis*, came from *Bengal*, and was destined for *Port l'Orient* in *France*. The clear weather and moderate wind gave us opportunities of visiting each other on the open sea. Our first supercargo dined aboard the aforesaid ship; and two gentlemen from the other *Swedish* ship which accompanied us, dined with us.

THE following days there was generally a calm, which likewise permitted the ships to keep company with each other.

The 26th of *May*, 35°. 24'. N. L.

BONETS and *tunnies* were caught for the last time; though we saw the latter in the following days. Now we took leave of the *Grafs-sea*.

The 28th of *May*, 38°. 24'. N. L.

STORM. Cloudy in the forenoon; but generally clear afterwards. In the forenoon we were on the latitude of *Fayal*, which, as well as the other *Azores*, belongs to the *Portugueze*. We then failed acrofs the longitude, till we faw the *Pico of Fayal*, on the 30th of *May* at four o'clock in the afternoon; but the 31ft we paffed the *Pico of Fayal* and *St. George*, which lie in 38°. 38'. latitude. The fhips had orders to ftop at *Fayal*, and to make enquiry concerning the ftate of *Europe*: but on account of the ftrong wind it was thought expedient to fail on. I therefore miffed of a great number of unknown plants, which are undoubtedly to be met with in thefe iflands, lying almoft in the middle between *Europe*, *Africa*, and *America*.

The 1ft of *June*, 41°. 10'. N. L.

CLEAR weather; and likewife cloudy. Brifk contrary wind.

TURDUS

TURDUS *Chinenſis, Diſſ. Lhin. Lagerſtr.* 11. is by the *Chineſe* called *Whammay* (*Linnæus* in his *New Syſtema Naturæ* calls it *Turdus canorus*), and might, on account of its ſtrong voice, be called the *Crying Thruſh*. It was ſold for a piaſtre at *Canton*, and died here: for which reaſon I put down the following remarks: the *bill* is angulated-conic, the back part of it ſomewhat angulofe: the *tongue* is as it were torn and emarginated before. The *whole body* of the *female* is ferrugineous, except three quill and three tail feathers, which for the greater part are white (this circumſtance is ſeldom to be met with in the other ſpecies of this genus): about and near the eyes is a ſhort white line: the *belly* is blueiſh: behind the *noſtrils* are ſome briſtles: the *bill, legs,* and *feet,* are whitiſh: it has twelve *quill-feathers,* and twelve in the *tail,* which latter are the ſame length with the body: in *ſize* it equals our black bird. It eats rice, moths, flies, and fleſh. To-day we met an *Engliſh* ſhip which had ſailed from *London* ſixteen days ago, and was bound for *America,* having both male and female ſlaves on board.

The 13th of *June*, 49°. 16′. N. L.

WITH the lead we found ground at ninety fathoms laſt night; it was a fine browniſh ſand.

The 14th of *June*.

CLEAR weather. Moderate wind.

WE at laſt ſaw the *Scilly Iſlands* in the forenoon. Theſe iſlands and rocks are very low, and therefore do not appear before one is quite up with them, for which reaſon many ſhips have been loſt juſt at the entrance of the *Britiſh Channel*, notwithſtanding there are two light-houſes erected for the uſe of ſeamen. The rocks diſcovered themſelves to us by the breakers. *Fucus divaricatus, veſiculoſus, et Zoſtera,* came ſwimming from the ſhore. *Engliſh* boats came from the *Scilly Iſlands* to us, with butter, lean ſheep, geeſe, ducks, chicken, eggs, plaiſes (*Pleuronectes Plateſſa* Linn.), rock-fiſh (*Labrus ſuillus* Linn.), potatoes in baſkets, turneps, cabbages, long and purple-red beet, ſallads, and (*Crithmum maritimum*) ſamphire; which latter, when cleared of its roots,

roots, coarfe ftalks, and the adherent *Nardus ftricta, ftatia armeria, Arenaria rubra et Lichenes fcyphiferi*, is put into falt-water for twelve hours together, and afterwards boiled with vinegar, alum, cloves, and ginger (which two fpices are however not neceffary).

In the afternoon we paffed the *Land's End*, the firft promontory of *England* in the *Channel*, where the tides make up for the lofs of wind. The tide met us at the *Lizard*, in the evening; a neck of land from which the *Englifh* generally count the longitude of places; as do likewife *Swedifh* feamen, who generally make ufe of *Englifh* books.

The 15th of *June*.

Clear weather. Little wind.

We failed by *Plymouth*. The fine fields hereabout, and grounds which are furrounded with quick-fet hedges, afforded a charming view. The chalk hills on the fhore made it appear white and high.

The

The 16th of *June.*

HEAVY rain, and contrary wind all day.

WE passed *Devonshire* and *Dorsetshire,* and came in the afternoon to *Dover,* that well-known *English* town and castle, which is exactly opposite to *Calais* in *France,* and is not far from it; so that both kingdoms may be seen at once, if you sail through the *Channel.* At *Dover* we went on shore, and purchased beef and mutton, cabbages and cauliflowers, cucumbers, carrots, sallads, parsley, sage, leeks, artichoaks, beans, beer, bread, &c.

THE people came on-board us, and offered men's cloaths, shoes, wigs, hats, stockings, watches, and such things, for money, or *East India* goods; preferring green teas to most other things: the brown teas are not reckoned of any great value with them. After we had taken in the necessary refreshments, we directed our course to *Gottenburgh.* On this voyage we met amongst several other ships an *English* one bound for *Petersburgh.*

The 25th of *June*.

AFTER a voyage of eight days, we happily got fight of *Jutland*.

The 26th of *June*.

WE faw *Marſtrand* and the *Gottenburgh Rocks*; and yet in the forenoon we caſt anchor under the caſtle of *Elfsborg*. After the cuſtom-houſe officers had put the feal to our cabbins, I went on ſhore again with great ſatisfaction and in perfect health.

WE loſt eight men on the voyage: of theſe one died of a dyſentery, one of the pleureſy, three of agues, and three loſt their lives by accidents. But thanks be to GOD, who has ſo fuccefsfully brought 124 men back to their own country.

LINNÆUS'S LETTER

TO

MR. OSBECK.

SIR!

I HAVE read your excellent book with pleasure and surprize. It cannot be disputed, that few books are so agreeable to the public as accounts of voyages, where something new is always found to gratify the reader's curiosity, and enlarge his understanding. But most of the voyages hitherto published, by imposing barbarous names on their discoveries, have rather sharpened our desire after knowledge, than afforded any real instruction. You, Sir, have every where travelled with the light of science: you have named every thing so precisely, that it may be comprehended by the learned world; and have discovered and settled both the genera and species. For this reason, I seem myself to have travelled with you, and to have examined every object you saw with my own eyes.

If voyages were thus written, science might truly reap advantage from them. I congratulate you, Sir, for having traced out a way in which the world will follow your steps hereafter; and, pursuing this career, will remember the man who first pointed it out.

CHARLES LINNÉ.

A SPEECH.

A

SPEECH,

SHEWING

What fhould be attended to in VOYAGES to CHINA,

DELIVERED BY

PETER OSBECK,

On his being chofen a Member of the ROYAL SWEDISH ACADEMY OF SCIENCES, at *Stockholm*, the 25th of *February*, 1758.

Gentlemen!

THE greateft rivers often come from the leaft fprings; and fo the leaft caufes may produce the moft confiderable effects. The ableft men in all fciences therefore pay great attention even to the minuteft information, which is defpifed by perfons of inferior abilities: they expect no fruit without a preceding flower, no fcientific knowledge without fimple but fundamental principles, and no experiments without previous introductions. To prove this at present is hardly necessary, when all you, Gentlemen, are living instances of the truth of my assertion; you protect even the slightest sketches, if the intention be good, and are continually labouring for after-ages. The honour you have conferred on me in particular, in chusing me a member of your *learned Society*, will raise my respect and veneration, and encourage me to proceed in the same career.

GIVE me leave now, Gentlemen, to begin with making a short discourse upon some *Instructions how far attention may be useful to the public in voyages from* Sweden *to* China.

ATTENTION has always its use, which in part appears immediately, and in part avails posterity. Whatever serves for food, or the amendment of health, is looked upon as useful by all without exception; they are two of the most considerable advantages; for the calls of hunger admit of no delay, and sickness is the first step to death. But our enquiries may be extended to other objects, which are considered as necessary. Each of our senses expects its peculiar gratification, and this sometimes

from

from the moſt diſtant parts of the world. That other nations may not run away with all the advantages ariſing from carrying merchandize from place to place, we are obliged to fetch foreign goods ourſelves by long voyages. It is advantageous to trade to take time, and to have a free uninterrupted courſe; and therefore we prefer going by ſea: to this the compaſs is not only uſeful, but abſolutely requiſite; yet it is probable that at firſt the effects of the load-ſtone were looked upon as trivial, and it is doubtful whether the inventor got a proportionable reward for its diſcovery: but time has ſhewn, that the firſt attention to this object has been of great and almoſt ineſtimable uſe. Our attention muſt therefore not merely extend to thoſe things of which we already ſee the uſe, but likewiſe to thoſe from which we ſtill may expect it.

Follow me therefore, Gentlemen, over the foaming waves to the *Spaniſh* ſhores, and over a boiſterous ſea to the riches of the *Indies*: but we ſhall here mention only a ſmall part of what will gratify a laudable curioſity, and confine ourſelves to domeſtick œconomy and natural hiſtory, which will be amply ſufficient

ficient to give birth to such reflections as may be useful to yourselves and your country.

Such a voyage is undertaken in the coldest season, in the stormy *November*, the dark *December*, and the following winter months. This regulation is made on account of fetching money from *Spain*, and lest the monsoons in the *Chinese* sea should be lost. I do not speak of those voyages which are made first to *Suratt*, and thence to *China*; for these are begun in the spring, and have only the voyage home in common with the other.

The exchange of a good warm room for a cold ship-cabin (for there is no other fire on-board except that by which the meat is boiled) is a most sensible change, when the body is not well secured against the rigours of the season; and especially to those who cannot keep in continual motion. The penetrating cold of the sea can hardly be kept off by any thing else than furrs. The most common cloathing of our sailors about this time are sheep-skins, which are bought of the *Danes* in the *Sound*, and are said to be so well prepared, that they do not lose their softness even if they are worn in the heaviest rains and snow. I should think

think they might be prepared in *Sweden* too: skins cannot be wanting in a country which is not only capable of, but obliged to breed sheep, and without which it cannot subsist.

For fear of missing the true entrance into the *Channel*, the ships chuse rather to go north about *Ireland*; for a secure road, though round about, is always preferable to a dangerous one though more direct.

Our *East India* ships should not wish to see the *Færoe Islands*, were it not to escape their foggy rocks. Yet there is no country but has its peculiar advantages. It is cold, but it has plenty of furs for cloathing. The sheep, whose delight are hills and dry pastures, grow very fat here. The want of bread is supplied by dried fish; a food which, with some others, might be introduced to great advantage in such places of our country where fisheries obtain, especially during these times, when every thing bears so high a price. The wise institutions of the Creator are glorious in directing nature to supply us with one thing instead of another which we want: if some places have barren mountains and dry hills, they are generally counter-balanced by fine rivers or seas swarming with fishes. But we deviate too far from our voyage; the providence of GOD, and the light we derive from that source, may well enrapture our senses, and for a time engross all our ideas.

WE left off at the seventeen *Færoe Islands*, but must haste from them to the *Spanish Sea*, and its majestic waves. On the way we meet with a species of whales called the *Grampus*, but are obliged to leave them to the nicer observations of those who may for the future find better opportunities of enriching the science with a perfect natural history of whales. The *Gothenburgh* merchant, Mr. *Peter Bagge*, who by means of this *Royal Academy* has offered to bear the expences of a natural historian that shall attend the *Swedish* whale fishery, deserves honour and thanks for so generous a design.

ON our voyage, *Spain* is the first continent where we rest: here is a considerable degree of warmth even in *January*. The finest fruits are then gathering from those trees which we keep in our hot-houses, and the fields are adorned with beautiful flowers. We meet with people who understand several languages

in

in the port towns hereabouts, of which *Cadiz* and *Port Mary* are the first we fee.

CADIZ, which in the times of the *Phœnicians* and *Romans*, and before its deftruction by the *Moors*, was very fplendid, may afford many objects of enquiry to an antiquary. The bifhop here might be able to produce feveral curiofities out of his own library, and perhaps fome remains of our ancient *Goths* in *Spain*. This is what I leave to others. The eating of flefh in Lent is allowed only to fuch invalids as have exprefs leave to do it. I could not during my ftay obferve that fafting was any way conducive to religion; but it might be a momentous circumftance with regard to diet and œconomy. The *Spanifh* meat is (at leaft about this time) very bad. By this they fee themfelves obliged to procure the more fifh, for which they have fufficient opportunities; but more efpecially to cultivate fruits, which are here fold in plenty. Perhaps fuch a periodical faft would put our gardens into a better condition, and prevent many difeafes, which if they do not arife from, yet are encreafed by, the fuperfluous confumption of flefh.

Cabinets of natural curiosities cannot be greatly enriched at *Cadiz*, if you except fishes; the exact enquiry into which requires some time and patience. If they are put into *Spanish* brandy, which is strong enough for the purpose of preserving, it would be too expensive to have each sort in a particular bottle; and it would likewise take up too much room; but if a thread is fastened to the fish, and a piece of lead or somewhat else with holes or numbers, hangs on it, you may put many into one glass, and mark the *Spanish* names on the leads. Quadrupeds, birds, amphibious animals, and insects, are not so frequent here, unless a cabinet of natural curiosities could be found at *Cadiz* by some future naturalist. Plants belonging to physic may here be examined in the apothecaries shops. Those who have bought our common fumitary (*Fumaria spicata*), which by our *East Indiamen* is used against the scurvy, and who probably profited by it much, can assure you that it is to be got here likewise; but I can ascertain its growth about *Port Mary*, in case it should not be found in the apothecaries shops. It is the same thing with many of our common remedies. *Ninsi*, the most valuable root, is brought

brought hither from the *West Indian* plantations. Such a fresh root, if it could be found and brought to *Sweden*, would be very well received in our hot-houses. As for stones, you find a great number of varieties of marble near the great church, which they have already been so long building. The stones with which the *Spaniards* build are compofed of shells, and are to be met with every where. If we go out of town, we find the flying loose sand most plentifully, which often spoils the finest spots of ground, and seldom leaves any thing but the *Spartium monospermum* behind it, which withstands its utmost fury, and the feeds of which lie in great quantity on the sand, and will keep for a long time. This plant is as yet unknown in our country, and might at least be made use of to furround beds containing tender plants.

On going from hence on the high road to the towns of *Chiclana*, *Isla*, *Port Real*, *Xerez*, and *Port Mary*, which an attentive natural historian ought to do, on foot, you are doubtful what to fix your eyes upon. A good company and *Spanish* drefs (I mean a white cap, a hat flapped down, and a thin brown great coat over the common cloaths) eafe the inconveniencies

veniencies of the journey. A bound folio with writing paper to put plants into, a box or two with pins to collect infects, a pair of fciffars, and a pocket book to write upon, may be hid under the great-coat. The fciffars muft fupply the place of a knife, which it is forbidden to wear. Books of natural hiftory would be very ufeful on fuch a journey; but, to avoid the fufpicion of their containing any thing againft the religion of the country, one is obliged to leave them on-board the fhip.

After we have feen thefe towns and what they contain, we at laft ftop in *Port Mary*, where we have more opportunities than at *Cadiz* of making collections from the neighbouring gardens, meadows, and fields.

The plants which are to be met with here about this feafon are mentioned in my voyage; but at other times more may be added. Each requires a particular attention, but I will only fpeak of one or two. It ought to be tried whether the *Coccus cacti*, the infect which gives us the cochineal, is to be met with on the *Cactus opuntia*, which here grows in the quick-hedges. Our flax, which grows fpontaneoufly here, takes fhelter under a little fhrub

(under

(under the *Palmito*): ought not we to follow nature, and to support flax as we do pease, especially in the open field, where it is apt to be damaged by the wind, beat down by the rain, and frequently rots while it is yet standing in the ground. I have seen that they put sticks among the flax in *Wingocker*, and have heard that the same was practised at *Wadstena* by the foreigners who live there, and work at the cambrick manufacture.

The lovers of insects find several very scarce beetles in the *Spanish* flying sand: these are *Scarabæus typhæus*, *Tenebrio muricatus*, *Meloe majalis*; and magnificent butter-flies, such as *Papilio rumina*, and several others.

The water requisite for the voyage to *China* is, for the most part, fetched from this town by our ships, and it is certainly exceeding clear; but in time it becomes so full of worms, that they creep about in it as maggots in cheese: by boiling, it gets a brownish colour, and always maintains a bad taste. In a country where lemons bear such a low price, it might be tried, whether the growth of these worms could not be stopped, by mixing the water with lemon juice as soon as the vessel is filled;

filled; perhaps the little eggs of the worms, which are undoubtedly already in the water, might be killed by it in the beginning, and by this means hindered from becoming *sea wood-lice* (*Oniscus aquaticus*), and other insects, which make the water nauseous and unhealthy. Such experiments ought to be tried before credible persons, and not be pronounced as good before they have been often repeated. If this expedient succeeds, we are delivered from a great inconvenience; and if it fails, it does not hurt the water, but makes it capable of assuaging thirst much better. We reckon lemon juice very wholesome for internal use: but, according to the account of our *Spanish* passenger, it occasions a pain in the hands if you frequently wash them in it.

But we linger too long in *Spain*: we must go past the *Canaries* and the Cape of *Good Hope* into the wide ocean, between *Java* and *Sumatra*, to *Canton* in *China*, there to employ our attention in those distant parts.

Of the fishes and birds which we meet with on our voyage, we ought to keep some, the former in *Spanish* spirits, and the latter stuffed with tow, though their entire drying requires

requires a long time and frequent care. Their manner of living ought likewise as much as poffible to be obferved.

The minuteft animals ought not to be forgot. We frequently find fome which fhine in water. The knowledge of thefe animals and of their place of abode may perhaps hereafter be as fure a mark to determine in what parts of the fea we are, as the trumpet weed (*Fucus maximus*) together with the cape pigeons are an undoubted token that we begin to approach the Cape.

It is more advantageous (if circumftances allow of it) to go on fhore in *Java* when we fail to, and not when we fail from, *China*; fince in the feafon of our return the rain ufually occafions many interruptions. We here meet with a collection of the moft magnificent productions of nature: the moft remarkable animals, the fineft infects, the prettieft fhells, the moft wondrous corals, the fcareeft plants, efpecially many forts of palm-trees, which might afford many a year's work for an admirer of nature. The civility of the inhabitants is no fmall encouragement to us: and we forget the fury of wild beafts, in confideration

of

of the rarities of this ifland. We admire, and are aftonifhed. The remarkable trade wind, which blows fouth-weft one half of the year, and north-eaft the other half (including the time of change), in the *Chinefe* fea, has obliged fome *Swedifh* fhips, which arrived after the fetting in of the contrary wind, to lie by half a year together at *Java*, or fome other ifland. If one attentive perfon fhould be found among fo many people, the difadvantage arifing to the company from this delay would be balanced by enriching Natural Hiftory and other fciences. The *Indian* medicinal herbs, and other things which the *Dutch* pour in upon us from *Eaft India*, whofe native foil we are in general unacquainted with, would, at leaft, in part become more known: but the traveller ought firft to be acquainted with an apothecary's fhop, and the writers on *Indian* natural productions. It is worth enquiring, befides, whether the *Dutch* take in natural faltpetre as ballaft at *Java*, refine it, and afterwards fell it to us and to others at a great profit.

Passing by *Sumatra*, we were all reminded of its gold mines, but probably may never have any opportunity to fee them. The inconftancy of the wind, the falling of the water, and a dangerous paffage between the neighbouring iflands, forced us frequently to caft our anchor. When we weighed anchor again, we pulled up fuch a quantity of fea worms with it, as are otherwife difficult to be found. The *Chinefe* fea is full of the fineft and moft curious fifhes, which may fometimes be procured during the trade wind.

On entering *China*, I remember the account a *Swede* gave me, who had failed to the eaft, and travelled from *Bocca Tyger* to *Canton:* this journey deferved all poffible care and expences, unlefs our eyes were prejudiced in favour of any other country; for we fhall fcarcely find fo careful an œconomy of foil in any other place as in *China*. The gathering of bones, hair, *&c.* which we throw away, and the extreme but well-rewarded trouble they take in tranfplanting, are certain proofs of the induftry of the *Chinefe*, and of their laudable difpofition to cultivate their country. If travellers would permit me, I would give them the following advice: forget if you will your expences, but never forget the leaft particular of the œconomy of the *Chinefe*; for they regulate their art according to nature, and

and modify it according to the situation of the place.

Foresight is necessary against the suspicion of the *Chinese*, and even the least opportunity ought not to be missed. A silent company is here necessary. An old interpreter would be of great use, if your finances allowed you to keep one. But with a people so totally governed by self-interest, you seldom arrive at the truth by direct questions.

We bring the *Porcellane* clay to *Sweden*; but are we sure that the *Chinese* give us a true specimen of that important manufacture? I either do not yet know this nation well, or I have great reason to doubt it.

A person who is able to bring them to his own terms when they offer their goods to sale, can best get the truth out of them unobserved, during the carrying on of the bargain. Such a merchant might, if he was besides acquainted with natural history, be of double use to his country.

Perhaps the *Porcellane* is not manufactured at such a distance from *Canton* as we are told

it

it is. The old *Porcellane*, the stone *Porcellane*, and the present *Porcellini*, seem to be made in different places, and of different materials.

Do we know what the brown or red ware is made of? Would it be impossible to get a little way into the country by means of money, and to be able to get a sight of such manufactures? Could we not get cotton (which is bought up in great quantities here by the *Armenians*) to *Sweden* by the way of *Turkey?* But we must dwell no longer upon such suppositions.

We may here get collections in all the kingdoms of nature. They sell birds, fishes, shells, and insects. They will also supply you with trees; among which the *Bambou* tree, and the *China* root, with many others, deserve to be brought to *Sweden*. The country is adorned with the finest trees and plants, and almost all of them are very different from those of *Sweden*. But, to make still more accurate observations, some courage is required, and a careful examination of all their accounts.

The quarry at the lion tower deserves a journey; though the stones which are dug there are worked in stone-cutters shops at *Canton*. There you may perhaps find another sort of stone, below, in, or above, the strata of sand stone. Even those who are not used to collect stones, might enrich our *Swedish* cabinets of natural history from hence; a piece of stone of the size of a chocolate-cake is easily wrapped up in a piece of paper, on which the place may be marked where it was found. Species of the earths, sands, and clays, of so distant places, would likewise adorn our collections. You may likewise enquire at *Canton* about *Ores*, viz. gold ore, from *Sumatra*, copper ore from *Japan*, *Porcellane* earth from the same place, *Tintenaque*, *Chinese* gold ore, &c.

MANY other articles there are, worthy our attention: but I need not try your patience any longer, Gentlemen; and what is here omitted may be supplied by the accuracy of the traveller.

I MUST once more mention *Java* and its neighbourhood, which we see again on our return. *St. Helena*, an *English* island, has formerly been a convenient resting place to us; *Ascension* likewise, where birds and fishes are caught with little trouble: the former on the heaps

heaps of stones, and the latter when the water throws them on shore. Stones, earths, sands, and in a word the greatest part of what is to be met with here, are uncommon in other places. I likewise pass over *Fayal*, with the other *Azores*, of whose natural curiosities, as far as I know, no satisfactory account has been as yet given. It is worthy our trouble to enquire whether they there make a sort of indigo from another plant, besides the *Indigofera tinctoria* of the *Indies*. I have seen these islands, but without any hopes of getting on shore. It is no wonder that I passed them with regret. That which gives life to all sciences is, a desire of knowing more.

THE ANSWER.

Given in the Name of the ROYAL ACADEMY of SCIENCES, by their President Mr. JOHN FREDERICK KRUGER.

SIR,

I BELIEVE it is an undoubted truth, that the advantage or difadvantage of travel into foreign countries depends principally on the inclination and abilities of the travellers. To travel in order to acquire wifdom, is the moſt dangerous of all undertakings, eſpecially when the traveller is raw and unprincipled, and not animated by the pureſt love of his country. The difadvantage would be but little, if the head of fuch a traveller could only return as empty as it fet out: for it would then comprehend only the loſs of the money ſpent. But if his mind is filled with foreign follies,

follies, the lofs is double: for the money is fpent, and our native virtues are adulterated by new-imported vices. This occafions a moral evil, which grows more incurable from time to time, fince there are fo few that are confcious of its baneful influence.

A NATION which does no honour to fcience, arts, and trade, can expect nothing but foreign fopperies from their travellers: for how can they be inquifitive in other countries about thofe things which are defpifed in their own? or, why fhould they with a great deal of trouble acquire fuch notions abroad, as will not be regarded or adopted at their return? And this is the principal reafon of the little benefit which *Sweden* has formerly reaped from its travellers. But, fince fcience has been equally efteemed both by high and low, we can boaft of thofe travellers, whofe fole view has been to improve their knowledge by frefh experience. The more foreign nations endeavour to conceal any wife regulations, the more is their laudable defire of knowledge inflamed. And as it is difficult to conceal any thing from a quick-fighted and wife man; fo it has likewife but feldom happened, that connoiffeurs (the purpofe of whofe travels has been the improvement

provement of sciences) have returned without having obtained their aim. 'I even venture to say, that as much as the useless travels of our restless youths have formerly proved to our disadvantage in trade, in regard to the balance of money with foreign nations; so much has been our advantage of late, by means of the travels of some *Swedes* into the most distant countries.

The discoveries which have been made in natural history, and the scarce collections of foreign plants made by *Kalm* in *North-America*, *Hasselquist* in *Palestine* and *Egypt*, and *Loefling* in *Spain* and in the *Spanish* parts of *South-America*, are of such a nature, that they are not to be found in foreign accounts of travels. It is therefore much to be regretted, that the two last mentioned gentlemen finished their pilgrimage in this world so unexpectedly, on the very travels they had undertaken for the service of science: a misfortune which cannot be remembered without regret, because it has occasioned an almost irreparable loss, not only to *Sweden*, but to the whole learned world.

If the Royal Academy had not made it a rule, Sir, to reserve the praise of its friends, to a time which it always wishes may be as distant as possible; I should find sufficient occasion here to turn my discourse upon the abilities you have shewn on your travels in foreign countries; but your own writings sufficiently explain my thoughts. Give me leave however to say, that the public thankfully acknowledges the courage you have exerted amidst so many difficulties, for the enlargement of knowledge; and reckons you among the small number of travellers, who have opened a field, (which before had never been attended to) and in a country too whose natural history has lain till this time in the greatest obscurity.

Your excellent journal, the curious treatises with which you have several times enriched the memoirs of the Royal Academy, and the speech which you have just now pronounced, undoubtedly shew, that I do not embellish mine with flattery. It is now a long time since you have acquired the friendship of the Royal Academy; but since it is desirous of obtaining your confidence more fully, and of employing that mature judgment (which you have by travel so considerably enriched)

…ished, it could find no better means to effect … than by assigning you a place amidst its … …ore whom I now offer you my hearty congratulations.

A VOYAGE

TO

SURATTE, CHINA, &c.

From the 1st of *April*, 1750, to the 26th of *June*, 1752.

By OLOF TOREEN,

CHAPLAIN to a Ship in the SWEDISH EAST INDIA Company's Service.

IN

A Series of LETTERS

TO

DOCTOR LINNÆUS.

THE author of the following letters, a perſon of quick parts, took a reſolution to leave *Gothenburgh* in the quality of chaplain to an *Eaſt Indiaman*. In order to qualify himſelf to make proper obſervations as a naturaliſt, whilſt on this diſtant voyage, he went to *Upſal*, that he might profit by the inſtructions of the celebrated *Linnæus*. On his voyage he collected many ſcarce plants, which he preſented to his inſtructor in natural hiſtory; who named the *Torenia Aſiatica* after its diſcoverer. After his return, he publiſhed in a ſeries of letters (from *November* the 20th, 1752, to *May* the 3d, 1753) this account of his voyage; but died near *Naſinge* in *Sweden*, on the 17th of *Auguſt*, 1753.

TOREEN'S VOYAGE

TO

SURATTE, CHINA, &c.

LETTER I.

SIR,

YOU will be so kind as to excuse my not complying sooner with your desire of seeing some account of my *East India* voyage. The causes of my delay have been owing to a necessary attendance on my own affairs and those of my family, and the bad state of my health. If what occurs to my memory can serve to amuse you in some of your leisure hours, I shall have more than sufficient reason to think my pains well bestowed.

THE

THE 1ft of *April* we fet fail on-board the fhip called *The Gothic Lion*, after the weft wind had continued to blow for five months together at *Gothenburgh*, and had almoft induced us to believe that there is a trade-wind in the *Scaggerac Sea*. The wind made *April* fools of us [a]; for we were forced to return before *Skagen*, and to anchor at *Rifwefiol*.

THE 8th of *April* we had better fuccefs. A fairer wind than the former helped us out of this corner, and we continued our voyage in company with many other fhips. We met with nothing extraordinary, except a *Danifh* fhip called *The Hereditary Prince*, which was bound for *China*, and had left *Copenhagen* the 4th of *December*, 1749; fhe had therefore a very perverfe wind from the time of her departure.

THE high waves of the *German Ocean*, and the *Flemifh Coafts*, hindered us from reaching *Dunkirk* before the 19th of *April*. I did not go on fhore, for but few had that liberty al-

---

[a] It hence appears that the fame practical wit of duping people on the firft of *April* obtains in *Sweden*, as among our wags in *England*.

lowed

lowed them. But the situation of the place naturally brought to my mind the reasons why *England* would not permit it to continue fortified.

THE town is situated on an open harbour: the entrance is difficult; and the pilot asked six hundred *French* livres for his trouble. But besides that the privateers in time of war can do a great deal of harm from hence, it is very conveniently situated for the *English* smugglers, who run the *French liqueurs*, &c. over to *England*, where there is a high duty laid upon them. Not to mention that the *Austrian Netherlands* can be provided from this place, as a free port, in great plenty, to the disadvantage of a neighbouring nation.

FROM hence we sailed, the 22d of *April*, with so good a wind that we were able to anchor on the south side of *Madeira*, at *Funchal*, the 4th of *May*. The ship happened to be so stationed that the country exhibited the finest prospect I ever saw.

IT rises like an amphitheatre: below is adorned with fine fields, gardens, and vineyards, to which nature has given an advantageous

tageous situation, both in regard to the rising and setting sun: at the top are steep hills covered with trees. Here and there are some country-seats, which make the prospect still more delightful: but below, as in a center, is the city of *Funchal.*

If you go on shore, you have a battery at the water's edge on the right, and a castle on the left. Whoever lands here must carefully decline meddling with the tobacco-trade, in the same manner as in *Portugal*; a single roll of tobacco is enough to bring both men and ship into danger. The best thing is, that the custom-house officers are satisfied with any excuse almost, if it is but plausible. The town has a rampart, within it a castle, and besides this a commanding fortress on a rising ground: but all these are without a *terreplein*, have only high banquets and very short flanks, as is usual when they are to be perpendicular to the curtains.

The houses are pretty good, and three stories high, but the lowest are generally uninhabited. I saw no windows in private houses, but instead of them, iron grates.

THE many processions hindered me from looking about as much as I could have wished. I once saw the *Francifcan* monastery. It is not a regular building, but convenient, and shews that it has large revenues. The good fathers had retired from the world like the moufe into the cheefe. I did not fee one that had the leaft employment. It is eafy to imagine that fo fine a country in the hands of the *Pertugueze* muft have nunneries and colleges of jefuits.

My landlord, Mr. *Timothy Dowling*, affured me that he would willingly ferve the *Swedifh Academy of Sciences* in what he could procure from *Madeira* or *Brafil*; and it might be worth while to put him in mind of his promife, fince he himfelf is curious. He had found fome petrefactions, and a plant which he would have to be the *Laurus* which crowned the heads of the ancient *Romans* [b]. The particular plants which I faw on my fhort walks were:

A *Cactus*, on a fteep hill. When this begins to ripen, I think it might be ufeful to ob-

---

[b] This is the *Alexandrian Laurel*.

serve with a good microscope whether the *pollen* goes down the whole *stylus* or not.

Musa Paradisiaca, which our *Swedish* sailors, together with the *Malacca* people, and the *Dutch*, call *Pisang*, the *English Plantain-tree*, and the *Portugueze Bananas*, bore larger fruit here than I have seen any where else; but a very lively imagination is required to see the figure of a cross in a plantain-tree.

Passiflora grew without the inclosures.

Some *Chesnut-trees* were preserved on account of their great age and fine shade.

The grapes of this island (which is scarce above ten *Swedish* miles [c] round) yield, as I was told, between 30,000 and 50,000 pipes of wine.

It would not be accurate to judge of any two nations by two of their cities alone; but since I have been at *Cadiz* and at *Funchal*, the difference to me seemed greater than could have been supposed, considering their religion, climate, neighbourhood, and language. A

[c] See note, vol. I. p. 2.

Sennor

Sennor at *Cadiz* is tawny: if he is not a monk, he wears a coat reaching to the feet, a linen cap, and a hat upon it; every thing is solemn: but in *Funchal* they had fine complexions, full faces, and did not affect so much gravity. Their dress was *French*, except the long black coats and surtouts.

THE *Portugueze* ladies are scarce ever in the streets; but as far as could be discerned when they opened their windows in order to see and to be seen, they displayed a fine fair complexion and lively eyes. I think I saw five at *Cadiz*, and these were thin and tawny. I observed that the Virgin *Mary* had correspondent airs, complexions, and shape in her pictures; and I judged from thence, that this was the taste of the nation with regard to beauty.

AFTER we had provided ourselves with wet and dry provisions, we set sail, the 11th of *May*, and made the best use of the uniform weather and wind that subsist between *Africa* and *America*, which forward the voyage to the *East Indies* with more expedition than that to *Hudson's Bay* and the *North Cape*; because the wind in those latitudes is more changeable.

South of *Brasil* we were forced to turn east. We had here, for some days together, a sea which would have frightened any one who was not used to it. I should not exaggerate more than some poets, if I say, that in one moment we were afraid of pulling down the Magellan clouds from the skies with our top-sails, and in another of crushing Neptune and the Tritons with the keel of our ship. It will easily be conceived by those who have been at sea, or know how the sailors measure the wind, with what force it blew, when I say that we ran eight knots with a reefed fore and main-sail, though the ship was deeply laden, and none of the best sailors.

CAPE *Pigeons* are a species of birds which are frequently seen in great numbers in these latitudes. Perhaps they get their name from flying in a circle, and the resemblance they bear to pigeons in regard to the size and wings. I could not examine them near enough, but took them to be *Procellaria Capensis*. Their colour is like damask, white and black; for which reason the *English* call them *Pintado-birds*, from the *Spanish*. When the wind was high, we sometimes saw the less dark-brown Storm-finch, which is called *Malefit* by the *Portugueze*,

tugueze, and *Petrel* or *Foul-weather-bird* in *English*; it seemed larger than that which I saw in 1748 in the *German Ocean* (*Procellaria æquinoctialis*).

BELOW the *Cape of Good Hope* the waves frequently dashed over our deck, as is common in these parts. Once they threw somewhat shining in the dark upon the deck; I ran to it, and caught up this seeming curiosity; but upon a closer examination, found it was only a little crab.

LETTER II.

BETWEEN *Africa* and *Madagascar* we found an *animalcule* in the water, which, whilst living in that element, resembled a worm; but when it was taken out and laid on a plate with water, all its articulations came asunder, and each moved by itself. We likewise caught a *By-the-wind-sailor* [d] (*Holothuria physalis*). Besides this, we likewise took an unusual sea animal of a slimy substance, which is difficult to describe, of which Mr. *Braad* has probably sent you a drawing.

We had already seen *Madagascar*, *Massota*, *Mobilla*, and the high *Comaro*, not without a longing desire of getting on shore; when we arrived in the *North-bay of St. Joanna*, on the 16th of *August*.

This country seems to be one of the most agreeable on the whole earth: and not only myself, but likewise far more experienced

---

[d] This is the name which the *Swedes* give to this kind of *Holothuria*. F.

travellers are of this opinion. The island is hilly and uneven; but this inequality only adds to its beauty, since both the little hills and steep mountains are covered with verdure. Cocoa-nuts, plaintain-trees, pine-apples, pomegranates, papayas, and other fruits, are in great plenty here. Oxen with humps on the fore-part of their backs, goats with pendent ears, common and *Guinea* hens, are sold at very reasonable prices.

THE inhabitants are *Mahometans*, and are descended from the *African Arabians*; but they are very civil, and more honest than any one could expect. As some of our people could speak *English*, they received us with their usual compliment: "*Englishmen*, come; all of " one brother, come." They are very different in colour. The chief officer in the village where we landed was almost quite black, but his nephew was only somewhat tawny: and the same difference is to be met with among the rest. Their hair curls (as the negroes) like wool, and will hardly become straight by cutting. They were but poorly dressed: a turban was very rare among them; and a great many could hardly afford to cover what ought to be covered.

WE here caught an animal (*Lemur catta* Linn. or *Macauco* of *Edwards*) whose colour was reddish, but its *back* of a greyish-brown: about the *ears* it looked like a fox: the *tail* was grey, with black rings, about one third part longer than the body, and is set an end by the animal like that of a squirrel; but has shorter hair: the *snout* was pointed. (The reason why I give this description, though so incomplete, is, because I fear that some might mistake it for a species of ape, to which the feet would lead one: for it has five flat round nails, but the thumb on the hind-feet is very large, and the first finger had a tapering nail [e]). The *teeth* were, as far as I could see, not like those of monkies; for I observed no canine ones: and when there was more than one serrated primary tooth in the upper-jaw, there were at least five little ones. Thus far I proceeded in my observations when it bit me. I was not present when it died and was thrown over-board. In curiosity and restlessness it was like a monkey; but it was more shy, not so

---

[e] I think it hath not been observed that the second toe of the hind-foot of *Lemur catta* has a bird's claw. This is perhaps a new species, *Linn.*

docile,

docile, nor so unseasonably officious. It lives in *Madagascar* and *Mauritius*. I might have had opportunity on this voyage of examining several more exactly; but they cannot be procured without paying for them.

THE most nauseous and troublesome animals are the lizards, which are, without any exaggeration, innumerable, and much more frequent than in *Madeira*: in one cocoa-tree of twenty yards high you may see at least sixty of them. In some places I could not advance a step without stirring whole troops of them, which sculked under the fallen leaves.

THE boats in this country are commonly single trees made hollow, and round at the bottom; and they have two out-riggers, which, by means of a board pointed at both ends fastened to them, prevent them from oversetting.

THE 20th of *August*, being provided with meat and water, we continued our voyage without hindrance; except that we were under arms on account of some *Portugueze* vessels.

THE

THE 16th of *September* we anchored in the harbour of *Suratte*, about a *Swedish* mile from the shore, because the sands prevented our nearer approach. It was some time before the trade in *Swedish* cottons could be settled with the people of the country. But this was more the fault of the Christians than of the *Mahometans*. Perhaps the owners of the *Swedish* iron, which was already laid up in our neighbours storehouses, could not relish that which was just arrived, because it was carried on a *Swedish* keel. The old accusation of our being pirates, was too stale to make any impression on the nabob. The *Arabians* had applied this opprobrious appellation to the *Portuguese*, these made use of it against the *Dutch*, who it is said employed it against the *English*. After several efforts, the gentlemen and *Myne heeren* ᶠ at last respected his Majesty's pass, at least they left us quite at liberty.

THE sea runs commonly very high both in ebbing and flowing at this place, and is full of

---

ᶠ Mr. *Toreen* seems to mean the factors of the *English* and *Dutch East India* companies here; *Myne heeren* signifies Gentlemen in *Dutch*. F.

sea-

sea-worms, which not only keep above water, but likewise eat the wood of the anchor at the bottom of the sea; and if their piercers were also strong enough to penetrate the paper, pitch, and hair, which compose the sheathing on the outside of the ships, they would soon sink them.

The nearest land is every where very flat, and consists of alternate plains and woods. On the fields millet was commonly sown about this time. The cocoa-trees are almost sacred here; their juice is drawn off by tapping, and therefore they bear no fruit.

Banian-tree (*Ficus Indica*) is that peculiar tree which shoots new roots from its branches which bend down to the earth. It seems to have obtained this name, because these idolaters look upon it as sacred. Perhaps, without this providential care, this sort of trees might be entirely destroyed. I observed very attentively, but could not find the least remains of fruit, flowers, or roots. It seems to grow but slowly; and I think the high broad tree which serves as a sea mark on the harbour is very old. It would have been extremely hazardous at the time that we were here to have undertaken

taken botanical excursions; for the attacks of the *Marattoes* and other nations were to be feared even before the gates of *Suratte*. What I was able to snatch up there in other places, (as the dog does the water of the Nile) is undoubtedly by this time in your hands.

The magnificent tombs in the country built with domes (which manner of architecture the *Mahometans* greatly affect) did not seem so extraordinary, when one recollects that pride subsists even beyond this life. Some exceeding deep wells, which were dug at a great expence, and with a great deal of labour, and had very good walls about them, deserved much more to bear the name of those who had thus supplied the inhabitants with so necessary an element. The water was drawn out of them by a rope and wheel, worked by means of two oxen; being then poured into leathern bags, it is brought to town on buffaloes and sold there.

The soil is none of the best. The earth proper for vegetation composes but a thin stratum: below is very good potters clay, which is of good use to the inhabitants, who,

like

like other *Afiatick* nations, make much ufe of earthen ware.

After rowing or failing from the anchoring-place, about three *Swedifh* miles, you come on the river *Tapti* or *Tapta* to the city of *Suratte*. The thing that firft ftrikes the eye is a confiderable building, called the caftle. It has formerly had four baftions, one of which is tumbled down; and the bad wall which has been built inftead of it feems ready to follow its fate. It has a good number of cannons on feveral terraces; but their muzzles are dropping, and they are fo ill ranged that often an eighteen pounder ftands clofe by a fix pounder.

The caftle is the centre of a low wall, which makes almoft a femicircle, and has angular baftions, and a dry ditch, which includes the city. Thefe are again furrounded by the fuburbs, which have the fame kind of fortification, and are faid to contain above a hundred thoufand inhabitants.

The fearch at the gate for the firft time feemed fomewhat rigorous to us, becaufe the cuftom-houfe officer would know how much

money

money we had in our pockets: for I was told there is a tax *per cent.* on the import of money. We escaped this tax; however, I could not sufficiently wonder at such odd politics.

LETTER III.

THE streets of *Suratte* are irregular, and many fine buildings have been destroyed by fire, which, according to the *Mahometan* doctrine of predestination, it is in vain to withstand. Street-pavements are unusual here; and though the owners and tenants of houses every day sprinkle the street before their doors, yet the dust is frequently troublesome. But should the streets be paved it would be in vain, for the rain which sometimes continues for half a year together would tear every thing up, and wash the whole work away. The houses are tolerably well built of bricks, mixed with wooden beams, but without braces: in the inside they are plastered with a fine white cement, which renders them as smooth as if they had been rubbed with pumice-stone. I was told that the cement was made of pounded egg-shells, and the dregs of sugar. Captain *Shierman* related, that he and the other captives had been forced to pound lime mixed with sugar dregs for the pirate *Angria*, which was probably for this use. In the lower stories are no windows, and but few in the upper. In my opinion this is done merely through jealousy, and not out of any well-grounded fear of thieves; for he who steals five bottles full of rosewater is punished by the loss of both his hands, which punishment must probably deter from the commission of this crime.

I HAD little opportunity of seeing the dispositions of their houses, further than in the *Swedish* factory. This house was exactly quadrangular, and had some beds with flowers instead of a yard, in which a fine *Althæa frutex* (*Hibiscus Surattensis*) was in blossom towards the end of *January*. Round about it were stone walks of two steps high, and on the four sides as many halls, open towards the yard, with niches on the other three walls reaching from the roof within three feet of the floor. In the corners are bed chambers, or the kitchen. Those who live in the lowest story, have air-holes in the walls for their refreshment in the great heat. At the top is a terrace paved with stones, from which you have a fine prospect. Cisterns and artificial fountains are considered as the greatest luxury, partly on account of their refreshing coolness, and partly on account of the necessity of their ablutions.

The

The ſtair-caſes are narrow and the ſteps high; as for the reſt, the foundation is extremely expenſive. We had in our quarters two wells twenty-four feet deep, neither of which afforded water that was drinkable. Under the *Swediſh* latti or warehouſe was a tank [g], that was arched over.

Their architecture is neither borrowed from the *Greeks* nor *Italians*; yet there is taſte and an agreeable proportion in their columns. Some ornaments on the capital and pedeſtal do not ſeem to be in the right places; but they have ſuch confidence in their architecture, that they would make one believe that an whole building is ſupported by leaves or feathers. The *Indian* architects have proved by the tomb of baron *Rheède von Drakenſtein* [h], that a building may look majeſtic without being either of the Corinthian or Tuſcan order. Engliſhmen have ſuch funerals here as a prince would not be aſhamed of.

The inhabitants are for the moſt part of three caſts, of which the *Malabarian* heathens are the firſt, which are called *Gentives*, Gen-

[g] A reſervoir of water.
[h] This is the author of the celebrated book, *Hortus Indicus Malabaricus*. 12 vol. in folio.

toos, or *Gentiles*. These are the most ancient inhabitants of the country, and divide themselves, as is well known, into certain principal families, each of which has its peculiar trade. The *Bramins* and *Banians* religiously observe the law not to kill any thing which has life and sensation. I have seen them make the most moving petitions, in favour of loathsome vermin. The soldiers are not so tender, even towards their fellow creatures.

Though the *Gentoos* eat nothing but milk, butter, and vegetables, yet they are rather fat. I have seen *Bramins* and *Banians* with very prominent bellies. Their persons are of a middle size, upright, and of an easy carriage; they have regular features, and an agreeable air, but are tawny.

Their women are generally very little, thick-set, and brown; I was told they marry early, but soon grow old. Their dress is somewhat singular: besides that their ears are quite full of rings, they have a ring with a ruby or garnet and two pearls in their left nostrils: a great number of rings are worn on the arms, both above and below the elbow; they have great silver fetters above the feet; and almost on every toe a ring of the fame metal. Their half-jacket covers no more than the breaſt; to conceal the lower parts, they tie a piece of ſtuff (generally red-ſtriped) about their middle, turn the two ends through between their legs, and faſten them before. On the head they have a cloth of the fame ſtuff, which goes over the left and under the right arm, and is faſtened to the girdle. All the reſt is naked. They go ſo upright, that even a dancing maſter could not give them a better air. Perhaps this erect carriage is occaſioned by their carrying water every day from the river, on their heads. A *Gentoo* woman can carry three pots one above another, without holding them with her hands, go backwards and forwards with them, turn about, ſtand and hold converſation, &c. Whether the ladies of quality and the rich are obliged to fetch their own water, I am not certain; however I have ſeen ſome coming with their pots, for the value of whoſe rings many a good farm might have been bought in our country. Their virtue is ſuſpected by many, becauſe all the dancing women of the *Mogul* empire are taken out of this nation.

I could not ſee their pagoda and religious ceremonies, but I obſerved their morning prayer in the river. They were obliged to wash themselves before this ceremony, clean their mouths, and with their faces towards the sun say a prayer. They use rosaries for this purpose, as is usual in all countries where it is laid down for a principle of religion, that the repetition of a certain number of prayers will atone for any offence. The *Gentoos* say their prayers on their fingers, beginning at the most extreme joint of the little finger, and counting on downwards; when they have gone over all the fingers in this manner, they lay both their hands flat together, bow before the sun, and then get up and are painted by a *Bramin*.

THE *Bramins* themselves have some cross strokes of ashes over the forehead, with which they sometimes paint their whole body. The *Banians* have generally a red spot just above the nose, about the size of a silver two-pence, from which two yellow strokes run down, and on each flap of the ear is a yellow spot.

WHEN they carry their dead, they run in full career, and cry *Beyram Rambolu*, which, as I have been told, signifies, *My brethren, call upon Rama*. The corpses are burnt by the river side without the city, but the widow is not

obliged

obliged to follow her husband into the fire. If we consider the great number of corpses that are burnt, it must necessarily follow that many thousand of *Gentoos* live in *Suratte*. They have likewise *Santons*, or living saints, who distinguish themselves from the multitude, and endeavour to make themselves pleasing to *Ram* and his brothers, by their ridiculous behaviour. Those fellows which *Bernier* has described and painted in all sorts of constrained postures, I have not seen; but you frequently meet with some who walk about more than half naked, and twist their long hair about their head in form of a turban, which must be very troublesome in this country. I once saw a novice of this order, begging in a very singular way. He placed himself before a shop, where he did nothing but stamp against the ground, and after he had very patiently lifted up and set down one foot after another, he quietly devoured the victuals he had received. It is peculiar that the hair of these fellows grows pale and turns straw-coloured; but I believe that they make it so by art; for those *Mahometan Santons* who do not cut their hair, preserve their black complexions, and have besides the advantage that they look like devils of the first order, for their hair stands an end like a juniper a juniper bush on their heads. It is said the *Bramins* have many curious secrets; especially it is here looked upon as almost certain, that the renowned *Pedra de Cobra* is a composition known alone to them: and it may be that the *Pedra de Goa* or *Gaspar Antonio*, and *Pedra de Porco* or swine, must come from the same hands. If their ceremonies are not sufficient to maintain a whole cast or tribe, they seek their livelihood another way. For this reason *Bramins* sometimes enter into the service of rich *Banians*: yet they keep their privilege; for the master is not allowed to touch the rice which his servant is to eat, because the latter would become impure by it.

LETTER

LETTER IV.

THE *Parthians* or *Perfees* (who are descended from the ancient *Perfians*) are the second nation which lives here. They have been driven out of *Perfia* long since, according to *Hamilton's* new account of *East India*. They adore the fire, the sun, the moon, and the stars. A *Persee* cannot be persuaded to put out a candle any other way than by blowing. I observed once a little boy, who sate a great while mumbling I know not what over a burning candle-snuff, which was purposely thrown on the ground: he snapt his fingers, and continued this till the last spark was extinguished. They ought not to be called *Gafres*, because *Gaur*, *Gause*, *Guebre*, or *Cafre*, signifies an heretic, unbeliever, or heathen. They have the whitest skins of any among the natives; are lively, indefatigable, and are generally employed in the meanest offices by the *Europeans*, induced perhaps to undertake them through necessity; for they are more oppressed than the *Gentoos*, get into no places of trust, and have not the resources which avail the *Banians*, namely, a thorough experience in a thousand sorts of little arts. Their women have been found to be less corrupted than most others in *India*.

In the state they are in, one would little expect divisions among them in religious matters. Nevertheless there was one of them who had read more than the others, and had found out that they did not celebrate the new year at the due time. He got a number of followers, but met with a great deal of vexation from the opposite party. And this is nothing uncommon; for formerly the disciples of *Thomas Aquinas* and of *Duns Scotus* could hardly ever part without cuffing and boxing. There was a time when a *Jew* was preferred to an *Arminian*; and a *Siamese* to a *Jansenist:* some reverend fathers will overlook many failings in a *Chinese*, and yet will excommunicate any one who differs from them in opinion, with regard to the conception of the *Virgin Mary*.

The third cast of people who frequent *Suratte* are the *Mahometans*, or rather, as the sailors call them, *Moors*, which may be contracted from *Mogors*, or *Persians*. Their colour is a medium between the other two. Their

Their religion is the reigning one, especially that sect which honors *Omar*. But *Ali* cannot be without a great many followers here; for at a procession which was undertaken the 26th of *November*, in honour of the two last *Persian Imams*, I think I saw at least two thousand men. At this ceremony a great many faquirs or begging friars were present, dressed in white jackets, to which were sewed several rags of different colors, and a cap resembling a sugar loaf. The *Dervises* generally officiated in the mosques and on other occasions. I observed a certain *Dervise* who was exceedingly well acquainted with the ceremonial part, and who was ordered to undertake a pilgrimage to the graves of the deceased *Imams*. He sauntered all the way along, and had besides his disciples several others about him, who beat a sort of drum, and sung *la allah*, &c. along with it. I saw a *Santon* who seemed to deserve a good thrashing for his sanctity. He did penance by going about the streets stark naked. He was by no means shunned; but on the contrary had always a reverend *Mahometan* with him, who received the alms and kept them for him.

BESIDES the aforementioned clothes of the *Bramins* and *Gentoo* women, they are almost all of them dressed in white cotton about the body. The parts of their dress are a pair of slippers which are pulled off at the door; a pair of trowsers; a short shirt which is open before, and above the breeches; and over this a coat reaching to the feet, which fits close to the body, and has folds below like a petticoat; it has long sleeves, which fold over the hands. The *Mohammedans* and *Heathens* observe this difference, that the former tie the fore part of their coat below the right, and the latter below the left arm. They tie a girdle about their waists of the same stuff of which the coat is made, or sometimes of richer; and in it they have a precious knife, or, according to the difference of customs, a dagger. The *Persees* have a string below the girdle, which seems to be a part of their religion; for at *Dombes* (a village near *Suratte*) I saw a *Persee*, who, before he saluted his guests, measured his forehead with this string, and made a bow to the moon.

THE turban is of all colours; the green here denotes nothing extraordinary in the rank of
the

the rank of the wearer. A turban of *Suratte* is eafily diftinguifhed from the *Perfian* and *Arabian*, for though it requires above thirty yards of cloth, it fits very neatly on the head, except a great bolfter which comes juft over the right eye.

The drefs of the women who are feen in the ftreets differs from the drefs of the men in regard to the coats, which are open before, and cannot be thrown back to the other fide; and their breeches reach down to the very feet. They only throw a loofe cloth over the head and fhoulders. Poor people of both fexes wear both fhorter and fcantier clothes.

Both fexes falute in the fame manner, namely, they lay the hand on the forehead or on the head. Some fay *Salam* or *Sala Maleck* with it. If they intend to exprefs fubmiffion, they firft lay their hand on the ground or floor, and then on the left breaft, and at laft on the head. On the aforementioned feftival in honor of the *Perfian* martyrs, I faw another method of faluting their friends; they firft put our heads on their left fhoulder, then on the right, and then again on the left;

left; then we placed their hands between ours, and put them at laſt to our foreheads.

The *Gentoos* make uſe of the *Malabaric* language; the *Moors* ſpeak a dialect of the *Arabick*, which the *Perſees* muſt learn; for which reaſon there are but few who know the language of their anceſtors. As for other people, ſome broken *Portugueze* is ſufficient in all the trading towns of the ſouthern *Aſia*. They eat ſitting on a mat, ſpread on the floor; and lay the table-cloth on the ſame place. Rice ſerves them inſtead of bread, and is either boiled in pots, or kneaded and baked on plates, like the thin bread uſual in *Bahus Lan* [1]. I am unacquainted with the drink made uſe of by the rich; but the common people ſatisfy their thirſt with water; if they will have any thing ſtronger, they procure toddy (or the juice drawn out of the cocoa-tree) at a very conſiderable price. Beſides this, according to the account of *Bonaventura*, the roots of millet will likewiſe intoxicate. A ſingular ſcruple ſometimes hinders theſe people from eating with others, out of the ſame diſh. A *Mahometan* can make a bargain of a hundred

---

[1] A province in *Norway* on the *Skaggerac*. F.

thouſand

thousand rupees with a *Banian*; yet he cannot eat with him, nor go home with him. All the vessels which a *Bramin* has in his kitchen are sacred, and must not be touched by any one that does not belong to that cast. An old complaisant *Persee* woman, who gave us some milk as we travelled by, would not let her bottle come within a quarter of a yard of our glass.

They have flesh in plenty, but such probably as is not very wholesome, especially to those who come on shore from long sea voyages; for, if they indulge their appetites, they are subject to vomitings and diarrhœas, and are in danger of losing their lives. It is probable that *Brama*, or whoever at first gave laws to the *Gentoos*, had discovered that these meats were very unwholesome to the *Malabarians*. *Mahomet* found his account in the frequent ablutions, which in some cases are indispensably necessary, in order to prevent the chopping and parching of the skin, and perhaps worse accidents. If you go in the morning into the suburbs and lanes, you very soon see how busy these people are in washing the children with the left hand.

BESIDES

BESIDES the aforementioned difeafe, fevers frequently attack *Europeans*. The *French* at firft loft a great many men by this diforder, and were at laft (according to their own account) obliged to have recourfe to the phyficians of this country, who reject the ufe of bleeding and of tamarinds in agues. Tamarinds are not half fo much in ufe in *Eaft India* as in *Europe*. The *red-dog* is a difeafe which afflicts almoft all foreigners in hot countries, efpecially if they refide near the fhore, at the time when it is hotteft. This diftemper difcovers itfelf by red fpots which look like meafles, itch and prickle, and then become little bladders, which, when they vanifh, take the fkin away along with them.

THE friction ufed among the ancients feems to have been very rational. A perfon of fome confequence in *Suratte* is always rubbed at night by his fervants, as an expedient of great ufe to promote the circulation of the blood.

THEIR mufic is but very mean. *Italian* pieces you are fure not to hear of in this country; but inftead of it, the noife of brafenbafons and little drums with one or two bottoms.

toms. Their wind inftruments are a fort of ftraight trumpets, four or five *Swedifh* ells long, which make a bleating found. Sometimes they make ufe of a great horn in form of an S, which is however only played upon when the nabob or fome other man of quality is coming. The reveille was played upon a flagelet from the caftle. Guittars and fiddles were the inftruments of beggars, who begged in verfe, and accompanied them with vocal mufic. A war-like mufic is generally in ufe among the fouthern *Afiaticks*, and this they want very much; for fofter tunes would make them more effeminate. Perhaps the *Spartans* had more than meer cuftom in view when they broke a ftring of the lyre which was above the ufual number.

THEIR jugglers are not to be compared with thofe of *China*, except that they can fafcinate in fuch a manner the *Cobra de Capello* (*Coluber Naja* Linn.) as to make it dance [k]. When the *Moors* or other people have a mind to divert themfelves according to the cuftom

[k] *Kempferi Amœn. Exotic.* Fafcic. III. Obf. ix. p. 565—573, gives the moft credible and curious account of thefe tricks with the *Cobra de Capello*. F.

of

of the country, they get a band of dancing women (for such is their name though they stand still for the greatest part), who sing amorous songs, with all sorts of wanton gestures. Such a diversion is often very troublesome to the neighbourhood, because the instruments generally used at it will allow of no rest all the night.

I HAD seen no blue eyes either in the southern parts of *Europe*, or in *Asia*, till I found an *Arabian* at *Suratte* whose irides were not the common colour. I was told, that they were not esteemed in seraglios, perhaps because they do not sparkle so well; but dark eyes seldom look serious.

THE arms of the *Moors* consist of muskets with matches, bows, sabres, and daggers, the latter of which have a singular shape: for the handle consists of two pieces of iron, which are so far distant as easily to afford room for the hand to take hold of two cross iron bars. The breadth of the blade, near the handle, is three fingers, or about two inches three-quarters, and its length one quarter and half a quarter, or thirteen inches and a half. They like glittering arms and silver hilted sabres.

Besides

Besides this, they have a round hollow shield of buffalo skin, a yard in diameter. The *pions*, or the people which go before men of rank in this country both for parade and security, carry their swords drawn, and their shields on the left arm.

THE advantageous situation of *Suratte* for trade appears from a map. The *Arabian* merchandize can here be very conveniently bartered against the *Indian* and *Chinese* manufactured goods. But it is unlucky that the government is not stable: the court is inactive at *Delhi*, while the governors at *Suratte* fight with each other.

THE continual rains from *May* to *September* frequently change the sands, and the gulph is as full of pirates as the *Baltick Sea* was in the time of the *Wickinger*. These three obstructions, together with some others, have induced some *Europeans* to have entertained sanguine hopes of getting this trade to themselves; which would not be difficult, if there was toleration in religious matters, if the government was less despotic, and the pirates were opposed with more vigor, who, it is said, have been purposely neglected by the powers which

which wanted to be sovereign in the eastern and western oceans. But, notwithstanding this, many thousand rupees pass through the hands of the merchants for *Persian* and *Chinese* silks, and white striped checkered cottons; likewise for camboya, agates, and *Ceylon* stones, which are always soft; also for diamonds from *Vija Poor* and *Golconda*, and for many other goods. The *Moors* get a considerable part of the profit, because they enjoy the greatest protection from the government; but the *Banians* are the most cunning merchants in all the world, which is nothing extraordinary, since they have for a long space of time improved and derived down their skill in mercantile affairs from father to son. If what I have been told is true, they must certainly be enormous usurers: for they are said to take one rupee interest per month for nine rupees. Hence it is certainly not to be wondered at that *Shah Abbas* should expell them out of *Ispahan*, in order to admit a far more honest people, namely, the *Armenians*. It is pretty plain that the merchants have opportunities of gaining considerable fortunes here, when one of them had nineteen ships at sea on his own account: but it was looked upon by the *Mahometans* as a clear proof of

the

the invincible power of fate, that he could never get to the twentieth. He is said to have been poffeffed of a whole *arip*, that is, 1000 millions of rupees; which is an incredible fum, when you obferve that the invafion of the *Mogul's* empire by *Nadir Shah* did not coft more, when every thing which can be eftimated by money was taken into the account.

OF the weights here ufual, a *candee*, or *candy*, is twenty *maunds*, and a *maund* is forty *feer* [l] : a *feer* is little different from a *Swedifh* grocery pound. Their lefs weights I could not get an exact knowledge of, but gold and filver they weigh by the feeds of the *Abrus precatorius* [m], becaufe they are light, hard, and durable. Their moft ufual coin is the *rupee*, which weighs about twenty-one pennyweights; and it is faid, its filver is finer than that of the *piaftres*, on which account the *Chinefe* take them fooner than *piaftres* [n]. A

[l] One *maund* is thirty-feven pounds and a half, and one *candy* is fix hundred wt. two-thirds. See *Rolt's* Dictionary, under the article of weight. F.

[m] Formerly a *Glycine*, but fince changed by *Linnæus* in *Ed.* 12th of his *Syftema Naturæ*. F.

[n] A *rupee* is about 2s 6d fterling. F.

rupee is valued at forty-eight *poise* or *pice*, and a *poise* at forty-eight *almonds*. The coining is performed with an hammer, which is directed by the hand. This is the reason that the *rupees* sometimes crack, which makes them found ill in the hand of a banker, and lowers their value. There is a species of *rupees* which has the honour of being mentioned by our connoisseurs in coins: but what I have read in their books, was different from the account which was given me in the *Indies*. If it is right, it is as follows: " *Nour Mahal*, " the wife of an officer, was once undesignedly " seen by the Great Mogol *Jehan Ghir*, who, " since he could not come at her by any other " means, made away with her husband, and, " after many solicitations, at last prevailed " upon the deeply-afflicted widow to accept " of his own bed. Her step-children felt " how well this beautiful lady was skilled in " politics. *Jehan Ghir* changed her name, " and instead of *Nour Mehal* (Light of the " Ladies), called her *Nour Jehan* (the Light " of the World, or of *Jehan*). He likewise " once gave her the liberty of having rupees " coined under her name; and added that " compliment to it that she might stamp the " elve heavenly signs on them." These

coins

coins are already scarce in *Indoſtan*: and the reaſon, as I was told, is, becauſe the *Mooriſh* ladies uſe them for necklaces; which is very probable, conſidering the great confidence the *Mahometans* repoſe in faſcination, amulets, the influence of the ſtars, taliſmans, &c. The rupees are current along all the coaſt of *Aſia*, but under different values. Thus a *Bombay* or *Pondicherry* rupee loſes four *per cent.* in *Suratte*; and on the other hand, a *Suratte* rupee loſes at *Mahee*. The orders of the magiſtrates ſeem to be inſufficient to ſettle this difference, for the *Banian* will give a greater value than perhaps would be ſettled by regulation, if from the pureneſs of the ſilver he finds he can be a gainer. We new-comers were not the only ones who ſuffered inconvenience from the change of value, but even thoſe who had already made a ſtay of ſome years here were not free from it. But beſides this four *per cent.* you likewiſe loſe two, three, up to four *per cent.* according to the ſum, if you give money to your ſervant to barter it, or buy ſomething with it. This he does not take clandeſtinely, but looks upon it as his perquiſite, which he thinks the buyer or ſeller muſt pay him without making any difficulties.

THERE are many forts of animals in this country, but this dry foil cannot fupport them in great numbers. The nabob had a very large and fierce tiger in a cage. In another place I faw a lefs one, marked with ftripes acrofs; but its fnout, gait, and eyes, gave him the appearance of a wolf. If you fleep in a farmer's room at night, it is not uncommon to hear the howling of the jackcall [*] (*Canis aureus* Linn.) round the houfe. The nabob had likewife fome elephants in his poffeffion, which are only made ufe of when he and his family have a mind to fhew themfelves on fome feftival. During our ftay we faw the gratitude of an elephant: a foldier in the *Dutch* fervice ufed to go into the governor's ftables, and to feed an old elephant with the rice which he had about him; he once came fo drunk to him that he tumbled down under the animal, and fell afleep between its feet; but the elephant guarded him fo carefully, that fcarce a fly dared to come near him.

HORSES are very rare and valuable animals in *Indoftan*. The beft horfes are brought

[*] For jackcall fee *Haffelquift's Travels.*

over

over sea from *Arabia*, where the *Arabians* sometimes esteem them above their wives and children I have been told, that sometimes they pay as much for the genealogy of a horse as for the horse itself.

We did not see many camels. The goats are of that kind which have pendent ears. The oxen have a hump on the back like those at *Madagascar*, *Joanna*, and as far as the Straits of *Malacca*. The sheep have bent snouts and pendent ears, their wool is more coarse and stiff than the goats hair, which plainly convinced me that a warm climate does not always produce fine and soft wool. Higher up in the country *Gazells* are to be met with: you must already have seen, Sir, that their horns have rings all the way, and are screw-shaped, by the offensive and defensive arms which I bought of a *Patan*, and which M. *Lagerstrom* undoubtedly hath sent you before this time.

Some *Germans* call the turkeys [p] *Calcutta* hens; for this reason I looked about for them here, and only found them in one place, and

---

[p] Turkies are altogether *American*.

to the best of my remembrance I was told that they were foreign in this country.

GREEN parrots with long tails (*Psittacus articularius*) are very numerous here. Their sagacity in knowing where to find a breakfast is remarkable: for the house of the *Shafdaar Khan* was built in such a manner, that through some holes contrived for that purpose the birds could get to the rice which was refused to the poor inhabitants.

THEY put oxen before their waggons and carts, and take as much care of them as a hackney-coachman of his horses. Their excrements are gathered, mixed with straw, and used as fuel; the ashes of it make the paint which the *Bramins* use. They want no whip to drive them, but in the *Portugueze* manner a stick with a spike at its end. Their carts are of a peculiar construction: the axle-tree is made of iron, and scarcely of the thickness of the last joint of the little finger; it is fastened to the axle-tree of the wheels: the wheel moves between an upright standing pole and two linch-pins, which, together with an arch, carry the *bamboo* net or cover on which one sits; this is either with or without curtains,

curtains. The *bamboo* sticks bend upwards near the thill, and make a seat for the driver, on which he rides as on a saddle. This is the carriage of the common people. The *Armenians* and *Europeans* rode in coaches, but they were of such a construction as I suppose might have been in fashion in the year 1500.

THE greater nobility are carried in a *palekee*, which looks very like a hammock fastened to a crooked pole. When the ladies are carried, they are shut up in a box twisted of *bamboo*, which is afterwards covered at the top with double cloths. On each side goes a stout black eunuch, with a drawn sabre in his hand.

THOUGH dogs are held in abomination by the *Mahometans*, yet the streets are full of them. The *Persees* have a certain veneration for them; and I was told, that in a famine which happened some years ago, alms were given to the dogs.

THE houses are not so infested with lizards here as in other parts of *East India*; but even the stone walls in the uppermost stories are not free from a sort of little brown ants. The *Gentoos*
take

take great care not to kill any one, and feed them with powder sugar, which they throw on the floor.

I was told, that the heat was still greater at *Gamron* and *Baſſora* than at *Suratte:* and if this is true, then it muſt be exceſſive; and I do not wonder that the *Dutch* have given up *Gamron*. Even in *October* the *Swediſh* thermometer roſe thirty-ſeven degrees. A *Florentine* thermometer was at half an hour paſt five o'clock in the morning at thirty-ſeven degrees, and in the afternoon it roſe to ſeventy-five degrees. Father *Bonaventura* has obſerved that the cold is greater three days before and three days after the new moon. It is ſomewhat ſingular, that notwithſtanding this place is but juſt north of the æquator, the time between the months of *May* and *September* ſhould be called winter, and other months ſummer, only becauſe it rains during the former.

The Chriſtians in *Suratte* are *Armenians*, of which the greateſt part were natives of *Julfa*, and have their *Archimandrite* here. They have ſeveral books in their language, printed at *Amſterdam*. They are known in trade on

account

account of their induſtry and cunning, and live very well on their profits. It is here neceſſary that a merchant ſhould cut a great figure, ſome of them dreſs quite in the *Mooriſh* faſhion, and wear a turban; others a callot and a velvet cap, with four prominent parts; the brim is two inches high, open behind and before. They have commonly their ſhroud from the ſepulchre of CHRIST ready at hand q.

THE *Portugueze* are the only Roman catholics who live here. It is remarkable, however, that, notwithſtanding the ſeverity of the *Portugueze* inquiſition againſt the *Jews*, the *Jew Kohen* has the management of the *Portugueze* affairs at *Suratte*.

THE *French* ſeem to endeavour to re-eſtabliſh their declining trade. Three *French* capuchin friars hired a houſe, and were forced to get their bread as well as they could. Their ſuperior father *Bonaventura* ſometimes gained ſome ſmall benefactions to the convent by his knowledge of medicine, though he was obliged to give many plaſters away gratis.

q A conſecrated ſhirt perhaps from the ſepulchre at *Jeruſalem*.

Theſe

These preachers of the gospel are obliged, by the commands of their despotic superiors, to continue here during their whole life.

The *Dutch* have a director, with a council and officers, as is usual with them in *East India*.

The chief factory of the *English* in these parts is *Bombay*; however, they have likewise a factory at *Suratte*, with the necessary officers. All the factories belonging to the *English* in the *East Indies* have chaplains.

Here are likewise *Jews* possessed of considerable wealth. One, by name *Moses Tobias*, was distinguished on account of his liberality towards people of all religions: he is said to have commonly distributed in charity forty rupees *per* month. A *cakan*, or scribe, told us, that the long-sought-for sceptre of *Juda* could still be found; and that he had certain accounts of a great number of *Jews* in *Africa*, to the west of *Abyssinia*, who still were subject to their own magistrates.

There is an admiral at *Suratte*, but he has the misfortune of having no ships under his command.

command. The *English* and the *Dutch* exercife the privileges of admiralty in the harbour, fo that not a fingle floop can get up to the town without their permiffion. Their greateft merchant fhips are built after the *European* manner. It is remarkable, that the older a fhip is, the eafier it procures a cargoe, becaufe it is thought to be lucky. The fhips which they make ufe of againft their enemies are called *goerabbs* by the *Dutch*, and *grabbs* by the *English*, have two or three mafts, and are built like our fhips, with the fame fort of rigging, only their prows are low and fharp as in gallies, that they may not only place fome cannons in them, but likewife, in cafe of emergency, fix a couple of oars, to pufh the grabb on in a calm. *Gallivates* are lefs, and are ufed, like the grabbs, in piracies and for trade. They have feldom more than one maft, and incline forwards fixteen or eighteen degrees: they have a fail, which at a certain diftance looks triangular, though it has four corners. The boats which are called *hurry* have the fame fails. The fhip floops, which are worked on with faddles, are like the preceding, fomewhat pointed before, and narrow behind. The planks of all thefe veffels are made fo oblique, that they lie one above another:

other; they are fastened with nails. Instead of tow and tar, they use cotton and a sort of thick oil, which is said to make them so tight that they have less occasion to use the pump than the *Europeans*. In the timber which they use to build ships of, iron does not rust so much as in oak; for which reason they are forced to clench the nails well on the inside, and therefore our short thick nails are of no use.

This nation has a peculiar agility in swimming; I saw one swim a good way, and hold above water eight pound weight in his hand. Practice does much towards this feat; but perhaps there is a sleight in it, for they only make use of the right arm and left foot, and then the left arm and right foot alternately. During the time of our stay here we were not attacked by pirates. On the 20th of *October* a pirate, who was called *Budgero*, anchored in the harbour accompanied by about two hundred great and small vessels, which made a good appearance at a distance; on their approaching and anchoring in part between us and the shore, we prepared every thing in order to receive them. However, they did not offer us the least insult, but after a day or two went their way

way and left us alone. Yet it muft not be fuppofed that they are always fo civil. In September fome *Gallivates* failed out of the port, having an *Englifh* fhip for their convoy. It was attacked before our eyes, and in the face of the other *Englifh* fhips, by eight or nine piratical *Gallivates* which kept up a continual fire for a couple of hours, without any body being able to give affiftance, on account of the tide. The end of this was, that the pirates fucceeded in taking two or three of the other *Gallivates*; upon which they left the *Englifh* fhip to purfue her voyage without any farther moleftation.

I AM unwilling to omit one or two accounts belonging to political intelligence, though I cannot be anfwerable for their truth. Towards the end of *April*, 1748, died the great *Mogol Mahomed*, of the venereal difeafe according to the Jefuit *Tiefenthaler's* account. His only fon *Achmed*, by a concubine, fucceeded him, and was then on his march returning from *Seranda*, where he had defeated the army of the *Patans*, who had undertaken an irruption into the empire from the mountains of *Kandahar*. Of the ftate of the *Perfian* empire, I had the following account. *Nadir Shah*

Shah put out his eldest son's eyes, from suspicion, and appointed his other son his successor. But after *Nadir Shah* was murdered on a hunting match, all his family were killed by his nephew called *Adel Shah*, only excepting *Sha Rock Shah* [r], who was *Nadir Shah's* grandson, and the son of the daughter of *Shah Houssain*. This *Adel Shah* is said to have been very mild towards his subjects, especially towards those who lived about *Ispahan*; for he not only freed them from paying any thing to the king for five years, but also gave them money to enable them to cultivate the soil. When he was visited by the law of retaliation, *Sha Rock Shah* took possession of *Kharazan*, and had, as I was told, the greatest part of the riches of *Nadir Shah* in his hands: *Solyman Shah*, who was formerly *Sha Rock's* servant, took possession of *Ispahan*, and *Cely Mehemet Shah* took *Tauris*; the undertaking of prince *Heraclius* we first learnt at *Canton*, where the *Armenians* told it with great expressions of joy.

We weighed anchor the 1st of *March*, 1751, after a stay of five months and a half;

---

[r] Mr. *Toreen* seems to be mistaken here, since there is a repetition of the word *Shah* in *Sha Rock Sha*. F.

during

during all which time I had no opportunity of being on shore more than twenty-three days. We sailed to *Mangulor* with land and sea winds, successively changing, and anchored there the 12th of the same month, with the same difficulty as at *Suratte*. After this, we did not anchor before we came to *Canton*. It would be but a small expence to make a good and convenient haven, behind a narrow inlet which would contain a whole fleet.

The town of *Mangulor* is open and large; and contains many gardens. The houses are low, and generally made of a reddish tophaceous stone, which, as I was told, is soft under ground and easily worked, but grows hard in the air.

The tiles are shaped as those at *Suratte* and *Cadiz*. The brickmaker forms a hollow cylinder about twelve inches long, and four in diameter; this is cut into two equal parts lengthways, and burnt in little kilns. They tile here by single rows, and when one row of tiles is laid so that the concave part comes uppermost, the next is inverted, and so covers the ridges. There is a constant saltness in the earth, both here and in *Suratte,* which eats away the lime near the ground.

I saw two waggons, which seemed to be intended to be carried about in a religious proceffion, befides a reprefentation of a white elephant, which was placed on wheels, as I fuppofe for the fame purpofe. The wheels of the waggon were of one piece of wood, three feet in diameter, and of a proportionable thicknefs; thus they are more than fufficient to crufh the poor people who expect to gain eternal happinefs under the facred wheels.

The inhabitants are heathens: they drefs like thofe at *Suratte,* except that the cottons with red ftripes are more in ufe here, and that they go barefooted, or bind a wooden fole under their feet like the friars of the order of *St. Francis.* When they ride on horfeback, they only put their great toes into the ftirrups.

Banian trees (*Ficus Indica*) are very numerous and large: they are taken great care of. Round about this place are great and open woods; but I was told, that if I entered them

them I should be lost, because they were the habitations of many fierce tigers.

I could only be twelve hours on shore. The 17th of *March* we left this place, and having nothing to do at *Cananor*, we sailed to *Mahie*, where we stopped the 19th of the same month.

This town or plantation belongs to the *French E. I.* company. It is near the shore, and the mouth of the river is so covered with a ridge of rocks above the water, that a stranger cannot get up with a boat. Several redoubts with high ramparts serve as a defence, which in this country are esteemed a considerable fortification. At the top of one of the redoubts, blocks of wood were erected, which at a distance looked like men. I forgot to enquire into their use, but they seemed to me very proper to fill the holes when the garrison was forced to be on the ramparts. This would be an invention, which in some cases might be as useful as blocks of wood instead of cannons. I have often heard that wooden heads are placed in the advanced stations; but that they are likewise used as blind works in sieges, I never knew yet.

The sun was exactly vertical to us; the thunder was heard to make an exceeding great noise, especially on the *Cardomom* mountain: the heat was so intolerable, that even the natives were forced to keep in during the middle of the day. The poison of snakes and of other venomous animals seems to be more fatal in hot climates than in cold; if the accounts we have in *Sweden* of the viper's bite, and in *East India* of the scorpion's sting, are true. The *French* therefore quite dissuaded me from going into the woods. Nor could I have made any useful observations there; for the person that undertakes to amend and explain the *Hortus Malabaricus* ought to be master of the *Portugueze* and *Malabaric* names, which Baron *Rhede* has confounded; and the time of one's stay here ought to be the whole rainy season; because at other times the burnt-up *Malabaric* soil is unable to produce either flowers or fruits; but this season is very dangerous for ships on account of the hurricanes.

It is impossible to examine a plant in such a scorching heat, without one knows all its characteristics as it were by heart: for while you hold it between the fingers for a moment

or

or two, it withers and becomes unfit for preſervation. I learnt this on my former voyage by very irkſome experience: and therefore, when I could not get ſeveral ſpecimens of the ſame plant, it ſeemed beſt to me to keep ſingle ones for our maſter. I here ſaw the thick bamboo in one place. Its height was ſcarce four fathoms, its ſtem, which is the thickneſs of a hand's breadth, is naked, and has only ſome digitated leaves at the top. Its numerous ears, which came out of their ſpathas on the middle of the ſtem, were then in bud. The other ſpecies of bamboo, grow to the height of ſix or ſeven fathoms, but they are not above an inch thick. They have branches on the ſtem, and thoſe have again pinnated leaves.

I HAD here an opportunity of admiring an elephant. Its maſter had let it for a certain ſum per day; its employment was to carry timber for building, out of the river, which buſineſs it diſpatched very handily under the command of a boy, and afterwards laid each piece one upon another in ſuch good order, that no man could have done it better.

If all the *Malabaric* oxen are like those which we got, I do not wonder, that those heathens will not eat their flesh. The mere description of them would make the most hungry lose their appetites. If we must derive the badness of their flesh from the *oestrus* [s], then either the cause or the effect is greater here than in *Sweden*. Perhaps this dainty meat was the occasion, or at least contributed to the following disease: viz. that many of our men were afterward exceedingly tormented by intolerable bloody ulcers.

The ugliest animals we saw were the *Gentoo* women, who were quite naked except their thighs. Their naked and jetty bodies were not in the least alluring.

In *Mahie* I obtained that curious insect, which has a long sinew between the thorax and body, and is in the little collection which I have sent you.

---

[s] The *oestrus bovis* deposits its eggs in the backs of cows, which turn to maggots as large as the end of one's finger, called in some counties of *England*, wornils. When cattle are pestered with these, they are always out of condition. See *Derham's Physico Theol.*

THOUGH I am not difpofed to judge of the *European* nations, merely by their behaviour towards each other in the *Eaſt Indies*; yet I cannot omit taking notice, that the *French* have every where been very civil to us. They always called us *leurs grands alliés*, that is, their great allies; and their civility extended fo far as to give us leave to bury one of our dead in their church at *Mahic*.

OUR fuperiors had made no regulations on ſhore; for which reafon, every one who went on ſhore was forced to procure as he could every thing for himfelf; which made it more advantageous to ſtay on board.

BESIDES the gold coin, called pagoda, which is valued at four rupees, their ſilver coins are rupees of which each contains five *fanno*. *Tar* is a copper coin of different values.

THE boats, which are made ufe of here and at *Mangulor*, have flat bottoms, like common boats, and are pointed at both ends. For fear of overfetting, one ought to know how to keep an exact equilibrium. I was told that the *Malabaric* rowers at *Mahie* were obliged

to

to give head for head, if an *European* was drowned in their boats.

AFTER we had provided ourselves with the aforementioned animals, which were only like oxen, and with other things, we set sail the 21st of *April*. Nothing particular happened, except our losing the main yard, and another yard. This damage was easily repaired; but we lost four ship boys on this occasion. Afterwards our voyage to *Queda*, in the straits of *Malacca*, was very fortunate; and we cast anchor there the 13th of *May*.

THE country is very low to a great distance from the sea shore, and every where covered with thick forests. Among the trees was the tamarind tree; the papay tree; the *Abrus precatorius* (the seeds of which the inhabitants of the *Malacca* coast put into rings for want of stones, because it is not usual among the eastern nations to wear mere gold rings); a tree, which I could not get to, but observed that it sent branches towards the earth from the top, different from its common branches. The *English* call it mangroves in the *West Indies*.

AN

An unfinished castle was situated on the mouth of a smooth river. The engineer seemed to be no disciple of *Vauban*. The faces were parallel to the curtains, and the walls so thin that half a dozen six pounders would have made a breach. In the inside were some houses, the roofs of which served for batteries. The cannons were most of them from an *English* ship which was lost just before the river, but so leisurely that there was even time to get those heavy goods out. Though this castle has such a miserable appearance in the eyes of *Europeans*; yet it is sufficient to keep the nations hereabouts in awe, merely because it looks *European*. I saw here some prisoners, whose necks and hands were fastened to a pole with willow-twigs. They had coined money, and seemed not to hope for pardon: but did by no means shew any fear; a foolish insensibility must be the effect of the doctrine of unavoidable destiny.

The other houses are generally built on poles, four feet above ground, on account of the high tide. The walls and floors are frequently made of bamboo sticks split in pieces.

MAHMUD

Mahmud *Houssain Basha*, who was master of the place, was a vassal to the king of *Siam*. He was exceedingly interested for the promotion of trade in his country. He was (as all the other *Malayans*) a *Mohammedan*; but tolerated heathens and Christians. He would not permit the widow of a *Frenchman* to go away; but made up matters so well, that she married a *Chinese* Christian, in order to have the *Europeans* who come there well received, for he wanted to ingratiate himself with them. We could not take in the quantity of tin that we intended, as he insisted on keeping some for the ships that were coming after us.

Oxen, buffaloes, and chicken, are very reasonable. The woods are the habitations of tigers, which are said not to attack men: but as they carry off the dogs from the houses, one dares not venture out far. Monkeys are very numerous; some are large, with very long tails, grey hairs, white beards, and black skin; some less ones have short tails bending upwards. A parrot (*Psittacus galgulus*) was no bigger than a goldfinch. Its colour was dark green on the back, and light green under

der the belly: the upper fide of the tail and the throat were red; the bill was black. Some had a blue fpot on the head. When they fleep, they always hang in the cage fo as to point with their head downwards. We obferved that their nefts were remarkable for their exceeding fine texture; but we did not fee the birds. If they had a different conftruction, the monkeys would be very mifchievous to them; but now, before they can get to the opening, the loweft part as the weakeft breaks in pieces, and the vifitor falls to the ground without any danger to the young birds.

THERE are feveral forts of crabs in the fea, befides various other fifhes. I fhould be forry if one-fpecies which I fent you by Mr. *Lagerftrcm* fhould be injured; its eyes were on long pedunculi, and it had peculiar feet (*Cancer arenarius*). While it was alive, its eyes fparkled in the dark, like cat's eyes. In and by the fide of the river are whole cart-loads of oyfters, and likewife crocodiles by hundreds. When the water during the tide fills all the ponds and ditches, with which nature has divided this low country, the crocodiles go up a good way into

into the woods; therefore, when a great motion is heard in these pools of water, the best way is to make off immediately.

TIN is not found in this *Bashaw's* country, that I know of: but he has the toll and custom of what is brought there. I am told, that in the places where it comes from, they do not fetch it out of the mountains, but dig it out of the ground, together with the sand. It is reckoned better than *English* tin, at least a *Chinese* likes it better.

THE coins are *rupees*. A *rupee* contains three *cupang*, and a *cupang* four *condorin*. They are all silver.

THE 27th of *May* we set sail: before *Salingor* we staid in vain from the 30th of *May* to the 2d of *June:* but afterwards we sailed among the many fine islands in the *Straits of Sonda*. On one of these islands is a species of stones very like the sand-stone from *Oland*, but it burst into little cubic pieces, scarce above one foot and a half long, and as much broad.

IN

MACAO. 1751.

IN the beginning of *July* we first saw *China*. We passed *Macao*, were searched by the custom-house officers, who are in the castle near the narrow mouth called *Bocca Tigris*, and anchored near *Wampoo* the 7th of *July*.

LETTER

LETTER V.

THE 17th of *March* I sent the continuation of my accounts by a friend. I will now relate what I have seen in *China*.

A person who for the first time visits this country, thinks he has a new world before him; for almost every thing looks different from what he has seen in other places, unless where climate renders some simularity of customs necessary.

The rocks and the shore, even a good way into the sea, are covered with fishermen and their tackle; which sight immediately leads one to conclude, that the country must be very populous. The naked and uninhabited islands hereabouts seem at first to occasion other thoughts; but, on advancing a little further, the plains and vallies speak the number and the industry of the inhabitants.

The lowest fields are sowed with rice, because it requires a great deal of water, which

it

it gets by the tide without any trouble to the hufbandman. Thefe fields are croffed by fuch great canals, that during the flood one may go in boats on them. Rice is fowed and reaped twice a year. During its growth, it is pulled out and planted into ferpentine lines, to admit the water more freely to the roots. Thofe who have not the advantage of the tide, are forced to carry or lead the water, or bring it up by machines, of which Mr. *William Chambers* made a drawing on a former voyage, and has probably communicated it to the fuperintendant Baron *Horlemann*.

THE high places are likewife employed to great advantage: for there are mountains whofe declivity amounts even to forty degrees; but they are divided into feveral terraces, on which are planted *Convolvulus Batatas* [t], *Dioſcorea* [u], *Goſſypium* [w], fugar-canes, and many other plants, according to the time of the year, or quality of the foil. When it rains, the rain water is preferved, and conveyed from one ftory to another. If it rains too much, a ditch is opened, through which the water may run away freely. The ufe of dung may be judg-

[t] *Spaniſh* potatoes. [u] Yams. [w] Cotton.

ed

ed of by the careful manner of gathering of it at *Canton*, and by the ftinking fampanes, or boats, which daily pafs by our fhips. But on the fields which were near the fhips, we feldom faw any other manure than the roots of rice, which, together with the clay fticking to them, are thrown on the higher foil, which is mixed with fpar.

THOSE places which cannot be tilled, are planted with trees, if the high fituation and dry foil will allow of it. But a great part of fuch places are deftined for burying-grounds; which practice would induce one at firft to fuppofe that the *Chinefe* acted againft their own principles, in leaving fo much ground for burying-places, and by that means making them unfit for ufe; fince the graves muft not be difturbed. But for this very reafon moft people are buried on fteep mountains, or other places which cannot be ufed for other purpofes. The refpect which children and pofterity fhew to their parents and anceftors, even after death, is to be confidered as a confequence of the implicit obedience to which they are obliged in their life time; and which is the foundation of their exceeding great fubmiffion towards the magiftrates, without which it

would

would be impoffible to rule fuch a number of unmannerly, ftubborn fubjects. Over their graves are generally little open ftone-buildings, which are almoft femicircular, and have a niche for a perfuming veffel. I only found one fingle grave more magnificent than the reft, on the northern fide of the town; it was covered by two round vaults, and fhut up by a wall.

On fome high hills there are towers. They have all of them eight fides, are nine ftories high, are almoft every where of equal breadth within, have every where windows, and terminating in a point. I was told, that in time of war they were ufed as watch towers: they are therefore fo difperfed, that the given fignals can eafily be feen from one tower to another. In the villages were lefs fquare towers, three ftories high; but the *Chinefe* faid, that they were *pagodas*.

One of the firft things on arriving here is to procure a *bancfhall*; this is, a great houfe conftructed of *bamboo* and mats on a place appointed for that purpofe, in which the ftores of the fhip are laid up, and whatever is not abfolutely neceffary on-board, or whatever would

would be in the way during the cleanfing, lading, and clearing of the fhip. The *Dutch* fay, that they will fpend no money in building a *bancſhal*; but others fay, that the *Chineſe* will not give them leave. Thoſe who have been confined to a ſhip ſo long as we had been, would eafily be attracted by the adjacent iſles to go on ſhore. The *French* iſland, where the *French* have their *bancſhals*, is almoſt the only one where we enjoy the liberty of burying our dead. It is dangerous for a fingle perſon to venture too far, becauſe he is in danger of being ſtripped to the very ſhirt. Though the curioſity of the *Europeans* may not be perhaps void of blame; yet the natives look as if they were glad to find a pretence to uſe violence againſt a ſtranger, eſpecially when they are ſure of over-powering him.

On the paſſage from the place where the ſhips ride at anchor to *Canton*, which is one *Swediſh* mile and a half, you are obliged to have your baggage vifited three or four times. The cuſtom-houſe officer, who lies in his boat continually, quite cloſe to the ſhip, gives an inventory of every thing you take with you; and all that you carry beſides is to be confiſcated according to the laws at the three cuſtom-houſes,

houses, where you are obliged to stop; except you go in a sloop with a flag. The river is at first on both sides bordered with rice-fields; and this is the fatal scene on which many lascivious *Europeans* have lost their health.

THE further you advance up the river, the more the number of both great and small vessels increased, part of which lie still, and part go up and down the river. Nearer to the town they have scarce room upon the river; but are forced to bear hard one against another behind and before; and to form, as it were, streets, length-ways and cross-ways. Those who in this manner spend their time on the water, are not all of them sailors or fishermen: the ferrymen, who come and set off at certain times, are in great numbers; but the rowers, or oar-men, are still more numerous. The others are tradesmen, such as carry on some sort of business; they keep wives and children, hogs, and chicken, together with all their utensils, in these boats; for which reason they need not come on shore: and there are particular people appointed by the government to overlook them. I can say no more of the city of *Canton* itself, than that its drawing in Lord *Anson's* Voyage round the

world

world is inaccurate, and taken from an old drawing which I had already seen in *Sweden* before Lord *Anson* left *England*; and the original itself is very faulty. It is surrounded by a smooth, round, high rampart, which has at the top loop-holes, or *crenaux*, very close together. In the river are three little islands, with castles in the same manner; with this addition, that in the inside a cavalier two stories high is raised, which commands the works within and without, and likewise serves as a retirade. The other redoubts on the neighbouring hills on the country side are of such a construction, as shews that the plan is designed for security, but not to shew their genius for war. A work like this might be defended for a long while in this country by good officers and valiant soldiers: but when a *Chinese* knows there is a place of retreat, he would hardly dare to perform heroic atchievements on the out-works.

The suburbs, in which the *Europeans* have their factories, are divided by many canals, and crowded with buildings as full as possible; for several of the houses are even a great way over the water, built on piles. The lodgings are spacious, and the yards narrow and long, and

and therefore they have been obliged to make shift as they can. Since they like to lead their soughs underground, the foundations of their houses must cost a great deal; but the superstructures are not very durable. Here and there you meet with open yards, in the midst of which the floors of lodging-rooms are laid, and covered with nothing else but a tile-roof. The stairs are under the same inconvenience with those at *Suratte*, *viz.* they are narrow, and the steps are high and likewise narrow. When the rooms cannot get light enough from the doors and open walls, they have windows of mother-of-pearl: for which reason the cathedral church at *Goa*, on account of such windows, need not be thought one of the wonders of the world. The walls are covered with fine white or painted paper, and ornamented with some *Chinese* or *European* drawings. The *Chinese* in their own houses fix up generally some tables of proverbs. Almost close to each room is a little garden, in which are some flower-beds, and scaffolds for flowerpots, and greater vessels for shells, goldfishes, &c.

THEIR pillars or columns serve only to bear the rafters. Mr. *Chambers*, I suppose, has already

ready given us the proportion of the parts. To judge by the appearance of a triumphal arch, the width of the middlemost portico seemed to be two thirds of the whole height: the side porticos were in the same proportion to the middlemost, with regard to height and breadth. The populace hindered me from taking a more exact measure.

You find no trees trained up by art, nor walks, nor flower-pieces of several figures, in a *Chinese* garden; but every thing is in an agreeable natural confusion. Instead of grottoes they throw a heap of a porous sort of stones together, which look like rocks and mountains. This taste of the romantic in gardens extends even to the small flower-beds, and flower-pots in houses.

ONE of the principal *pagodas* is in a fine wood in the suburbs; on the outside it is like the others, but it is higher and more spacious. I was told, that it formerly belonged to the jesuits. The structure and stories are entirely according to a correct *Chinese* taste. In the lowest division, or in the hall, were four gigantic statues, one of a white, one of a brown, one of a black, and one of a red colour,

colour, in the attitude of flourishing about them with their swords: this has no *Chinese* appearance; for, even supposing they knew the complexion of the *Americans* (of which, however, I greatly doubt), they would most probably be of opinion that the honour of attending upon the gods belonged to themselves alone, exclusive of all others. These statues have likewise wider eyes than are to be met with among the *Chinese*. Perhaps they were intended to shew the universality of the church of *Rome*, about which they give themselves more trouble than about all its other qualities. In the back-parts is a court surrounded with low buildings; before it stands an high, open, large house, which is broader than long, as is usual in *pagodas*. Steps surround the whole building, as is usual in the South of *Europe*. Nobody is allowed to pass through the door, for reasons unknown: therefore I decline advancing any uncertain surmises concerning the idols, which could hardly be discerned in so dark a room. On advancing somewhat further, you again come to a yard, which is divided by a canal, and has likewise a *pagoda* of two stories high on the other side. In the lower story a squat, fat, half-naked idol, is seated upon an altar or sofa; it seems to be

breaking

breaking out into an horſe laugh; and is ſitting on one leg, and holding up the other knee: in ſhort, it is in a very indecent poſture. Before it ſtands an iron perfuming vaſe, on which matches made of wood-ſhavings are burning. In the upper ſtory is a female figure, ſitting with her legs acroſs, and ſmiling very decently with downcaſt eyes. Both ſtatues are of a gigantic ſize, and gilt all over. Out of town, in the outward apartments of a *pagoda* ſituated on a hill, are two white equeſtrian ſtatues. In the moſt outward room is a little ſtatue repreſenting a woman with a child in her arms; in the inner room is a larger idol on a chair, which, after the *Chineſe* faſhion, has a long beard; and before it are four other ſtatues. In each houſe, and aboard all ſhips and ſampanes, is a little chapel on the larboard ſide, in which they burn incenſe, or put orange-trees, &c. Sometimes the whole chapel conſiſts of painted, ſometimes of torn, paper, and a veſſel with aſhes and matches.

The ſailors, and even ſome books of voyages (as may be ſeen from *de Uris's* notes), call the *pagodas, Yoſs-houſes:* for, on enquiring of a *Chineſe* for the name of the idol, he anſwers, *Grande Yoſs,* inſtead of *Gran Dios.* I have not ſeen

seen the deformed idols of which *Pinto* speaks. The *bonzes*, who minister in the *pagodas*, wear long grey cloaths, reaching down to the feet, with wide sleeves; their heads and beards are shaved; their caps are black and round. On the other side the river is a great *pagoda*, where near 100 *bonzes* are kept. They have such a great field, that they are not only able to sow the necessary rice and fruits for themselves, but likewise to keep cattle; which, it is said, they only feed and bury. They have all the necessary tradesmen among themselves, wherefore they do not seem to be troublesome or chargeable to others. Processions with idols, masks, plays, and jugglers tricks, are frequent enough. As for the rest, the *Chinese* trouble themselves very little about their gods and *pagodas*.

THE people differ very much in size, but are seldom tall. The men have a yellowish skin; the ladies are fair, but the common women tawny. The bone above the eyes projects very far, and forms a triangle with the chin. Most of them never quite open their eyes: and I am told, that the custom of bearing the children at their backs, with their heads hanging down, occasions as it were a
swelling

ſwelling of the eye-lids; for the orbits are the ſame with them as with other people. Their noſes are ſomewhat flat: their lips middling; and their looks, when they hope to gain any thing, as ſweet as poſſibly can be.

The children are at firſt ſhaved, that their hair may grow the thicker; afterwards one or three locks are left. The men, as is well known, are obliged to ſhave their heads, excepting a tuft of hair on the crown, which they plait into three traces. Their high value for their locks of hair ſeems to abate in ſome meaſure; for at *Queda* I ſaw two *Chineſe*, who, living there, and having laid aſide all thoughts of ſeeing *China* again, had ſhaved their heads: whereas their neighbour, who was likewiſe a *Chineſe*, had all his hair tied in the old faſhion. Their beards do not grow well; but perhaps they chuſe to have a thin beard. If a *Chineſe* is aſked what ſum would induce him to part with his tuft of hair? he again aſks, what you would take for your head? And no wonder that they are ſo very careful of an ornament which they have perhaps nouriſhed for twenty, thirty, or more years together. The women tie their hair above the top of the head; and to make the

tuft

tuft of a confiderable thicknefs, they faften
fome falfe hair to it, and ftick as many and as
coftly pins or bodkins in it as their circumftances will allow of They take a great deal
of pains to have fmooth and gloffy hair; but
this is perhaps the reafon why their hair wears
off and becomes thin, and ftraggling when
they grow old. Both fexes let their nails grow
as long as poffible, if they do not interfere
with their bufinefs.

You fee many blind men [x] in the ftreets;
and they are the only beggars which are to be
obferved. The alms which the *Chinefe* give
them, confift of a fpoonful of rice. The moft
common difeafe here is that which naturally
proceeds from promifcuous luft. A grave
Chinefe afferted that they cure this difeafe in
a hundred days, *per* τεκνοφαγίαν *alternis die-
bus, alternis jejunio.* I cannot be anfwerable
for the truth of this account; but fo much I
know, that it is poffible to procure a fufficient
quantity of this food. A *Chinefe* would like
better to take money for his children, than to

---

[x] Perhaps the blindnefs of the *Chinefe* is for the greateft
part the effect of their voluptuous irregularities; there may
be alfo other caufes. Compare with this *Tiffot de febr. biliof.*
p. 187. 189.

be

be obliged to throw them into the water for nothing. I have no reason to doubt of the fact I hint at; since I have seen several children floating on the water: but I cannot pretend to say whether they are destroyed with or without the permission of the magistrate.

Their cloaths are wide and long, generally consisting of gawze or other thin stuffs. Their boots are embroidered, and made of a species of silk, have thick soles and no heels. Their head is covered with a hat plaited of canes and lined with tiffany; the hat is cone-shaped or like a cover of a dish. On the top of it is a tuft of red silk, which covers the hat on all sides; and on the tuft is a button, by which is distinguished the quality of the wearer, as father *Du Halde* mentions. In winter they wear round caps of black velvet or sattin, with a shallow brim, on which is a tuft of red silk threads: they likewise wear warmer cloaths. The common people wear coarser stuffs, stockings of nankin, shoes without buckles of the same stuff, and go generally bareheaded. The poorest of all wear only breeches. The women go bare-headed; their cloaths fit somewhat closer to the body, but stays are unknown among them. An *Englishman* had his wife

wife with him at *Canton* this year: but the *Chinese* could find no proportion between her spacious hoop-petticoat and her waist. Their shoes are pointed; and have high heels, on which they go crippling as upon stilts; because the unnatural position of the foot takes off all the strength and use of the toes. The poor only wear a short petticoat over their breeches.

THE whole world knows how difficult a matter it is to learn the *Chinese* language; but you can have no true idea of it, till you hear it spoken yourself. Their various accents occasion the great difficulty. They pronounce one word as if they were quarrelling, and prolong the next as if their tongue was fixed to their gums. Their strong aspirations, even before the initial consonants, cannot be pronounced by every tongue. The *European* languages are not very difficult to the *Chinese*, if only the D and R could be rejected. For they say instead of *doctor* and *padri, locta* and *pali*. They can in some measure avail themselves of the D, but as to the R it is too difficult for them. They generally converse with the *Swedes* in broken *English*; and sometimes in broken *Portugueze, French,* and *Dutch:* and
some

some of them speak a few words of *Swedish.* A *Chinese* merchant being asked whether he had any stockings? Answered, *no habó.* A person pointed to a pair of stockings and said what is that? *Oh,* said he, *telumbo, tclumbo.* When he is to say great or small, he says *grande* or *galande,* and *pequenini;* and so in other instances.

Of their genius and character, others have given accounts. I can but wonder that the missionaries, when they speak of their reigning vices, such as avarice, voraciousness, great and petty thefts, should mention nothing of their beastly lust. It is incredible to suppose them not to have known any thing about it. Though the *Chinese* are too cautious to boast of their irregularities, like some *Europeans;* yet, if you have resided some time at *Canton,* you will understand the *Latin* bard, who imagined that he tasted the waters of *Aganippe,* while he was drinking something which should not be named. Some perhaps may think that such sins are looked upon by the missionaries as peccadillos or little offences, which are of small account; but that would be judging too hardly of the reverend fathers. Without doubt, they did not chuse to discredit the nation,

tion, and mention such disadvantageous circumstances. But be this as it will, yet we cannot attribute this vice to the climate, as we might have been rashly led to do: for the whole argument falls to nothing, when it is seen that the *Persees*, which are patterns of chastity at *Suratte*, are in the same climate with the *Moors*, and have a warmer air than the *Italians*.

THEY are courageous only when they are set on stealing; for then they venture their backs, and even their lives. They are, however, revengeful and malicious, like all narrow minded people. You look in vain among the greatest part of them for disinterested gratitude, pity, placability, and a generous manner of thinking. Had *Rochefoucault* been born and bred among the *Chinese*, he would probably have denied the existence of virtue: yet with all these faults they are very civil, and are obliged to be so, because private ceremonies are the object and business of one of the most considerable colleges of the empire. The following is the manner of saluting among them. They clench their left fist, put the right hand on it, drop it down, bow, and lift it up again. Those who have accustomed themselves to

the

the more free manners of the *Europeans*, only clench their fifts, and fay *kin*, *kin*. They ufe much ceremony at coming in; and before they fit down, will be entreated to do it feveral times. If you vifit them, they entertain you with tea, comfits, and even with *European* and Cape wine, adapting every thing to the expectations they have of the traffic you are to carry on with them. You are at liberty to walk about their rooms, but muft not approach their females: for the *Chinefe*, like all nations among whom polygamy prevails, are jealous. All that I have faid relates only to merchants and tradefmen. How it is with the noblemen, I know not: for what the common people fay of them is not to be relied on, and travellers are apt to add fomewhat of their own invention.

LETTER VI.

AS I have acquired some knowledge of botany by your kind assistance, and have heard and read of the merits of Baron *Rheede* in this branch of learning, I should have been inexcuseably negligent if I had passed over his epitaph in silence. As it was inconvenient for me to keep pions, I experienced on this, as on many other occasions, the difficulty of waiting till I could get company: but even these would not always stop, when I met with any thing which according to my judgement appeared remarkable. When I came the second time to Baron *Rheede's* grave, I found the shutters fastened. Therefore I could not copy the whole epitaph [y], but only the principal things, which I should have communicated long ago, had I thought they were not known.

I HOPE I shall be able to say openly in *Sweden* what they make no great secret of in that country, namely that he had been poisoned: nor is it unlikely; for so great power in the hands of an honest man must be very dreadful

---
[y] The translator does not think the epitaph interesting to an *English* reader.

to some people. If you were to hear some anecdotes told in *East India* of the *Dutch* manner of governing there, you would by no means be astonished to find that the interest of the company is but seldom trusted to any but those who have given undeniable proofs of the good attachment to their own. One is apt to expect that the magistrates will take cognizance of these things: but they bring this excellent maxim with them out of their own country, *leven en leven laten* [z]; which keeps them from making any strict enquiries.

With your leave, I now intend to proceed to describe our voyage, and add the rest of my observations on the behaviour of the *Chinese*.

They are either incapable of, or not used to, an habit of intense investigation. Many *Europeans* are likewise obliged to confess with father *Loubere*, that one is incapable of thinking much in hot climates. On the other hand, their application to trade is so much the greater; they pursue gain, without being tired; and as their expectations are frequently boundless, so bankruptcies are frequent among them. All men here traffick; and

[z] To live, and to let others live.

when a journeyman comes from his work, he goes about felling trifles, or ftolen goods. They have in common with many other nations, the art of cheating in accounts, in meafure, weight, and quality of goods; and likewife know how to raife the price of their goods at certain junctures. At the arrival of the fhips from *Embden*, the exchange never fails to alter.

THEY are always ready to fell or to exchange; but they feldom pay away any filver, except for provocatives, of which there is a great fale. It is very peculiar, and one would hardly believe, that they fhould fet fo great a value on antique paintings, and *Porcellane*. I once afked a merchant the price of a common tea-pot, which would hardly have coft three dollars of copper money in *Sweden*, but he demanded ten pieces of eight, and fhewed me a ftamp at the bottom of it, according to which, he faid, it was made in the times of fome emperor, who lived four thoufand years ago: as if fuch poor frail veffels had at that time been made ufe of to affift chronology. The occafion of this high price is, probably, becaufe the government efteems antiquities.

HERE

HERE are many artists who are diligent, and reasonable as to their prices, especially if you do not suffer yourselves to be cheated, as frequently happens to new comers.. Their open shops have this advantage, that no trade remains a mystery, or is looked upon as difficult by the people passing by: this is certainly a great advantage to the inhabitants of the south; and might probably take effect in the north, if that custom was established, that no one must come into a shop who does not intend to make some purchase. I am almost led to believe that this stubbornness and suspicion comes from the usages of the artists [a].

THE *Cantonese* take great pains to make their goods strike the eye, and sell well: but they do not take the same care to make them good and strong; nor do they offer them as the best and finest; for when they have a mind to praise their goods, they say that they come from *Nanking*, viz. *Nanking* silk, *Nanking* ink, *Nanking* fans, and even *Nanking* hams.

[a] In *Sweden* and in many northern countries the artists and tradesmen have often certain silly customs and ceremonies, through which the apprentices must pass, when they are to be declared journeymen. F.

THEIR painters would acquit themselves very well, if they knew how to shade. You meet with very fine drawings painted on paper and glass; and likewise the very worst. Japanned wood and enameled copper is seldom to be got elsewhere at the price which it bears here. I have not heard of any carvers in wood or stone; but images and busts of clay are cheap.

THE joiners copy almost every thing that is shewn them. They have but few tools; and what should they do with a joiner's-bench, when their foot serves the same purpose? The chief strength of their joints is from the glue. Nor do the smiths undertake any great pieces of work: for when they intend to make rings or buckles, they do not beat them round, but cast the metal.

BOTH weavers and such persons as prepare silk and cotton are in great numbers. Here are likewise goldsmiths, pewterers, *Porcellane* painters, and tinkers, together with many others. Those persons who cut peoples nails and corns make use of an instrument, which is like that of a turner.

Their barbers have an exceeding light hand at shaving; but a person who is not used to their customs, will be astonished when they afterwards pull him by the nose, and begin to thump his back with their clenched fists.

Their physicians seem to be very attentive, because they spend an hour in feeling the pulse; but they must likewise make use of quacks tricks, when they pretend to tell by it the number of stools which the patient has had.

The dropping and weak eyes of the *Chinese* are occasioned by the rice, which is their most usual food, as the *Europeans* say. Next to rice, their most usual diet is bacon and salt fish; both are cut into little bits, and eaten together with the rice: they convey the victuals to their mouths with a couple of sticks. People of higher quality feast upon birds-nests[b], sinews of deer, and the like corroborative dainties. Between meals they make use of tea, sweetmeats, betle, and tobacco, which is almost as small as snuff, and is smoaked in brass tobacco pipes by persons of both sexes. The *Chinese*,

[b] See note, p. 258, vol. I.

as well as all other eastern nations, love opium, though it is strongly prohibited.

They love to play with dice, at a sort of draughts^e, and with wooden cards, &c.; yet the liberty of playing is under some restrictions among them. Their jugglers are exceedingly dexterous; one of them produced a piece of wood, and after some *hocus pocus* brought a living snake and a tortoise before us. They act plays in the streets, between two of the upper stories, or in other places where there is room for the spectators. In the representation of their plays, they run into many gross absurdities; such as representing two armies by eight or ten persons, who, instead of climbing up rocks, get upon chairs, and so on. However, the companies, which consist merely of little boys, possess a wondrous fluency of language; for they often act whole days together without stopping, making grimaces without end, now singing, now speaking, and all together keeping exactly in time. When they fight and wrestle, they must exactly know how to hit the

---

^e This is perhaps the *Chinese chess* or *siang-ki*, of which, see *Hyde Syntagma Dissert.* vol. II. p. 143. *seqq.* et tab. ad p. 144. F.

blow,

blow, and to throw themselves down with as exact cadence as in a dancing school. They can represent some passions as well as if they were real. One boy was once representing a very suspicious man, who was however to be very submissive to his wife; and another a wife who was somewhat of a coquette, yet knew how to make use of her power, and was very artful. At first they came to blows; but when madam began to sob, cry and sigh so that her whole body shook, the husband could hardly make her pardon him, though he fell down on his knees several times; and the articles of peace seemed to be very disadvantageous to him. The musical instruments usual on this occasion are first a couple of pieces of wood half a foot long, tied together at one end, and put across the thumb; which when shaken, make a clattering noise like castanets. Besides these they have little drums, great and small kettle drums, *gungungs* or round brass basons like frying pans, flutes, guittars, metal hautboys, strait horns, and an instrument which I sent over formerly, and which consists of a hemisphere to which thirteen or fourteen pipes are applied, catching the air blown into the cavity by valves. If the pastoral flute of *Pan* was not made in this manner, I do not know how

how he could exprefs thirty-two parts. How bad foever their mufical tunes may be, yet they put a higher value on them than on thofe of *Corelli*: and they deferve fome commendation for their fkill in keeping time, for when five or fix play together you fcarce diftinguifh more than one.

LETTER VII.

THOUGH I have taken care not to mention what I have already found well described in other authors, yet I see from the *Stockholm* gazette, that I have either relied too much on my memory, or on the heads in the *English* collections.

THE *Chinese* ell, or cubit as it is called, contains about fourteen inches three-fifths. I doubt whether they have any solid measure; since they weigh every thing, even wood and water. A *pekul* is about 142 pounds and a half, *Swedish* weight: 100 *katty* make one *pekul*: with this they weigh heavy goods. Gold, silver, and the like, are weighed by the *tel*, of which sixteen make a *katty*. A *tel* contains ten *mefs*; ten *kanderins* make one *mefs*, and a *kanderin* weighs ten *kas*. Father *Du Halde* mentions yet eight gradual less weights; so that a *fun*, which is the least of all, seems only to be of use to those who will try by cutting and weighing whether matter is infinitely divisible. They have, as is well known, a brafs coin of the fize of a *Swedifh* piece of two groats, which has a fquare hole in the middle. In value it is proportionable to the *kas* of filver; however, at prefent, they only give eight fuch brafs *kas* for a *kanderin*; in the fame manner as gold for fome reafons is always valued fourteen times and a half more than filver on this voyage.

THEIR *fimpun*, or table of accounts, is a fquare frame, which is longitudinally divided by a fmall piece of wood, not exactly in the middle. In it are 11, 13, 21, or more wires, on which roll little balls, namely, two on one, and five on the other fide: the latter fignifies 1, 10, 100, &c. and the other two oppofite to thefe five fhew the units, tens, &c. They go on very readily with adding and fubtracting; but as for the reft, it will not do fo well. I now am forry that I cannot draw; but if I remember right there is a drawing of the *fimpun* in *Loubere's* Defcription of *Siam*, and befides that, I fent you fuch a *fimpun* the laft time. They write with a pencil, which they hold perpendicularly, between the thumb and the two laft fingers, and only lean their hand on the table, or on the paper. One would be led to think that they muft write very flow-

ly;

ly; however, their pencil runs as quickly as the pen of one of the readiest *European* clerks. They have likewise a current sort of writing, which they only make use of when they write fast.

To keep 900,000 *Cantonese* in order, no measures can be so effectual as those taken by the *Chinese*. Justice is done very speedily, especially when the fact is quite recent; but injustice as frequently takes place. It sometimes happens that several objections delay their giving satisfaction to the *Europeans*. The *Europeans* do not easily give up any of their privileges; but when they cannot succeed, the fault is in the *Chinese* officers, who do not take a right cognizance of the affair. Of this you find examples in Lord *Anson's* Voyage. But if one threatens to apply for justice in higher courts, they are afraid that their superiors will punish them with heavy fines. The sale of the lowest places of trust, even that of a *mandarin*, is so common, that every one speaks of it, and they venture to mention it in the most public manner. A surveyor, who lay along-side our ship, took a considerable sum of money from the master of the boat, with whom he lodged, for the money which

the

the fellow could make from our crew: and the furveyor faid, that he was forced to pay money to the cuftom-houfe officer: and fo it feems to go round. It often happens here juft as I was told it does in the *Portugueze* regulation of the cuftom-houfes, namely, that the revenue from it looks well on paper, but actually is worth little or nothing. The police, however, is excellent: for it keeps every thing quiet at night both in the town and on the water, where an officer goes his round regularly. The gates in the ftreets, which are fhut up at night, are always open near the factories, for the convenience of the *Europeans:* and in thofe places where in day time you muft be on your guard for fear of pick-pockets, you may pafs without danger in the night time.

If you go further up into the town, they call you names, and pelt you with ftones, which fly about your ears as thick as hail. If you intend to go out of town, you muft have company, walk faft, and carry a good ftick.

Both petty larceny and theft are punifhed by a certain number of lafhes with a *bamboo* ftick. The prifoners are fo fettered about the
head

head and on one hand, that they cannot lift it to their head. In *August*, in the year 1748, they difpatched fome rebels at *Canton* by tying a rope twice round them, and faftening a horfe to each end, and fo cutting the body quite through. And as both high and low officers are the fovereign mafters of their vaffals, criminals are obliged, even for trivial faults, to fuffer with the greateft fubmiffion; and on their knees to hear themfelves reprimanded, and to fuffer themfelves to be fpit on.

As for wild beafts, tigers are faid to frequent the mountains over which the northern roads pafs: for fear of them it is, that in winter nights you fee hundreds of lanthorns carried before the travellers. Their dogs can do no more than bark, little dogs efpecially. *Spanifh* ones are the delight of the *Chinefe* ladies; and their hufbands pay dearly for them: and I think there is fome hufband-craft in it; for the affections muft be fixed on fome object.

HERE are buffaloes, oxen, and fheep whofe tails are a hand's breadth long, and very broad. Swine are numerous, and their flefh is daily eaten. Here are few horfes, nor

do

do they want any, becaufe people of quality' are carried in chairs: and thofe commodities which cannot be carried in boats, are borne on mens fhoulders: and on this occafion the feeble *Chinefe* fhews the advantage of a knack· or fleight: they have an eafy fmooth ftep; and always lay the poles obliquely on their fhoulders, by which means the collar-bone is left unhurt. They can very eafily change fhoulders, and three of them know how to fhare an equal part of a weight too heavy for two, and too light for four perfons.

CATS are very neceffary, on account of the number of mice. The *Chinefe* judge of the goodnefs of a cat by the colour of her eyes, and their changes; for they fay a cat changes them twice a day.

QUAILS, geefe, and chicken, are plentiful. I likewife faw fome *Siamefe* fowls, which have a double back-toe. Ducks are bred by hundreds in one boat, and at certain fignals either go out or come in. *Cockado* is a fpecies of white parrots, with a yellow creft (*Pfittacus criftatus*). They often expofe rare birds and animals to fale in the factories: but I am

I am not fond of looking at what I cannot buy.

Though the *Chinese* drefs ever fo light, yet they are troubled with infects. The gnats, or *mufquitos*, are fo troublefome to the *Europeans* at night, that they muft be kept off by curtains: for the place which they fting becomes painful, and fwells. A fpecies of *blattas*, called *cockroaches* in *Englifh* (*Blatta orientalis*) are brought to *Europe* in great numbers.

As you are better acquainted than I am with the vegetables hereabouts, I fhall only remark that I faw no cocoa-trees about *Canton*: perhaps they will not grow fo near the tropic; for if they could be planted here, the *Chinefe* would certainly not forget to do it. We took two tea fhrubs with us on our return: both of them died, notwithftanding all our care. The one was *Ankay*, and the other *Soatchun*: the former had oblong, and the latter lanceolated leaves.

The fmaller veffels of the *Chinefe* are called *fampanes*. They have a flat bottom, without a keel, are broad, and not very deep in proportion to the length. They have feveral divifions, divisions, and are so convenient that you are secure from rain and sun shine under the reed-mats, which are spread like an awning over the boat, and are supported with *bamboo* sticks. Such boats as these would be very useful in many places of our *Malar Lake*. They are rowed in a peculiar way, by one or more persons: the oars are neater than could be expected from people who have no theory in their mechanicks: in the middle it is composed of two pieces, but somewhat obliquely, and turns on a swivel, so that the oar turns both on the swivel and in the water; and the rower need only direct it. The part of the oar which goes in the water is very broad, such as is necessary to flat vessels, which have no keel to cut the water, but must only float on it. On the larger *sampanes*, besides this, is a stiff oar fixed to the bending of the *sampane*, with which they may be easily turned, even when they are deep laden. Their anchors (as is well known) are made of wood, sometimes plated with iron on the ends; and have frequently only one arm. Instead of the stern, they fasten a piece of wood crofs-ways to the arm, which answers the same purpose, as the angle grows sharper by the conjunction. The sails consist of mats, which are expanded by poles,

poles, on the ends of which are ropes which come together in a knot; so that all the parts of the sail may be pulled at the same time.

Their merchant ships, which are destined for long voyages, are deep, pretty short, and will carry about 200 *Swedish* tons. We call them *junks* [d]. They are likewise without keels; and have generally three masts, of which the greatest is six fathoms long from the deck, without the top-masts. The standing ropes are made of twisted canes; the sails are up. The space under deck is divided into several partitions; and each partition is so close, that if even a leak should spring, the ship would not be in danger. Instead of tow, they make use of a cement, which to me seemed to be mixed with ground *bamboo*. As the *Chinese* greatly admire the figures of dragons, and prefer the most ugly ones, their pendants have the same form. If you go on board them, or take leave of them, they play on the *gungung*; but they know nothing of striking their colours, or of what is to be done on that occasion. The sailors climb and tie what is needful with canes instead of hempen ropes.

[d] See Lord *Anson's* Voyage round the Word, Book III. Chap. 10. Table xxxiv.

WHEN the whole naval force of the *Chinese* Emperor is eftimated at 9999 fail by his fubjects, a great part muft be at *Canton*: but at that place are only great boats, which would fink with ten twelve pounders. Nor are any larger fhips of war required, while the *Chinefe* government has no intentions of making conquefts by fea.

FIVE or fix of the above-mentioned boats lie about the *European* fhips, to prevent acts of violence and fmuggling. Their arms are fhields of the ufeful *bamboo*, little fabres, halberts, bows, pikes of a tremendous form, for their point is almoft a yard long, and exactly like a *Weftrogothic* knife, and little flings which ftand on a kind of bow.

IT is however very amufing (at leaft for a perfon that finds pleafure in obferving the difpofitions of men, and their univerfal vanity) to fee fome place-men row by each other: every one who goes up or down the river has his flag and his diftinction, by which the others immediately know his rank: and if he who lies in the river, or paffes by, is of a lower quality, he muft beat his *gungung* firft, to

which

which the other anfwers with the fame inftrument; after which they wifh each other an happy voyage.

The *Chinefe* can certainly make gun-powder: neither do they feem to be miftaken when they difpute the invention of printing and of making gun-powder with *Holland, Italy,* and *Germany*. But their powder will hardly ferve for any thing but fireworks; for though it gives a report, and foon takes fire, yet it leaves a good deal of the charcoal on the paper, and feems to have but little ftrength. It is very peculiar that fky-rockets, fquibs, &c. and even air-guns, may be purchafed at very reafonable prices at *Canton*; while the people themfelves are fo afraid of fire-arms, that they would even run from a black *bamboo* ftick.

If any body had told me before-hand, that water would freeze naturally at twenty-three degrees and an half of latitude, I could not have believed it. But now I had the teftimony of my own eyes, and the *Swedifh* thermometer. Having ftaid eighteen months in this hot climate, the cold was fomewhat troublefome in the open harbour, where we were expofed exposed to the north east wind. We got clear of this and other inconveniences when we sailed through the passage at *Bocca Tigris*, the 4th of *January* 1752. We were provided with a *Chinese* pass-port and pilot, and accompanied by many white porpoises; and, on the 6th, we quite left the *Chinese* shore. On the 19th of this month we were so happy as to reach the place which the *English* call *New-bay*, which is situated on the south-west of *Java*: there we were to take in a store of the good water of that place. Half a quarter of a *Swedish* mile from the shore is a little island, called *Cantaye* in the *French* charts, which I proposed to myself to visit in our return: but, unluckily, the only time that I was allowed to go on shore, the water was so high that I was forced to wade up to my middle; and for all my trouble got nothing but a great piece of a *millepora*. I was therefore obliged to content myself with sitting and observing the *Javanese*, who are *Mahometans*; they speak the *Malaic* language, are of a tawny complexion, and let their hair grow about as low as their shoulders, and tie it with bast of trees. They chew *betle* in plenty, and are ready to run a mile for a little piece of opium. Their boats have large sails, and on the larboard a bamboo stem, which is fastened to two outriggers, and keeps the boat from oversetting, as it otherwise would do on the account of its lightness. The *Javanese* brought cocoa-nuts, plaintains, citrons, lemties or lemontyes (as the *Dutch* and our sailors call them), on board. The latter of these fruits is found to be very plentiful in all southern *East India*, and is like a citron; I never saw its flower, but both Mr. *Osbeck* and myself have always found the fruit to be ten *locular* [e]. Besides this, they had a sort of coarse brown sugar made of palm-trees, which the crew was forbid to purchase, because it occasions strong dysenteries; they likewise brought fowls, fishes, tortoises, sertularia, and some daggers of good workmanship, the blades of which were undulated, and, as I was told, poisoned.

The 21st of *January* we left this place, and experienced the weather at the Cape in *March*, which as usual was very disagreeable, and shifting from storms to calms. We here saw one of those tortoises called *Hawksbills* by the

---

[e] The same is observable in lemons: and this number of *loculi* seems to be the most natural in proportion to the *petals* and *stamina*, though they are also found eight and twelve *locular*. D. S. See vol. i. p. 306.

English;

English; its head is flat, and the upper jaw like the bill of an hawk. Its shields lie above one another almost like scales; on the fore paws are three nails, and on the hind feet are two. The shell is thicker and more variegated than that of any others, for which reason it serves for all sorts of work. Further on we saw *whales*, and a *zoophyte*, which the *Swedes* call *by-de-wind-seglare* (*Holothuria physalis*); the *English* call it *man of war*; the *Dutch besantyes*; and *Dampier*, if I am not mistaken, *cutlers* [f]. The body is half round, stands directly upwards, has many long and many short *tentacula*, is slimy, transparent; somewhat blueish; shines in dark nights; is poisonous, as I myself have experienced; and so light that it will scarce sink in *Spanish* brandy. Beyond the Cape they are small, in the ocean they are larger, and very numerous especially in *March*. The old sailors who have often been to the *Indies* affirm that they have seen what *Thevenot* calls *Carnasse*. I cannot determine whether these or the men of war are the true *Baharras*, which, according to your desire, Mr. *Lagerstrom* enjoined me to look for.

[f] *Linnæus* places this animal among the *Mollusca* class of his worms; and therefore I cannot account for the author's mistake in calling it a *zoophyte*. F.

On our approach to the tropick, we again saw flying fishes. I must remark that all the flying fishes which I saw eastward of the Cape had short *pectoral-fins*; and their *ventral-fins* were expanded while they flew, because they could not otherwise have preserved an *equilibrium*. There is yet another sort of flying fish, which has *antennæ* §, and a vessel containing an inky matter; but I cannot tell whether it is the *Sepia loligo*.

This time we did not touch at *St. Helena*, but bore for the Island of *Ascension*, where we anchored the 6th of *April*. This country has no other fresh water than what the rain sometimes affords; for which reason it is dry and barren, and only seems to be destined by Providence to be the habitation of tortoises, and to serve as a place of some refreshment for seamen. Goats, pelicans, and many sea birds breed here, notwithstanding the intolerable heat of the day, and the coldness of the night. The few low shores where we can land are covered with a loose pearl-sand, in which the tortoises bury their eggs. I did not see how

§ Not *antennæ*; but, as *Linnæus* calls them, *tentacula*. F.

much the tide falls, nor could any eftimation be made, on account of the ftrong breakers; thefe are likewife fo violent againft the wind, that in 1749 a floop with four men funk very near the fhore.

I FOUND nothing particular in the *Sargaffo*, befides that peculiar animal, the drawing of which refembles a fpider: perhaps this was only the fkin which fome animal had caft off.

THE 22d of *May* we fpoke with a *Frenchman*, who had received accounts from *St. Helena* of fuch events as had happened during our abfence. It was peculiar, that an officer from the *French* fhip afked us whether the *Swedes* believed in the Apoftles Creed? When a *Frenchman* has fuch mean thoughts of a *Lutheran*, the *Spaniards* and *Portugueze* may well think us *Turks* and Heathens.

THE 30th of *May* we faw the weftern iflands, or *Azores*, on which every one of us expected to breathe fome frefh air; but the refolution was changed, and we failed for *England*. In the mean time the fcurvy had attacked fome of our men. It was very happy that they were

were all *Swedes*. The 14th of *June* we saw *England*; and after we had bought some refreshments and greens, we left *Dover* the 19th of *June*. The 26th of *June* the *Gothenburgh* rocks were the most agreeable sight we had met with during a voyage of twenty-seven months.

OLOF TOREEN.

Stromstad,
the 3d of *May*, 1753.

A SHORT

ACCOUNT

OF THE

CHINESE HUSBANDRY,

By CHARLES GUSTAVUS ECKEBERG,
Captain of a Ship in the Swedish East India
Company's Service.

A SHORT ACCOUNT OF THE CHINESE HUSBANDRY.

FEW countries can boaſt the poſſeſſion of ſuch a variety of different natural advantages, as not to ſtand ſometimes in need of the aſſiſtance of others.

THIS imperfection ſeems to be the only tie by which civil ſocieties are kept together: but in *China* nature ſeems to have followed a different mode, for of this empire we may juſtly ſay, that it can exiſt by itſelf.

Its situation is so happy, that its northern parts are no more incommoded by the cold, than the southern ones are by the heat. Both are temperate for the inhabitants; the weather in the country, in the intermediate space, is mild, uniform, and accordingly pleasant to live in, convenient for health, and apt to produce all kinds of plants.

The trade-winds, which are peculiar to the southern and warmer regions, are no small advantage; for the northern one clears the air, by carrying away all the unwholesome vapour raised by the heat; the southern one, on the other hand, cools the scorching heat of the warm season. The greatest part of the *Chinese* frontiers are watered by extensive seas, which make good bays and harbours at moderate distances. While nature seems to have here set bounds to navigation, it opens new channels for it by means of navigable rivers, which extend to the innermost parts of the empire. The tide, which goes up a great way into the country, five *Swedish* miles above *Canton*, renders navigation more convenient; and gives the best opportunity to the several towns of communicating their advantages to each other,

by

State of the Country in General. 271

by an univerſal liberty of trading with one another.

THE ſoil is ſo fruitful, that though the hills and deep moraſſes may look ever ſo unpromiſing, yet they repay abundantly the work of the labourer: for the ſpecies of corn, of roots, and fruits, which in an infinite variety ſucceed each other, perfectly well reward their planters with continual harveſts.

THE great extenſive foreſts afford ſeveral fine and precious woods, uſeful juices, bitumens, baſt, and leaves, beſides the ſeveral ſorts of timber and wood for other purpoſes. They are likewiſe the habitations of many wild creatures, which afford food and cloaths for the inhabitants. Metals, ſtones, earths of many ſorts, ſalt, gold-ſand, pearls, corals though not of the beſt ſort, and innumerable kinds of fiſhes, which are very plentiful near the ſhores of this country, ſhew that nature has likewiſe not been ſparing in regard to them. The fowls, which are found every where in great flocks, delight the eyes, ears, and taſte. In a word, the empire of nature is found in the greateſt perfection in *China*; the fineſt views, ſituations, and conveniences of all ſorts, which

could

could not be brought to higher perfection by the utmost stretch of human invention. They have all the necessaries of life, without wanting any thing from other countries: from all which we however must except those things which may be reckoned among unnecessary luxuries.

As the welfare of a country depends greatly on good order and industrious inhabitants, so this empire likewise vies with many others in this particular. The industry of the *Chinese*, and their skill in all sorts of trades, has not only been observed in all the descriptions of this empire, but we likewise know it from the several goods which our ships fetch from thence. The raw materials for these trades are produced plentifully in their country.

I INTEND here shortly to relate, as a proof of the exceeding great industry of the *Chinese*, what I have observed during a stay of fifteen months, at three different times, concerning their constant and particular œconomy.

AGRI-

AGRICULTURE.

IN the fouthern parts of *China*, bordering upon the fea, rice, a fpecies of corn which grows beft in low and wet ground, is the principal food, and in almoft all the eaftern countries. There are fpecies of rice, which will fucceed in a higher, dry ground, as we fee here and there in *Java*, and on fimilar high places. This fort of rice is made ufe of by the provinces which are next to *Canton*, and have a dry and hilly ground; but in *Quantung*, or in the fouthern low provinces, it would be a lofs to fow it; becaufe its grains are fmall, and it takes half as much time again in ripening as the other fpecies does: and, on the other hand, the other fpecies has larger grains, grows better and quicker, and can, without any damage, ftand continually under water. Of this fort there is a more coarfe variety, which looks reddifh, and is eaten by the common people, and likewife ufed to diftill the brandy from, which they call *famfu*.

I HAVE been told that the further you go to the north, the more you find the culture of rice decreases; and that rye, barley, wheat, beans, pease, &c. are cultivated instead of it; for which reason, the inhabitants of the northern parts, where rice will not grow at all, are said to be well acquainted with the management of the last mentioned different species of corn.

The southern provinces likewise produce some wheat, beans, small pease, and lentils, which the inhabitants either make use of themselves, or sell to foreigners. But rice is sown more plentifully; and as it is used instead of bread about *Canton*, I shall speak more particularly of it.

It has already been frequently demonstrated, that *China* is exceedingly populous. Most parts of the country are so crowded with habitations, that you are amazed to see the land able to produce sufficient corn for so many millions of inhabitants; and especially as they are not supplied with it from other places, except by a few *junks* from *Cochin China*, or *Malay*, and sometimes (but rarely) by a few *Dutch* ships. But when one comes to reflect upon their almost incredible industry in cultivating and using every thing which can be

made

AGRICULTURE.

made ufe of, and on their fparing and temperate way of life, it is a convincing proof that a country can never be too full of fuch inhabitants, fo as to want the neceffaries of life. Rather, it is the number of induftrious men, that contributes to the riches of the country, and to the comfortable fubfiftence of its inhabitants; for every induftrious labourer, efpecially a hufbandman, always produces more from the grateful foil than he wants for himfelf.

THE pitch to which agriculture, and efpecially the culture of rice, has been carried in *China*, is the principal foundation of the happinefs of this country. Husbandry is much refpected here, and has the greateft encouragements. The emperor himfelf, to fhew the value he fets upon it, and to exhibit an example to his fubjects which deferves to be followed, goes annually, on a certain folemn day, into the field, attended by the noblemen of the court, takes up the plough, prepares and fows a piece of ground, and afterwards reaps the corn with his own hands. But I muft confine myfelf only to the environs of *Canton*.

E A R T H S.

THE foil is as different at *Canton* as in other places, according to the fituation. All low grounds are covered with clay and black mould; but the higher the ground rifes, the more a yellow and reddifh ochrous earth, glimmer, and fand, prevail: when fuch a foil has been left uncultivated and untouched for a while, it acquires, by the viciffitudes of rain and fun-fhine, as it were a petrified furface. Notwithftanding this, pines, and other bituminous trees, grow very well on it; and fome not very tender plants, which in our country grow on old walls, and on high rocks, ftriking their roots into the cracks: this fhews, that the earth on the hills, which is expofed to the winds and heat, is difpofed to produce plants, though the rain wafhes away its manure.

THE river *Ta*, or *Taho*, which runs into the fea below *Canton*, the water of which is hereabouts a mixture of frefh and falt by the tide, divides the country for the diftance of fome miles round about the town, into many greater and lefs iflands, whofe fhores are

broad,

broad, flat, and fo low, that for fome hours, when the flood is at higheft, they look rather like great feas than like corn fields. This continual humidity muft naturally make the clayey ground fwampy and moraffy, and accordingly the husbandmen muft be up to their knees in it when they work, before they can get a folid ground.

It fhould feem that a foil which is every twelfth hour under water, muft be entirely deprived by it of all fatnefs and power of producing corn, and become unfit for cultivation: and that even when the water fhould bring fomething on it, it would again be wafhed away when the water runs off; and that therefore manuring would be of no ufe. And indeed the wet rice-fields get no other manuring than the ftumps of the rice, which are dug in and left to moulder. Notwithftanding this, thefe fields annually produce a very plentiful crop. As often as the water overflows the fields, it leaves behind it a flime which makes the foil fruitful; for the tide, which comes up from the fea, is more faline and dirty than the ebb, which is clearer when it runs off; befides this, the ebbing retires at firft but flowly, and is already run off from the rice-fields before it quickens its pace; confequently the faline flime, which has fettled itfelf and becomes manure to the fields, cannot be wafhed off again.

RICE-FIELDS.

The rice-grounds are fo foft in fome places, that the flood carries away the foil from the fhores: to prevent this, they are planted with cypreffes, whofe roots being twined among one another give a confiftence to the earth. And as each great rice-field is feparated from the river by broad ditches, thefe long rows of cypreffes make a very fine fhew, efpecially when the field is under water.

They have a different fort of rice-fields in higher places, fuch as cannot be watered by the flood. About each of thefe fields they make, for the fake of watering, a dyke two or three feet deep, within which they either colle&t or let the water run off in the rainy feafon, as they think proper, but in the dry feafon they convey it to thefe fpots. The foil of thefe fields is a mixture of a ftrong clay and mould: and as the annual produce thereof may be double that of the others, they

they are supplied with several sorts of manure, and are better taken care of.

Besides this, the *Chinese* make rice-fields from swamps and brooks; but since these cannot be kept uniformly moist without great expence and trouble, they generally miscarry in dry years. Some persons of credit among the *Chinese* have told me that the river in the province of *Tockian*, which discharges itself at *Schangthey*, forms great flat shores, and that the inhabitants (displeased that such a considerable piece of ground should be useless) built rafts, spread mats over them, and carried soil and laid upon them, and then planted rice, to their great advantage. When the winds shifted, they suffered sometimes from storms: but this contrivance was reckoned very advantageous, because they had always a uniform degree of moisture from below, both in the dry and wet season; and in the latter season they did not suffer by the rain, because it ran off soon. This is an invention and a proof of their industry, which deserves admiration.

The preparation of all the afore-mentioned rice-fields is effected either with the plough, or with a beck-hoe to break up the ground. Both

Both methods have the same effect, since the whole business required is to remove the old rice stumps, and turn them under ground; for, as the ground is always so soft that the labourers must wade up to the knees in it, the work is very easy. Their plough is very simple, and is drawn by an ox; but with the beck-hoe they can likewise penetrate as deep into the soil as they think proper, without much trouble. By the next tide the ground is made as even as if it had been rolled; and as the continual humidity of the soil hinders the ground from binding together, they want no other tools. All other sorts of arable fields are prepared in the same manner, since they choose that time for cultivation when the ground is most softened by the wet, and accordingly can be most easily managed.

They manure, plough, and prepare a little part of a field, about 60 feet square, either more or less, which must be as the other ground, wet and swampy, but at such a distance from the river as not to be exposed to inundations when the water is high in the river. They sow it very thick with rice, which is first soaked in water, in which lime and dung had been previously put. When the

the rice begins to come up, they keep the field about a hand's breadth deep under water; and after thirty days the rice plants are ready to be tranfplanted into larger fields.

THEY are not very curious in tranfplanting, to place the plants in ftrait lines; but very careful that every rice plant has the neceffary room, which is generally about eight or nine inches from one another. The tranfplanting itfelf is tranfacted (as all their other bufinefs is) with great eafe, and in fuch a manner, that they crop off about two inches from the top of the plants, and plant each by itfelf: but when they are too fmall, they plant feveral together fo deep into the foft foil, that the roots immerfe full two inches. When the rice is tranfplanted in this manner, they do not meddle with it any more, except that now and then while it is yet tender, they examine whether the worms and little crabs do it any damage: in which cafe, they fupply the place of the deftroyed plants with frefh ones, and afterwards fpread fome lime, which annoys thefe animals.

MONSOONS and WEATHER.

The southern parts of *China*, within the tropick of *Cancer*, are so much influenced in their weather by the neighbouring monsoons, as to have the year divided into two seasons, the wet and the dry. When the sun in *September* goes to the southward of the equinoctial line, the air cools by degrees, and *October* and part of *November* are generally wet, with fogs and drizzling rain. As soon as the wind turns N. E. the sky clears up, and becomes free from vapours till this wind again is quite settled. In the following months the weather is more constant, till the sun again returns from his winter course, and passes the equator in *March*, going to the north.

The heated air, which has by little and little drawn up a quantity of moisture, returns it again in heavy showers, which alway grow stronger in *May* and *June*, and are so continual that sometimes you can count twelve or fourteen rainy days one after another. These very heavy rains are generally attended with violent thunder and lightning, and hurricanes from south to west. Though the sun begins in *June* to go to the southward again, yet he leaves behind him in these places a greater heat than what he caused when he was perpendicular to them. The weather however begins to be more constant, and the number of fair days rather encreasing, notwithstanding the heat declines more sensibly than before by the inconstant weather, attended by clouds and intermittent winds. *August* is more temperate, but has changeable weather, sometimes calm, sometimes foggy, till towards the beginning of *September*, which continues till the other wind settles. According to this view, their rainy months are *April, May,* and *June*: for the rain then falls more plentifully, and in such quantities that the water in great rivulets rolls down the steep places, and opens new roads and ways for itself in the rocks. On account of the dryness which may be expected in the following months, the inhabitants conduct this water into their rice-fields. We must here remark, that the shifting of the winds about the time when days and nights are equal, seldom happens without a sort of violent storm, which generally blows two days before or after the change of the moon. The lower air then grows exceedingly thick and full of fog, which on account of the violence

of

of the wind cannot become rain, but is hurried about with great violence. The storm increases as the wind tacks to the westward; and when it is become quite westerly, neither trees nor houses are always secure: it changes still from one point of the compass to the other, till after twenty-four hours it begins to abate. Such tempests seldom pass over without doing some damage among the fields, boats, or houses; for which reason the *Chinese* call it *tay fong*, or the great wind.

THE *Chinese* know how to avail themselves of this periodical weather, to the great advantage of their agriculture. They work the soil when it is wetted by the autumnal weather, and is yet soft for planting, or receiving the winter-seeds; this happens about *December:* and the air being then cooler, the water cannot dry away so soon, but that it must forward both the growth and the crop, so that the latter may be perfected in a hundred and twenty days, that is, in *April.* The ground which is then again soaked by the rainy season is manured a little, ploughed, and made ready for the second reception of the seeds, or planting: the usual time for the second preparation of the fields in the same year, is either towards the

the end of *May* or beginning of *June*. One should imagine that the viciffitudes of rain and warmth would now more forward the growth of the rice, than at the time of the firft crop: however, they are obliged to wait longer this time, and to count a hundred and thirty days from the planting to the reaping of the rice; for which reafon the harveft falls out in *September*.

THE low grounds are planted with rice-plants, towards the end of *April* or beginning of *May*. This crop requires as many days to ripen as that on the other fields; and the crop generally becomes ripe in *September*. After this, the ground is not ufed till *April*, during which time the *ftumps* and roots of the rice-plants are fo mouldered, that they quite become earth at the time of ploughing.

As foon as the rice begins to grow white, it is cut with fickles, (the blades of which are dentated like faws), bound up in fheaves, and carried to high dry places, where it is dried and put under cover till it is to be threfhed. The threfhed rice is yet in its hufk, and is called paddy; it is either ufed for feed, or as fodder for the cattle; but before the people use it, they pound it in stone mortars with wooden pestles, and cleanse it from the loose chaff by winnowing.

Some husbandmen, who have larger fields than they choose to cultivate, let a part of them to poor people at a certain rent. These tenants are not men of substance enough to be able to till the fields with ploughs and oxen: for which reason they make use of the beck-hoes, buy of others the necessary rice-plants for transplanting, thresh the reaped rice under the open sky on naked rocks and hills, cleanse it, and pay the rent to their landlords with it.

DUNG.

In order to have a sufficient quantity of dung, where agriculture is so extensive, many poor people get their livelihood by gathering all things fit for manure; the excrements of men and beasts, in the streets and about the houses, and likewise along the shores of the river, which they collect in little sampanes. They sell what they have got to others, who again sell it to the husbandmen who are in want of it: and for the same reason they collect

left urine in proper veffels which they keep in their own houfes. If the crop has been good a pekul of the firft fort of manure cofts two mes; and the fame quantity of the latter, only half that price. Befides this, every hufbandman takes care to make ufe of the excrement which his beafts drop on the paftures: children and fuch people as cannot do other bufinefs, gather it. They likewife pick up all bones, burn them, and fpread their afhes, together with the afhes of burnt plants and boughs, over the fields, to promote fertility.

Such fields as are moift, but higher than thofe whereof we have till now been fpeaking, and confift of deeper mould, are manured, ploughed, and laid very fmooth. In fuch a field they fow wheat very thick together, having before foaked it for fome days in the filthy water of a dunghill; afterwards they tranfplant the plants. Sometimes this foaked wheat is grain by grain planted over the whole field, fo that each grain may ftand four inches from the other. The foil is thrown up in ridges towards the grain. In a great drought a little water is brought over the fields, by which means the deep furrows occafioned by cafting the foil up towards the wheat, receive the water,

water, and give moisture to the plants, without drowning them. The true time for transplanting is towards the end of *December*, and though the air is then very cool, and it sometimes freezes in the nights, yet the seeds thrive, and the plants stock out in a fortnight; each of which brings forth in *March* seven or nine stalks, with ears and straw, rather shorter than ours; and in *May* there is a plentiful crop. I have been told that wheat produces a hundred and twenty fold; which increase plentifully rewards the husbandman's labour and trouble.

As rice is what the *Chinese* chiefly subsist on, and what they use instead of bread (as has been before mentioned), they employ but small spots of ground for the culture of wheat. They only use it in their sugar cakes, a great quantity of which are requisite for the pagodas on their holidays; and some they make for themselves. Foreigners eat the chief part of this corn; and because that which is raised in this province is insufficient, large quantities are brought from the northern parts.

I saw some barley on a little field in *June*; it grew very well, and shot out exceeding fine ears:

ears: but becaufe it was fown too late, the encreafing heat made it thrive too faft, fo that it grew pale before it could fet the grains, and only contained fhriveled hufks in thofe fine ears. If it had been fown like the wheat in the cooler feafon, it would undoubtedly have afforded a plentiful crop. From thence I concluded that as thefe fpecies of corn fucceed exceedingly well, when fown and tranfplanted in a well-prepared moift field; fo the cool weather muft be more ufeful to the growth than the hot.

THE manner of threfhing rice and wheat is the fame, and is performed as in our country with flails. The wheat after it is threfhed is paffed through a kind of fcreen for cleanfing it, which carries off all the duft, before it is ground. If the mills at *Canton* were made as convenient as thofe machines, the people might fave a deal of trouble; but the method of grinding with hand-mills is exceedingly troublefome. It is peculiar, that the *Chinefe* have many pretty inventions to make little works more eafy; but in greater works, fuch as fawing, grinding, and the like (which require greater powers), they do every thing by the hand; though they have fufficient opportunities

tunities of making machines, both on rivers and hills.

In the afore-mentioned manner they till all flat and low places, and find little trouble with the foft ground, which they always keep pretty level. The general produce is a hundred from one; but when irregular weather happens, and it is either too dry or too wet, a fterility enfues, in the fame manner as in other countries: but in this country it is attended with worfe confequences. A little increafe of the value of rice frequently occafions a murmuring among the lazy and poor, which at laft, if the number of malecontents increafes, turns into a rebellion againft the *Tartarian* government; as happened in 1751, when the famine was accompanied by an epidemic difeafe, which carried off a great number of people.

ARABLE FIELDS on RISING GROUNDS.

The natural fituation of hills and of declivities would make them incapable of producing any thing: for either the continual rain in the wet feafon would drown or wafh away all the feeds; or the plants, when deprived of earth by the wafhing of the water, would be too much expofed to the following heat and drought. To prevent thefe inconveniencies, the *Chinefe* have endeavoured to reduce the hills into plains, or at leaft to make them fimilar to plains, by terraces, whofe height and breadth are adapted to the declivity. Thefe terraces they employ for feveral forts of plants [h]; and to each they give fuch a fituation as beft correfponds with its nature. Thofe which can bear the greateft drynefs are difpofed at the top; the more tender ones at the bottom. When the rain has foftened the foil in the upper terraces, the water is conveyed by canals into the lower ones; which therefore, befides the rain which falls upon them, receive likewife the fuperfluous water of the upper ones.

The terraces, which are fometimes four or five feet above one another, acquire fuch hard folid banks by rain and funfhine, that they would ftand for many years. However, they have planted them with feveral trees, whofe

---

[h] In this manner did the *Jews* in the *Holy Land* cultivate their hills. See *Maundrel's* Travels.

roots twisting together keep up the borders; and the trees themselves shelter the plants from winds and sunshine, and so give a very fine appearance to these decorated terraces.

When the soil of the terraces is dug up by a little plough or spade, and made smooth with a little rake, they at the same time put so much dung as the plants require: yet in this case they likewise are very sparing. The dung is generally soaked in water in round cisterns sunk in the ground; and the seed is moistened with this filthy water. Sometimes when they plant or sow they lay a handful of ashes on each grain, because in their opinion the dung which lies between the plants does no good.

The beds which are made on the terraces, or in other places, scarce lie still one month; but soon after the ripening of one plant are prepared to produce another; and are annually employed three times. The husbandmen regulate the business according to the nature of the plants; and each plant, which either loves wet, cold, or dryness, obtains the most convenient season to grow in; and all the roots come in autumn.

The

The species of seeds which were generally sowed on the aforementioned terraces are the following:

A COARSE species of a plant with thin roots, whose leaves, flowers, and seed capsules, were like those of radishes. These were sown in the beginning of *December*; when they had levelled a field, they dug furrows of a foot broad, and of half that depth, making long narrow beds of half a foot broad at the top. By means of these furrows the superfluous water runs off, when it has supplied moisture enough. The seeds were put an hand's breadth deep, and seven or eight inches distant from each other; allowance being made for spreading in their growth. As this is done in the dry season, they water the plants at first. In *February* they were all in blossom; but in *April* the seed capsules turned yellow, and then the plants were plucked, dried, and the numerous seeds beaten out. From the seed they press an oil, which they turn to many purposes in œconomy; but especially they burn it in lamps, and dress several dishes with it while it is fresh. The oil is so fat that it cannot be used in painting, because it will not dry.

dry. The foot, which comes from the lamps in which this oil is burnt, is ufed in making the well known *Indian* ink.

Commonly the feeds of cotton (which they call *minfoo*) fucceed to thofe oily feeds. The foil for it is prepared as before, and the feed is likewife put into the fame forts of narrow beds, a foot afunder; it muft be obferved, that according as the plants either thrive or fpread more or lefs, the beds likewife are made either narrower or wider; and alfo either further from or nearer to each other. They are fown in *April*, over each feed they throw a handful or two of afhes of the oil plant or of other plants: and this is all the manure the field has at this time. They are watered in dry days till the fourth leaf appears. Warmth and rain change the flowers, which appear in *July*, into pods in *Auguft*, which open in dry weather, and fhew the cotton; they are then broken off, the feed feparated from the cotton, and preferved for the next year. Too much wet is hurtful to the cotton plants, both while they grow and while they ripen; and the cotton capfules hang mouldering on the ftalks during a continual rain: and for this reafon they feldom have fo plentiful a crop of

this

this as of the former. This feed is a delicate repaſt for mice; they not only ſeek for it when the pod is expanded, but likewiſe feed on it when in its capſules.

POTATOES (which they call *fowcec*) make the third and laſt crop which they plant on the terraces. The cotton crop being over, they prepare the ground as before, and place the ſlices of potatoes about one foot and a half aſunder. As this plant is not ſo tender as the former, grows ſlowly, and bears the cold, ſo they leave it to increaſe for the remaining months of the year. Theſe potatoes are in ſome reſpects different from ours. The roots have red peels, are longer, yellow, ſweet, and agreeable to the palate; but the leaves, &c. are like thoſe of the *European* potatoes.

THEY do not always ſow oil feeds, cotton feeds, and plant potatoes, exactly in ſucceſſion one after another; but ſometimes ſupply the place of cotton with lentils, beans, locktaw, and calvanſes: but they commonly begin the annual cultivation of their terraces with the oil feeds, and finiſh with potatoes. They always prepare the ground as has been before mentioned; nor do they ſow a ſingle feed which has

has not for a day or two been foaked in the water of a dunghill, or in lime water.

Yams, which they call *ootaw*, are planted like potatoes; but the ground fuitable to them muft be different: for thefe roots are fet in fwampy wet places which are unfit for other ufe, and fometimes on a rice-field which has already been cropped, and which is not worth fowing again with rice the fame year. The longer the roots ftand in the ground, the larger they grow; they are generally taken up in *November*.

The roots of the fugar-cane cut into pieces, (each of which had a fhoot or two) were planted more than half a foot deep into the ground; and two feet fpace was left between every two rows. They planted them both on the higheft terraces, and in the loweft places. In *March* and *April* thefe roots were planted in the low places, and in the rainy feafon on the hills, which occafioned two different crops. Thefe canes were by no means tender; for they throve in fhade and funfhine, wet and dry, heat and cold. When the canes began to grow yellow, they were cut; for when they ftood longer, they grew mouldy at the root. They

grow

grow from eight to twelve feet high. Some fampane cargoes of canes are brought together to a convenient place on the river fide; there they build a hut of bamboo and mats, at one end of which they make a furnace with two great iron-boilers; and at the other an even floor of a confiderable fize laid with planks, over which two oxen draw an angulated roller of hard wood. The canes, which are difpofed in layers under the roller, are crufhed; and the juice, which by means of a canal is conducted to the end of the floor, is there collected in a great veffel. The remaining juice in the canes is entirely boiled out in one of the boilers, is mixed with the expreffed juice, both are ftrained through a cloth, and boiled into a brown fugar in the other boiler: the leaves and ftalks ferve as fewel. When no canes remain in the place where they are, they remove the houfe again, and proceed further with all their implements. Thefe fugar-bakers travelled about in the country, and boiled the fugar out of the country people's canes, leaving it to be refined by other fugar-bakers, and made into fine and coarfe powder-fugar.

K I T-

KITCHEN GARDENS.

My account of kitchen gardens will not be so compleat as I could wish, because I have had no opportunity of seeing any besides some very indifferent ones. What I can assert relating to them is, that they generally choose low clayey spots to make them in, and that they manure them well. The known plants were *sallads, long and short cucumbers, leeks, white onions, spinage, celery, carrots, orach, a species of watery turneps, long radishes, gourds, and water-melons:* these they cultivate in the gardens, having procured the seeds from the *Portugueze.* But besides these we meet with several fruits, whose names and shape are quite unknown to us. Purslane grew wild; they did not use it themselves, and therefore made no account of it. They kept a coarse sort of water-spinage in ponds about half a fathom deep, in which it grew so plentifully, that it quite covered the surface of the water; this is one of their most usual pot-herbs.

THEY plant pieces of ginger in a clayey soil about a hand's breadth deep; this they do

KITCHEN GARDENS.

in *February* or *March*; for when it is done later, the heat forces the ſtalk and leaves too much, and makes the roots more ſpungy and ſmall: in other reſpects it bears both cold and heat.

THEY call tobacco *yeen*. The cultivation of it is the more advantageous in *China*, as it is there more eſteemed than in any other country; they therefore neither ſpare pains, nor think any ſoil too good. In *March* the plants are ſet a foot and a half aſunder: in *Auguſt* the tobacco is ripe, and then they pluck it, make it ſweat, and manage it as is uſual with us. This tobacco does not ſeem to be the beſt; for though it looks like ours, yet both its ſmell and its taſte are diſagreeable: the *Chineſe* prefer it to that of *Manillas* and *Aynam*, which in goodneſs equals the *Braſilian* tobacco. The dried brown leaves are laid one upon another in a preſs, and afterwards are cut into ſmall ſtripes, with a broad iron plane; and in this ſhape they ſmoak the tobacco here: when it is ſmoaked, it leaves behind a viſcid ſtinking oil; it burns better when it is cut into greater pieces. The ſale of this commodity is ſo great, that a large quantity

quantity of it is fent to the neighbouring parts.

They had fet a plant unknown to me, called *Fockyong*, not unlike mint, but with paler leaves; it was planted on broad beds in rows, and it was a foot high in *March*. The culture feemed very tedious; for on account of the heat it had been fown in the cold feafon, and was at that time quite furrounded with mats. They valued this plant very highly, and fold a *pekul* of it for 50 *tel*. They pretended that it was of exceeding great fervice in confumptions.

The greater and lefs *Palma Chrifti* (the lefs in particular, *Ricinus*) were planted every where, without any order, in the gardens at *Aynam*. The kernels being preffed, afford a white clear oil in plenty, which they deprived of its fatnefs by minium, quick lime, and vitriolic earth, and boiled it into varnifh, which when laid on, dries foon and gives a fine glofs.

Instead of cabbage, they ufed a plant with great coarfe leaves, like thofe of burdock, all iffuing out of a little root. The yellow

yellow flowers, the ftalk with the pods, and the feeds themfelves, were like cale. They daily ufe this plant, and therefore it went off fo faft, that they immediately fowed the void beds with it again. It grew very faft in all feafons. They half boiled it, dried it, and took it with them upon fea voyages. Befides this, the *Tartars* of *Pekin* had a fpecies of white *cale*, with long narrow heads, which was not yet very much in ufe, and therefore was fcarce.

THE CULTURE OF TREES.

THOUGH there are many good fruit-trees here, I could not obferve that the *Chinefe* did much regard their culture. They had planted feveral trees, and among thofe likewife fruit-trees, about their gardens and terraces; and likewife had made great orchards, which they looked upon as very magnificent; for which reafon, they were generally planted before the *pagodas* and places of diverfion. But few of the fruit-trees, or other trees, are known to us.

Sweet *orange-trees* (which have been brought to *Europe* by the *Portugueze*) were found bearing good large fruit: and it was said, that they came to still greater perfection in *Fockien* and about *Amoy*. Here are several sorts; some of the size of a walnut, others of the size of an apple, others were angular and reddish, &c. In a few places only, I found those trees placed in some order, in rows, and managed as they ought to be. But, if they were guarded from strong winds, they succeeded without any further care, and bore fruit plentifully. *Fockien* and *Quantung* are obliged to send annually a considerable quantity of fruit to the court at *Pekin*.

Leicki is a species of trees which they seemed to reckon equal to the *sweet orange trees*; there are several sorts of it, such as great, small, and wild ones. The fruit was of the size of nutmegs, surrounded with a coarse, knobby, reddish shell, and growing in bunches like grapes. The trees grow as high as pear-trees, and are furnished with narrow, cuspidated, prickly leaves: they preserve the berries dried, and eat them as raisins. It seems hardly credible, that the country about

Canton

Canton (in which place only this fruit grows) annually makes a hundred thousand tel of dried *leickis*.

TEA (which they call *cha*, and which hereabouts grows only upon an island directly opposite *Canton*) is esteemed for strengthening weak lungs: the island is called *Honam*, and the tea therefore has the name of *Honam* tea. The bushes, which were two or three feet high, stood in rows on dry sandy hills. The light-green soft leaves were plucked in *March*, and roasted in iron kettles, and rolled up as other teas are [i]. The harsh dark-green leaves were left hanging. It seemed as if they had taken too little pains with these shrubs, for near one half of them were dried up.

THE *areca tree* cannot grow far off *Canton*, as I should imagine by the fresh nuts which were exposed for sale. At *Aynam* were several plantations of this tree, standing in ground that was moist and fat. The trees themselves are not unlike cocoa-trees, and have strait stems. When the fruit was ripe, the shells assumed a burnt yellow colour, and then the nuts, which are like nutmegs, are taken out, dried, and sent to the north.

[i] See note, vol. I. p. 250.

THE

The *betle* bushes were likewise not tender, for they grew spontaneously without being planted, wherever they found a convenient place: its leaves, being covered with chalk and rubbed with a piece of areca nut, compose the known *pinang*, which this and many other eastern nations chew with great relish.

The *mange* tree grows high, with expanded branches, like the ash: the leaves are like those of our (the white beam) *cratægus aria*, and the fruit is reckoned the most wholesome of all the fruits in the *Indies*.

Citrus *decumanus* (the shaddock, *pompelmus mcift. itin.*) is a sort of great sweet citrons; the tree is like the citron-tree, but the leaves are broader. There were also little four citrons, *longan*, and other sorts of fruits; and likewise *otomkhoo*, from which, as *Le Comte* relates, they get the resin for their varnish. There are olives, pear and apple-trees, and likewise grapes, all which it would be tedious to mention and describe. It cannot be said that any of them enjoy the preference in regard to culture; for they are all of them left

CULTURE OF TREES.

to grow of themselves, as if they were wild: in some sorts of trees they make use of grafting, at which they are very expert.

GARDENS for DIVERSION.

As great a difference as there is between the taste of the *Chinese*, and that of other nations in their customs, dress, and other things, it is full as great with regard to flower gardens and those intended for diversion. They take very little care about flower-pieces, hedges, covered walks, and symmetry; they are better pleased with a naked place, laid with stones of different colours and sizes in the figure of dragons or flowers, than if they were adorned with pretty designs, and the spaces filled up with plants or grass. Their walks must likewise not be open; but generally they are inclosed with walls, on the sides of which vines and other climbing plants are planted; which being strained from wall to wall on poles, by this means form a covered walk. The benches made in those walks are not lined with walls on the sides, and, by the peculiar construction of the stones, they are provided with several holes in which they place pots with different flowers. The walks have many bendings;

sometimes

sometimes they pass over a little smooth place covered with stones, and lead to an open summer-house, on which there are flower pots; sometimes they form arched walks, which are doubly twisted with thin bamboo, but in an irregular way; and between it a sort of bushy ever-green is planted, which twines in among them, and makes them look like a green wall. Besides this there are many various scenes: hills covered with bushes, below which run some rivulets, surrounded with close standing shady trees; buildings which are three or four stories high, and generally open on the sides; towers, rough grottoes, bridges, ponds, places sown with beans; thick and wild bushes or little thickets, and other varieties which afford a fine landscape. Sometimes they have low stone seats under the shade of some great trees, from whence they can survey a great part of the country.

Though their gardens are very large, yet they appear still greater by their winding walks which turn backwards and forwards. From as much as can be judged of their taste, it appears that no part must be similar to another. In some gardens they dig ditches, round which a walk leads to all the above-mentioned

mentioned places; near them they have many summer-houses, which are all of them of a different construction, and are commonly near a pond on one side, that they may catch the fishes contained in it through the great windows. In the summer-houses they have gold and silver fishes in little ponds; and besides them, birds and other animals, flowers, figures of dragons, with many other objects more pleasing.

BEASTS and BIRDS.

The people about *Canton* and on the sea coasts have seldom any stock of great cattle, because they do not reckon them so necessary as in the northern and adjoining provinces; for they can till their ground with very little trouble, and without cattle; and they travel and transport every thing by water, being much assisted by the tide. Beef is not a very agreeable dish among them, and the plenty of fish supplies its place. But few people have horses, except the *Mandarins* and soldiers. They use only oxen and buffaloes in tilling the ground, especially in places at a great distance from the shore; they keep cows only to preserve the breed, becaufe they feldom make ufe of the milk. Some years ago they made little account of great cattle; but fince the *Europeans* have been more numerous here, and ufe every year a good quantity, not only in *China* but likewife on their return; they have been induced to keep more great cattle, on account of the flefh and the milk.

SHEEP are not fo numerous about *Canton* as in the neighbouring provinces. Their fkins and wool are ufed as cloaths in the cold months; they are however dear enough, fince every body cannot keep cattle, efpecially fheep.

ASSES are not fo common about *Canton* as they are higher up the country, where they are ufed for working and travelling. The *Tartars* have fuch a great liking to affes flefh, that they have introduced the cuftom of killing them, and eating them as they do horfes: I have likewife feen them fell this fort of meat here.

ALTHOUGH they greatly neglect the laft mentioned animals; yet they efteem the lefs animals much more, which they can keep with lefs trouble, and more advantage. Long experience

perience has taught them to manage them to
so much advantage, that little families have a
sufficient, and even superfluous, maintenance
from this business.

They keep plenty of hogs, whose flesh they
eat daily in great quantity and with great relish, and the species in this country is very pro-
lifick; for the sows farrow before they are one
year old, though they do not produce so many
young ones at the first time, as the third or
fourth, when the sow brings forth generally
seventeen or eighteen pigs at once. The dif-
tillers of samsu, ricestampers, and those who
have mills, always keep many swine: though
not so many as the people on the shore, and
the fishermen, who feed them with fish without any expence to themselves: but this food
gives them a fishy taste. Besides this, every
little family in the sampanes keeps hogs for
their own use, and for sale. It can hardly be
imagined how a sufficient number can be bred,
when you observe what quantities of pork they
carry about the streets, and daily consume
(since their principal dish is prepared of bacon); and likewise that they sacrifice large
whole roasted swine in the pagodas, and use
them on holidays; besides consuming many on

their

their sea voyages, and likewise by selling them to the *Europeans*. The pigs of the first and second breed are always small, like the sows which pig early; and for this reason the female pigs which are destined to be killed, are castrated.

They keep many chicken, but more for foreigners than for themselves, and are well skilled in making capons. They leave the chicken to be hatched by the hens, and do not make use of ovens. The warm weather and the many eggs which the hens lay, greatly contribute to their constant success.

Though there are pheasants about *Canton*, yet they are not so numerous as higher up the country, where they are very fine, and of several colours. They are brought to *Canton* as rarities, and are sold at a great price.

Turkeys are not bred in *China*; and though some of them are annually brought from the *Malabar* and *Coromandel* coast [k] (which is the native country of those birds), yet they have not taken pains to introduce them.

[k] Mr. *Toreen*, in his fourth letter, has shewn that these birds are not natives of those places. F.

ALL sorts of pigeons succeed and multiply greatly here.

THE geese thrive well: they are less than ours, and like our wild geese; so on the contrary their wild geese are like our tame ones.

THEY are perfect masters in the management of ducks. The breeding of these birds is a thing of the next consequence to the breeding of swine, which the *Chinese* take so much pains about: and as ducks are a daily dish at the tables of people of quality, the great consumption thereof requires a great breed. The continual warmth of the weather, and the conveniencies of the river, greatly promote their growth: for they can be fed at a trifling expence, with little fry, and crabs which remain on the rice-fields after the water is run off. Many people at *Canton* earn their subsistence merely by bringing up ducks; some buy up the eggs and trade with them, others hatch them in ovens, and others attend on the young ones. They lay an iron plate on a brick hearth; on this they place a box full of sand

half

half a foot high, in which the eggs are put in rows: the box they cover with a sieve, over which they hang a mat. To heat them, they make use of the coals of a certain sort of wood, which burn slowly and uniformly: at first they give them but little warmth, and increase it gradually; and it becomes a strong heat by the time the eggs are hatched. Sometimes, when they increase the heat too much, the young ducks are hatched too soon; and in that case they generally die in three or four days. The hatched young ones are sold to those who breed them up, and these try in the following manner whether they are hatched too soon or not: they take hold of the little ducks by the bill, and let their bodies hang down; if they sprawl and extend their feet and wings, they are hatched in due time; but if they have had too much heat, they hang without any struggling. The latter often live till they are put to the water (which is generally eight days after they are hatched), which turns them giddy; they get cramps[1], throw themselves on their backs, and die with convulsions. The owners then take them out

[1] Ducks hatched in *England* after *Midsummer* usually get cramps, sprawl about in an odd manner, and throwing themselves on their backs die of convulsions.

of the water and dry them; becaufe they will fometimes recover: but they frequently die of fuch convulfions if they get wet again. When the tide goes off, fome little crawfifhes and crabs are gathered, boiled, and cut to pieces, and given to the young ducks by themfelves at firft, but afterwards mixed with fome boiled rice, and minced with herbs. When they are older they are fhifted into a larger fampane, which has a broad bottom of bamboo, with a gallery round, above the river, and a bridge declining towards the water. The young ducks get an old ftep-mother, who leads them when they are let down to graze by means of the bridge. The old duck is fo ufed to the fignal from the fampane in which they are affembled at night, that fhe haftens, half fwimming, half flying, to her lodgings. The *Chinefe*, as occafion ferves, removes his fampane to another place, where he finds more food for his ducks, and lets them out daily on the fhores among the rice-fields. One cannot fee without aftonifhment many fuch fampanes furrounded with greater and fmaller ducks: and it is very peculiar that when many fampanes feed their ducks in the fame place, and call them home at night, each knows how to find the right fampane. The *Chinefe* are always

ways employed in bringing up ducks, except in the three cold months; and though this bufinefs requires a deal of attendance, you feldom fee them employ any particular care, for as foon as the young ducks are a fortnight old, they are able to get their own fubfiftence.

The filk worms, which, confidering their ufe, ought to have a place among the fmaller animals, fhould, together with their management, be defcribed: but as we find accounts of them in other *Swedifh* writings, I pafs them over, and fhall only mention that the *Chinefe* eat the *aurelias* with great appetite, after their filk has been wound off; and that they either boil them frefh, or dry them; the catty cofts eight or nine kandarins.

Up towards *Chingchiu* is faid to be a fpecies of very large filkworms, from which fo coarfe a filk is gathered, that at firft it looks like hemp; the inhabitants however make a fort of ftuff of it, which when new looks like unbleached linen, but by ufe and frequent wafhing acquires a glofs and better look. It feems that this filk will not take a dye, for they

they always wear it undyed, but it is said to be strong beyond credibility, and is called *Chingchiu* from the place it comes from.

THE FISHERY.

THE *Tahoa* is a very long river, and wide at its mouth, and abounds more with fish than any in this country; remarkable as the shores of *China* are for this commodity. It may perhaps be thought that the tide is a hindrance to any fishery, especially in places which are inconvenient to be drawn with nets: however, they catch a multitude with those implements. The most common manner of catching fishes is, they drive in on the sands at a distance from the shore, long poles or rather posts a fathom asunder; between these they place black coloured nets of strong yarn, into which the fish enter and are caught. This manner of catching fishes corresponds to ours of catching them with junkets placed in the river.

THEY have likewise a number of baskets which are formed of bamboo and willow sticks, a fathom and a half long, and like our baskets. They make use of these when

the

the water rifes more than ordinary; they place them along the fhore, but leave openings on both ends of the row of bamboo bafkets, where they lie quite ftill with their fampanes or boats, fo that the fifhes which fwim along the fhore may not be ftopped from entering them; but in the infide they meet with a row of bamboo bafkets, which are placed crofsways towards the fhore, and ftop them from going back. As foon as the water again begins to run off, they fill up this fpace with the like bafkets, the fpace of ground grows dry when the water has left it, and then they go down and gather up the fifh. They likewife make ufe of a fwimming net faftened between two boats, with which they go up and down and catch the fhoals of fifh coming in their way during the tide.

They likewife ufe great nets faftened between two bamboo poles, with which they fifh both on their fea voyages and in the river.

They ufe worms and crabs as baits on their hooks, with which they catch eels and fmall fifh. They likewife make ufe of long, low fampanes with white coloured boards on the fides; in thefe fampanes they keep a little fire

at

at night, which makes the fiſh, which purſue the fire, leap into the ſampane. This kind of fiſhery is generally undertaken on account of a ſpecies of fiſh called mullets, which leap in the dark towards the light of a fire.

BETWEEN the rocks and the ſhore the fiſhery is very great with nets and hooks: they catch a great quantity of fiſh, and ſell them ſalted or dried in the neighbouring towns and villages.

AMONG the many ſorts of fiſh there are ſome like thoſe known among us; namely carps, perches, and ſea perches; but I cannot with certainty ſay that they are the ſame: thoſe that are well known to me are eels, crabs, ſhrimps, oyſters, muſcles, and lobſters: a very large ſort of the latter is caught in plenty on the rocks of *Macao.* They do not only burn lime from the oyſter ſhells, but likewiſe make uſe of the largeſt in their buildings inſtead of bricks.

FAUNULA SINENSIS:

O R,

An ESSAY towards a CATALOGUE

OF THE

ANIMALS OF CHINA.

FAUNULA SINENSIS.

MAMMALIA. *Quadrupedes.*

I. PRIMATES.

Homo 1. SAPIENS monstrosus, macrocephalus, capite conico, *Chinensis:* thus does Dr. *Linnæus* rank men amongst the animals, and calls the *Chinese* with their large conic heads, *monstrous* men.

Simia 1. Ape. Great, black ones; their features are like the human. In the province of *Haynan. Du Halde* I. 118.

2. Gray, very ugly and very common apes. *Du Halde* I. 118. Brisson, p. 145? spec. 18. with yellow

yellow hair, resemble dogs, and have a shrill cry. In the province of *Quangsi*. *Du Halde* I. 121.

Vespertilio 1. Bat. As big as hens, which the *Chinese* eat, found in *Shensi*. *Du Halde* I. 108.

II. BRUTA.

Elephas 1. *maximus*. Elephant. In *Quangsi* and *Yunnan*. *Du Halde* II. 224.

Manis 1. *pentadactyla*. In Formosa.

III. FERÆ.

Canis 1. *familiaris*. Common dog. Dog's flesh is eaten in *China*. *Du Halde* I. 314.

2. *Lupus*. Wolf.

Felis 1. *Tigris*. Tiger. Very large and very common, called *Lou-chu* by the *Chinese*. *Du Halde* II. 336, and *Muller's* Collections for the *Russian* History, vol. III. p. 587.

2. *Pardus*. Leopard, called *Poupi* by the *Chinese*. *Muller's* Collections, vol. III. p. 587.

3. *Catus*.

SINENSIS.

3. *Catus.* Cat, eaten in *China. Du Halde* I. 314.
β. angorenfis. *Du Halde* I. 65. In the province of *Petcheli.*
4. Animals in *Shenfi* refembling tigers, *Du Halde* I. 108. perhaps it is a *Tiger-cat* which is found in the *Tartarian* defarts, is very fierce, about two feet long without a tail; this I faw at *Petetfburgh* in her Majefty's elephant houfe.

Viverra 1. *Zibetha.* Civet-cat.
Muftela 1. *Martes.* Martin.
 2. *Zibellina.* Sable, in the mountainous part of the *Chinefe Tartary,* to the north of the river *Amur.*
Urfus 1. *Arctos.* Bear.
 2. *Meles.* Badger.

IV. GLIRES.

Hyftria 1. *criftata.* Porcupine.
Lepus 1. *timidus.* Hare.
 2. *Cuniculus.* Rabbet.
Mus 1. *terreftris.* Moufe.
 2. *Rattus.* Rat.
Sciurus 1. *vulgaris.* Squirrel.

V. PECORA.

V. PECORA.

Moschus 1. *moschiferus.*
Cervus 1. *Alces.* Elk.
      2. *Elaphus.* Stag.
      3. *Dama.* Fallow-deer.
      4. *Capreolus.* Roe-buck.
      5.   Stag no taller nor larger than a common dog; in *Yannan.* Du Halde I. 122.
Capra 1. *tatarica.* Saïga. Yellow goats. Du Halde.
Ovis 1. *Aries laticaudata.* Sheep.
Bos 1. *Bubalis.* Buffalo.
    2. *Indicus.*

VI. BELLUÆ.

Equus 1. *Caballus.* Horse. Horse-flesh is eaten in *China. Osbeck.*
Sus 1. *Scrofa Chinensis. Chinese* hogs are a variety.
Rhinoceros 1. *unicornis. Du Halde* I. 120, in the province of *Quangsi.*

AVES.

A V E] S. *Birds.*

I. ACCIPITRES.

Falco. Falcons, excellent, but the species not mentioned.
Lanius 1. *Schach.*
2. *jocosus.* Sinensibus *Kow-kai-kon.*
3. *fauftus.* Amœn. Acad. 4. p. 241. among the *Chinenfia* Lagerftrœmiana.

II. PICÆ.

Psittacus 1. *Alexandri.*
2. *criftatus.* Cacatua.
3. green and red. Edw. 231.
4. *Galgulus.* Parroquet. *Calao* Sinicè. Amœn. Acad. 4. p. 236.
Buceros 1. *bicornis.*
Oriolus 1. *Chinenfis.* Linn. fyft. p. 160.
Cuculus 1. *Sinenfis.* Linn. fyft. p. 171.

III. ANSERES.

Anas 1. *Cygnoides orientalis.* Muscovy-goose. Swan-goose.
2. *Anfer.*

2.   *Anser.* Goose.
3.   *Boschas.* Duck.
4.   *galericulata.* Linn. syst. nat. 206.

Pelecanus 1. *Carbo.* Corvorant.
        2. *Piscator.* Booby.
Sterna 1.   *Stolida.* Sea-swallow.

IV. GRALLÆ.

Scolopax 1. *Rusticola.* Woodcock.
Fulica 1.   *Porphyrio.*

V. GALLINÆ.

Pavo 1.   *cristatus.* Peacock. *Du Halde* I. 113, is found in *Quan-tong.*
    2. *bicalcaratus.*
Phasianus 1. *Colchicus.* Pheasant.
    2. *Argus. East-India* pheasant.
    3. *pictus.* Gold pheasant, by the *Chinese* called *Kinki*, or *golden hens. Du Halde* I. 15.
    4. *nycthemerus.* Silver-pheasant.
Tetrao 1.   *Perdix.* Partridge.
    2. *Chinensis.* The bill is pale-blue. The head deep-brown edged with black, above the eye is a white line. The neck is dusky and most elegantly marked with numerous minute circular spots of white and

and pale-brown. On the belly are larger ones of white only. The beginning of the back has others of pale-yellow. The rest of the back, wings, and tail, are pale-brown, spotted here and there with minute dusky specks. Its legs are blue.

3. *Coturnix.* This and the foregoing species are made use of, by the *Chinese* of quality, instead of muffs.

VI. PASSERES.

Columba 1. *Sinica.*

Sturnus 1. *viridis.* The green Stare. On the forehead and chin is a tuft of black and white feathers. Above the first is a spot of white: beyond the eye another. The whole upperpart of the body is green. On the scapulars are two white spots. The wings and tail are green, the outward webs of the first are white; the shafts of the wings and tail are also white. The underside of the back, breast, and belly, pale-blue, the legs cinereous blue.

2. *olivaceus.*

2. *olivaceus.* The brown Stare. The bill is whitish red. The eye lodged in a long stripe of pale cœrulean. The whole body, the wings, and tail, light olive brown; on the belly faint, and tinged with yellow. The legs are pale red, the tail is long.

Turdus 1. *canorus.* By the *Chinese* called *Whom-mai.*

2. *Sinenfis.* Linn. syst. nat. p. 295.
3. *Chinese* black bird. Edw. 19.

Loxia 1. *Cardinalis.* Cardinal bird. Amœn. Acad. 4. p. 242.

2. *Dominicana.* Amœn. Acad. 4. p. 242.
3. *Maia.*
4. *flavicans.* Amœn. Acad. 4. p. 244.
5. *oryzivora.* Cock-paddy, or Rice-bird. A sort of cross-bill, has a green and long forehead, and the crown is of pink colour. The hind part of the head, cheeks, the hind part of the neck, wings, breast, and belly, are white. The chin, throat, and fore part of the neck, black, with

long

long pendent feathers over the breaft, the tail is black, the legs green. This bird haunts the rice grounds, and lives on it.

6. *Malacca.*
7. *Sanguini roftris,* Amœn. Acad. 4. p. 243.
8. *cyanea.* Amœn. Acad. 4. p. 244.
9. *fufca.* ibid.

Tanagra 1. *militaris.* Amœn. Acad. 4. p. 241.
Fringilla 1. *Melba,*
2. *Sinica,*
3. *Chinefe* fparrows. Edw. 43.
4. white breafted *Chinefe* fparrows. Edw. 355.

An Fringilla? a fmall bird; the head, back, coverts of the wings are purple; the prime quill feathers and tail of a fine blue, the fecondary quill feathers are green; the whole underfide yellow, on the ears is a white fpot.

Another like the former, only the back and tail are purple.

Another with a green head, purple breaft, and the tail of the fame colour.

A fourth

A fourth with a light green breast. The head and less coverts are brown.

A fifth has the head, back, and coverts of the wings of a fine deep brown. The tail is of the same colour; the underside of the body and the under coverts of the wings are of a fine crimson.

Each of these five birds had the white spot on the ears; but the head of the fourth was so placed in the drawing, that one could not see this spot.

Hirundo 1. *rustica.* Chimney swallow.
2. *esculenta.* The nests of these birds are eaten as a dainty by the *Chinese,* and for that reason are very dear. They are made of the sea-worms of the Mollusca class. For a further account, see *Kæmpfer's* Amœn. Exotic. p. 833, and *Du Halde* II. p. 201 of the octavo edition.

AMPHI-

AMPHIBIA. *Amphibious Animals.*

I. REPTILIA.

Rana 1. *Chinenfis*, palmis tetra dactylis fiffis, plantis hexadactylis, digito indice reliquis longiore. *Ofbeck.*
2. *Bufo.* Toad. *Bradley's* Works of Nat. p. 165, fays toads are eaten in *China*, and are found in the middle of ftones and in oaktrees.
Lacerta 1. *Chinenfis*, cinerea, cauda ancipiti, corpore paulo longiore, pedibus pentadactylis omnibus unguiculatis. *Ofbeck.*

II. NANTES.

Lophius 1. *hiftrio.* Amœn. Acad. 4. p. 246.
Baliftes 1. *Monoceros.*
2. *Vetula.* Amœn. Acad. 4. p. 247.
3. fcriptus. *Ofbeck.*
4. nigro punctatus. *Ofbeck,*
5. Sinenfis. *Ofbeck.*
Tetrodon 1. *hifpidus.* Amœn. acad. 4. p. 247.
ocellatus, called *de Opblafer* by the *Dutch.* A decoction of this fifh

fish is made use of by the *Chinese* and *Japanese* as a poison, and a branch of the *Illicium anisatum* or *Badian-tree* boiled, with this decoction, makes it still more poisonous. vid. *Kæmpf.* Amœn. Exot. p. 880, 881.

PISCES. *Fish.*

I. APODES.

Trichiurus 1. *Lepturus.* Linn. syst. p. 429,

II. THORACICI.

Gobius 1. *niger.*
      2. *Eleotris.*
      3. *anguillaris.* Linn. syst. p. 450.
      4. *pectinirostris.*
Chætodon 1. *pinnatus.* Amœn. Acad. 4. p. 249.
      2. *argenteus.* ibid.
Sparus 1. *nobilis.* Mandarin fish. *Osbeck.*
      2. *Chinensis.* Lesser Mandarin fish. By the *Chinese* called Kya-yo. *Osbeck.*
Labrus 1. *opercularis.* Amœn. Acad. 4. p. 248.
      2. *Chinensis.* Linn. syst. p. 479.
Scomber 1. *Trachurus.* Horse Mackarel or Scad. Amœn. Acad. 4. p. 249.

III. ABDO-

III. ABDOMINALES.

Clupea 1. *Thriſſa.*
       2. *Myſtus.*
       3. *Sinenſis.* Linn. ſyſt. p. 525.
       4. *lanatus.* Amœn. Acad. vii. 502.
Cyprinus 1. *auratus.* Gold fiſh.
       2. Cantonenſis. *Oſbeck.* very probably a variety of the *Cyprinus Griſlagine* of *Linnæus*, as Mr. *Oſbeck* himſelf ſeems to intimate.

INSECTA. *Inſects.*

I. COLEOPTERA.

Scarabæus 1. *Moloſſus.* Linn. ſyſt. p. 543. This ſpecies is made uſe of in the *Chineſe* apothecaries ſhops.
       2. *laticollis.* Linn. ſyſt. nat. p. 549.
Caſſida 1. *cinerea.*
       2. nigra, oblonga, faſciis duabus tranſverſis teſtaceis, punctis quatuor ad baſin. *Oſbeck.*
Coccinella 1. *ſeptem punctata.*
       2. *quadri puſtulata.*
Bruchus 1. *pectinicornis.* Linn. ſyſt. p. 605.

Lampyris

334 FAUNULA.

Lampyris 1. *Chinenfis.* Linn. fyſt. p. 645. & *Ofbeck.*
Bupreſtis 1. *gigantea.*
Meloe 1. *Cichorii.* Muf. Lud. Ulr. 103. & Amœn. Acad. 6. p. 137.

II. Hemiptera.

Blatta 1. *Orientalis.* Cock roaches.
Mantis 1. *pectinicornis.* Linn. fyſt. nat. p. 690.
Fulgora 1. *Candelaria.* Chinefe lanthorn-fly.
Thrips 1. *paradoxa.* Linn. fyſt. p. 743, & Amœn. Acad. 6. p. 401. n. 48.

III. Lepidoptera.

Papilio 1. *Paris.*
2. *Helenus.*
3. *Troilus.*
4. *Deiphobus.*
5. *Pammon.*
6. *Memnon.* Linn.
7. *Agenor.* Linn.
8. *Agamemnon.*
9. *Philoctetes.*
10. *Demoleus.*
11. *Mneme.* Amœn. Acad. 6. p. 403. n. 54.
12. *Thallo.*

SINENSIS.

12. *Thallo.*
13. *Braffica.* Linn.
14. *Napi.* This species is twice as big as the *European* variety.
15. *Pyrene.* Linn.
16. *Euippe.*
17. *Glaucippe.* Linn.
18. *Hecabe.* Muf. Lud. Ulr. 249.
19. *Trite.*
20. *Pyranthe.* Linn.
21. *Midamus.*
22. *Plexippus.*
23. *Chryfippus.*
24. *Mineus.* Linn.
25. *Almena.*
26. *Aonis.*
27. *Oenone.* Muf. L. U. 274, 275.
28. *Lemonias.* Muf. L. U. 277.
29. *Orithya.*
30. *C. aureum.*
31. *Leucothoe.*
32. *fimilis.*
33. *affimilis.* Muf. L. U. p. 300.
34. *diffimilis.*
35. *Niphe.* Linn. *P. Hyperbius* Amœn. Acad. 6. p. 408. n. 75.
36. *Augias.* Amœn. Acad. p. 410. n. 80.

37. *Lintingenfis,* fubtus pallide luteus nebulofus, fupra nigricans, luteo impraegnatus. *Ofbeck.*
38. *argyrius.*
39. *Pyrene.*

Sphinx 1. *Atropos.*
   2. *Auxo.* Linn.
   3. *Procellus.*
Phalæna 1. *Atlas.*
   2. *Mori.* The *larva* of this Moth is the filkworm.
   3. *lectrix.* Linn.
   4.   feticornis, fpirilinguis alis planis, fuperioribus caerulefcentibus, margine exteriore duabus maculis luteis. *Ofbeck.*
   5. *nigrella.*
   6. *altica.*
   7. *bicincta.*
   8. **macrops.*

IV. Neuroptera.

Libellula. 1. Chinenfis. *Ofbeck.*
    2.   fufca, capitis lateribus viridibus. *Ofbeck.*

V. Hyme-

V. HYMENOPTERA.

Apis 1. lævis, flavo, fulvoque varia, abdomine lineis, tranfverfis undatis nigris. *Ofbeck.* The *Chinefe* call them *Quong-fong.*

VI. DIPTERA.

Culex 1. *pipiens.* Mofquitoe.

VII. APTERA.

Termes 1. *fatale.* Linn.
Pediculus 1. *humanus.* Loufe.
Aranea 1. *ocellata.* Linn.
Cancer 1. *Grapfus.* Amœn. Acad. 4. p. 252. t. 3. fig. 10.
    2. Chinenfis. *Ofbeck.*
    3. Oryzæ. *Ofbeck.*
Scolopendra 1. *morfitans.*
Julus 1. *ovalis.* Amœn. Acad. 4. p. 253.
   2. *craffus.* ibid.
   3. *fufcus.* ibid.

VERMES. *Worms.*

I. MOLLUSCA.

Nereis 1. *cærulea.* Amœn. Acad. 4. p. 254.
Holothuria 1. *Priapus.* Amœn. Acad. 4. p. 255.

Medusa 1. *Porpita*. Amœn. Acad. 4. p. 255.
t. 3. f. 7, 8, 9.
Asterias 1. *pectinata*. Amœn. Acad. 4. p. 256.
2. *Luna*. ibid.

II. Testacea.

Chiton 1. *punctatus*. Amœn. Acad. 4. p. 256.
Lepas 1. *Mitella*. Linn. *Balanus Chinensis striatus*. Petiver. Gaz. t. 1. f. 10.
Voluta 1. *monilis*. Linn.
Ostrea 1. Chinensis. *Osbeck*. The *Chinese* call it *Hao*.

III. Lithophyta.

Madrepora 1. *polygama*. Amœn. Acad. 4. p. 258.
Corallium 1. Chinense. Amœn. Acad. 4. p. 258. tab. 3. f. 11. seems to be the *Madrepora polymorpha* of *Linnæus*.

IV. Zoophyta.

Sertularia 1. confervæ formis. *Osbeck*.
Vorticella 1. *conglomerata*. Linn. Hydra conglomerata. Amœn. Acad. 4. p. 257. t. 3. fig. 1.
Pennatula 1. *phosphorea*. Amœn. Acad. 4. p. 256.
2. *mirabilis*. Amœn. Acad. 4. p. 256.
3. *Sagitta*. ibid.

FLORA

FLORA SINENSIS:

O R,

An ESSAY towards a CATALOGUE

O F

CHINESE PLANTS,

FLORA SINENSIS.

MONANDRIA.

MONOGYNIA.

Canna 1. *Indica.* Indian cane.
Maranta 1. *Galanga.*
Curcuma 1. Chinenfis. *Ofbeck.*

DIANDRIA.

MONOGYNIA.

Nyctanthes 1. *hirfuta.*
        2. Orientalis. *Ofbeck.*
Jufticia 1.   *Chinenfis.* Linn. fyft. nat. tom. 2. p. 60.
        2.   *purpurea.*
Gratiola 1. Virginianoides. *Ofbeck.* Probably a variety of the *Gratiola virginiana.* Linn.
Utricularia 1. *bifida.* fee tab. iii. fig. 2.

Verbena 1. *nodiflora.*
Monarda 1. Chinensis. *Osbeck.*

TRIGYNIA.

Piper 1. *Betle.*

TRIANDRIA.
MONOGYNIA.

Valeriana 1. *Chinensis.*
Tamarindus 1. *Indica.* the *Chinese* call it *Tcham-paboo.*
Ixia 1. *Chinensis.* Linn. spec. pl. p. 52.
Commelina 1. *communis.*
           2. Chinensis. *Osbeck.* Perhaps it is the same with the *Commelina nudiflora.* Linn.
Cyperus 1. *haspan.*
           2. *Iria.*
           3. *odoratus.*
           4. *glomeratus.*
Scirpus 1. Chinensis. *Osbeck.*
Nardus 1. *ciliaris.*
           2. articulata. *Osbeck.*

DIGYNIA.

Saccharum 1. *officinarum,* by the *Chinese* called *Ki-æ.*
           2. pluvia-

SINENSIS.

           2. pluviatile. *Ofbeck.* Qu. Is not this a variety of the former?

Panicum 1. *alopecurodeum.*
           2. *glaucum.*
           3. *Crus galli.*
           4. *brevifolium.*
           5. *arborefcens.*
           6. *patens.*
           7. diffectum. *Ofbeck.* Perhaps the P. *dimidiatum.* Linn.

Alopecurus 1. *Hordeiformis.*
Agroftis 1. *Indica.*
Aira 1. feminibus hirfutis, ariftis terminalibus, flore longioribus. *Ofbeck.*
Poa 1. *anguftifolia,*
      2. *Malabarica.*
      3. *Chinenfis.*
      4. *tenella.*
Briza 1. *elegans,* fpicis oblongis, valvulis carinatis. *Ofbeck.*
Cynofurus 1. *Ægyptius.*
Arundo 1. *Bambos,* the Bamboo-reed.

           TRIGYNIA.

Eriocaulon 1. *fexangulare.*
Mollugo 1. *pentaphylla.*

TETRANDRIA.

Monogynia.

Hedyotis 1. *herbacea.*
Spermacoce 1. *verticillata.*
Ixora 1. *coccinea,* by the *Chinese* called *Kœn-long-faw.*
Plantago 1. *Afiatica.* Linn. spec. pl. p. 163.
Oldenlandia 1. *umbellata.*
Ammania 1. *baccifera.*
Trapa 1. *natans,* by the *Chinese* called *Ling-konn* or *Leng-ka.*

PENTANDRIA.

Monogynia.

Convolvulus 1. *hederaceus.*
           2. *Batatas,* called *Fauciy* by the *Chinese.*
           3. *biflorus.* Linn. sp. pl. p. 1668.
           4. *reptans.*
           5. *hirtus.*
           6. *Pes Capræ.*
Ipomœa 1. *Quamoclit.*
Nauclea 1. *orientalis.*
Morinda 1. *umbellata,* or *Pa-cock-faw* of the *Chinese.*
           2. *citrifolia.*

Muffænda

Muſſænda 1. *frondoſa.*
Mirabilis 1. odorata, *Oſbeck.* Perhaps M. *dichotoma.* Linn.
Datura 1. *ferox.* Linn. ſpec. pl. p. 255.
Nicotiana 1. *fruticoſa.* Linn. ſp. pl. p. 258.
Solanum 1. *diphyllum.*
   2. *Æthiopicum.* Linn. ſp. pl. p. 265.
   3. *Indicum.*
Capſicum 1. *frutescens.*
Lycium 1. *barbarum.*
Rhamnus 1. *lineatus.* ſee tab. vii.
   2. *œnoplia.*
   3. Thea, *Oſbeck.* The leaves of this ſhrub are made uſe of by the poorer *Chineſe*, inſtead of tea.
Mangifera 1. *indica.* The *Chineſe* call the fruit *Quai-mao.*
Achyranthes 1. *aſpera.*
   2. *lappacea.*
   3. Chinenſis. *Oſbeck.*
Celoſia 1. *argentea.*
   2. *criſtata.*
Gardenia *florida*, or the Cape Jaſmine. *Calyx* monophyllous, quinquangular, divided in five ſections, *Corolla* monopetalous, has a long cylindrical tube, the ſections of the

the flower leaves divided into five ovated fegments. *Antheræ* feated within the tube; the *Piftil* is below the flower, the flower ftem filiform, divided, and clavated; Stigma is bilobous, ovated, obtufe and great.

Seed Veffel egg-fhaped, ribbed from the defcending wings of the flower-cup, and within divided into two cells by a thin membranaceous partition.

Seeds numerous, compreffed, and furrounded with a mucilaginous fubftance.

Arbufcula Sinenfis, myrti majoris folio, vafculo feminali hexagono, ad fingulos angulos alis foliaceis munito, quæ porrectæ vafculi coronam efformant. Umki Sinenfibus dicta. Plukn. Amalth. p. 29.

Umky alias Umuy; cujus fructum ad colorem efcarlatinum tingendum infervit; florem fert rofaceum, album, hexapetalum. Plukn. Amalth. p. 212. tab. 448. fig. 4. Frutex cynofbati fructu alato, tinctorio,

barbulis

barbulis longioribus coronato. Petiv.
Muf. p. 498. Ray. Hift. III. p. 233.
Jafminum foliis lanceolatis oppofitis
integerrimis, calycibus acutioribus.
Mill. Dict. n. 7. Mill. fig. 180. Jafminum? ramo unifloro pleno, petalis
coriaceis. Ehret. tab. 15. E. N. C.
1761. p. 333.

Gardenia Jafminoides. Ellis Phil.
Tranf. 1760. p. 929. tab. 23. Gardenia Jafminoides. Solander Phil.
Tranf. 1762. p. 654. tab. 20. The
variety of this plant with double
flowers was brought from the Cape
of *Good Hope* in the year 1744, by
Captain *Hutchenfon*, and prefented
by him to *Richard Warner*, Efq. of
Woodford Row, Effex. Mr. *Ellis*
procured for Mr. *James Gordon*
fome fhoots, which turned very be-
neficial to Mr. *Gordon*, for he by
his ingenuity brought three fhoots
to grow, and afterwards multiplied
them fo much that they are now at
prefent in all the gardens of *England*. The plant with fingle flowers
was found by Mr. *Cunningham* in
China,

China, and in the *East Indies*. Some gentlemen have lately seen this shrub on the coast of *Coromandel*. The *Chinese* call it *Umki*, and dye with the seeds scarlet, it may perhaps, if properly enquired into, turn out a great improvement in the art of dying, and therefore deserve the attention of the commercial part of the public, and become an article of importance in commerce, if planted in the *English* colonies in *North America*.

Nerium 1. *Oleander*.

DIGYNIA.

Periploca 1. *Græca*.
Chenopodium 1. *scoparia*.
Gomphrena 1. *globosa*.
Hydrocotyle 1. *Chinensis*. Linn. spec. pl. p. 339.
Athamanta 1. *Chinensis*. Linn. sp. pl. p. 353.
Sium 1. *sisarum*. Linn. sp. pl. p. 361.
    2. *Ninsi*. ibid.

TRIGYNIA.

Rhus 1. *Javanicum*, by the *Chinese* called *Taisha*.
    2. Chinense.

SINENSIS. 349

  2.   Chinenfe. *Ofbeck*. by the *Chi-
      nefe* called *Mon-khi*.
Sambucus 1. *nigra*.
Bafella 1. *rubra*. The *Chinefe* call it *Tang-
      foy*.
  2. *alba*. Linn. fp. pl. 390.

TETRAGYNIA.

Evolvulus 1. *alfinoides*.

PENTAGYNIA.

Aralia 1. *Chinenfis*.

HEXANDRIA.

MONOGYNIA.

Narciffus 1. *Tazetta*.
Dracæna 1. *ferrea* ; in the *Chinefe* lan-
       guage *Tat-fio*. Irontree.
Convallaria 1. *Chinenfis*, foliis linearibus, co-
       rollis fexpartitis. *Ofbeck*.
Hemerocallis 1. *fulva*. Linn. fp. pl. 462.
Loranthus 1. *fcurrula*. Linn. fp. pl. 472.

DIGYNIA.

Oryza 1. *fativa*. Rice. The *Chinefe* call it
    Vo-a whilft it is growing, and *Vo-
                Kock*

Kock before it is ground. The raw groats they call *Mai*, but when boiled they give it the name of *Fann*.

OCTANDRIA.

MONOGYNIA.

Osbeckia 1. *Chinensis*; by the *Chinese* called *Komm-hoeong-lo-aw*. See tab. ii. fig. 1, 2, 3.
Daphne 1. *Indica.*
Bæckea 1. *frutescens*; called *Tiong-mazu* by the *Chinese.* See tab. i.

TRIGYNIA.

Polygonum 1. *barbatum. Ka-yong-moea* in the *Chinese* language.
2. *orientale.* In the *Chinese* language *Yong-moca.*
3. *Chinense.*

ENNEANDRIA.

MONOGYNIA.

Laurus 1. *Camphora.* The *Chinese* call the tree *Tiong-sio,* but the Camphire extracted from it they call *Tiong-No-o.*
Cassytha 1. *filiformis.*

TRIGYNIA.

Rheum 1. *undulatum.* Linn. fpec. pl. p. 531.
2. *palmatum.* ibid.
3. *compactum.* ibid.

DECANDRIA.

MONOGYNIA.

Caffia 1. *Sophera.*
2. *procumbens.*
Juffiæa 1. *repens.*

DIGYNIA.

Dianthus 1. *Chinenſis.*

PENTAGYNIA.

Averrhoa 1. *Bilimbi,* by the *Chineſe* called Sam-nim.

DODECANDRIA.

MONOGYNIA.

Lythrum 1. *fruticoſum.* Linn. fp. pl. p. 641.

TRIGYNIA.

Euphorbia 1. *neriifolia.*

OCTA-

Octagynia.

Illicium 1. *anisatum.* Linn. spec. plant. pag. 664. The fruit of this tree is probably the *Badian* or *Star-Anis*; and a branch of this tree, boiled with the *Tetrodon ocellatus*, makes the broth of it still more poisonous.

Psidium 1. Guayava, *Osbeck.* Probably P. *pyriferum.* Linn.

ICOSANDRIA.

Polygynia.

Rosa 1. *Indica.*
Rubus 1. *parvifolius.*

POLYANDRIA.

Monogynia.

Nymphæa 1. *Nelumbo.*
Lagerstrœmia 1. *Indica. Isjin-kin* of the *Chinese.*
Thea 1. *bohea*, with six petals. *The leaves stand alternately on the stalk, are elliptical, smooth, somewhat obtuse, and serrated*

or *sawed in such a manner as to make the outstanding corners obtuse.* The footstalks *are short, round below, and gibbose. It has no* stipulæ. Linn. syst. nat. tom. ii. p. 365.

2. *viridis,* with nine petals, *Linn.* The variety of tea which is called *green tea* with nine petals, is enumerated by Dr. *Linnæus* only upon the authority of Dr. *Hill's* Exotics, tab. 22. but it is quite incredible that *green tea* should be a shrub so different from the *bohea tea,* that it should differ in the petals: of which the latter species, according to *Kæmpher,* Amœn. p. 611, has six, which he himself saw in *Japan:* and what is more remarkable, *Kæmpher* says the green colour of tea depends only upon the manner and care taken of it in drying. For some roast the leaves in a large iron pan two or three times only, which sudden roasting makes them brown, and tinges the infusion with the same colour; but on the other hand others preserve that vivid green in the

leaves (and confequently in the infufion) by a flower roafting; and repeat the operation five, fix, and even feven times. Between each roafting the tea-leaves are rolled in one direction on a table covered with a bamboo or rufh-mat: but never is this operation performed backwards and forwards. The pan muft be fo hot, that by putting a frefh leaf in it, it may make a hiffing noife from the expelled juice. The leaves are continually ftirred by mens hands, till their heat grows intolerable; and then they are taken out with a wooden rake, and rolled as above on mats. The *Chinefe*, to take off the narcotic power of the tea-leaves of the firft collection, foak them for half a minute in boiling water. In curing the beft forts of tea, the pan is wafhed, and cleaned with boiling water after each roafting. This is however true, that there are many varieties of tea, differing one from another in the fhape and quality of the leaves: thus the *Tea-Ankai* has oblong leaves, the

Tea-

Tea-Soatchoun has lanceolated leaves and the tea *Linkifom* has hoary or rough leaves.

Captain *Eckeberg* brought a little tea-shrub, the third of *October* 1763, to *Sweden*; which is the first that ever came to *Europe*, for all sorts of trees die on the voyage: but the way to obtain them is to put the fresh seeds into pots in *China*, a little before the ship sails. And as a tea tree, according to *Kæmpher's* account, attains its full growth of about six feet high in seven years, it is probable that Dr. *Linnæus's* tree is now in full vigour. He intends to multiply this sort of tree, and to expose it then to the open air; as the tea-shrub grows as high as the latitude of *Pekin* in the open air, where the winters are far more severe than in *England* and in the south of *Sweden*. It is therefore highly probable that this attempt will succeed: and so it would in *England*, but not in the *American* colonies, for want of such a quantity of hands as the cultivation and preparation of tea require.

Clematis 1. Chinensis. *Osbeck*; it is perhaps a variety of the *Clematis Vitalba,* Linn.

DIDYNAMIA.
Gymnospermia.

Hyssopus 1. *Lophanthus.* Linn. spec. plant. pag. 796.

Leonurus 1. *Sibiricus.* Linn. spec. plantar. pag. 818.

Ocymum 1. *gratissimum.*
Scutellaria 1. *Indica.*

Angiospermia.

Gerardia 1. *glutinosa.* See tab. ix.
Torenia 1. *Asiatica.*
    2. β. *glabra.* Osbeck.
Capraria 1. *crustacea.* Linn. syst. nat. tom. ii. p. 419. & Mantissa, p. 87.
Buchnera 1. *Asiatica.* Linn. spec. plant. 879.
Ruellia 1. *crispa.*
    2. *ringens.*
    3. *antipoda.*

Barleria

Barleria 1. *criſtata*, in the *Chineſe* language *Ab-keyfaw*. See tab. viii.

Volckameria 1. *inermis*.

Clerodendrum 1. *fortunatum*, by the *Chineſe* called *Ka-tag-nong*. See tab. xi.

Vitex 1. *Negundo*.

Columnea 1. Chinenſis. *Oſbeck*. By the *Chineſe* it is called *Pange-ká*.

TETRADYNAMIA.

SILIQUOSA.

Braſica 1. *Chinenſis*, or the *Kai-lann* of the *Chineſe*.
2. *violacea*. Linn. ſpec. plant. 932.

Sinapis 1. *juncea*. Linn. ſpec. pl. 934.
2. *Orientalis*.
3. *Chinenſis*. Linn. ſyſt. nat. tom. ii. pag. 445, & Mantiſſ. plantar. pag. 95.

Raphanus 1. *ſativus*. Linn. ſpec. pl. 935.

MONADELPHIA.

POLYANDRIA.

Sida 1. *spinosa.*
Urena 1. *lobata.*
   2. *procumbens.*
   3. *Chinensis,* caule erecto, floribus majusculis. *Osbeck.*
Gossypium 1. *herbaceum,* or the Chinese *Minfu.*
Hibiscus 1. *mutabilis.*
   2. *ficulneus.*
Camellia 1. *Japonica,* by the *Chinese* called *Fo-kaï.*

DIADELPHIA.

OCTANDRIA.

Polygala 1. *Chinensis.* Linn. spec. pl. 989.
   2. *ciliata.*

DECANDRIA.

Abrus 1. *precatorius.*
Crotalaria 1. *Chinensis.* Linn. spec. pl. 1003.
        2 *juncea.*

SINENSIS. 359

2. *juncea.*
3. *sessiliflora.* Linn. sp. pl. 1004.

Phaseolus 1. *radiatus.* Linn. sp. pl. 1018.

Dolichos 1. *Sinensis,* by the *Chinese* called *Ta-o.*

Hedysarum 1. *maculatum.*
2. *styracifolium.*
3. *Gangeticum.*
4. *triquetrum,* by the *Chinese* called *Ka-song-soe.*
5. *pulchellum.*
6. *biarticulatum.*
7. *heterocarpon.*
8. *triflorum.*
9. *lagopodiodes.*

Indigofera 1. *tinctoria.* The *Chinese* call it *Tong-ann* or *Vaw.*

Astragalus 1. *Chinensis.* Linn. spec. plant. 1066.
2. *Sinicus.* Linn. syst. nat. tom. ii. pag. 499. & Mantiss. p. 103.

A a 4   POLYA-

Citrus 1. *Medica.*
2. *Aurantium.*
3. *decumanus.*

POLYANDRIA.

Hypericum 1. *monogynum.* Linn. spec. pl. 1107.
2. Chinense. *Osbeck.*

SYNGENESIA.

POLYGAMIA ÆQUALIS.

Cacalia 1. *sonchifolia.* Linn. spec. pl. 1169.
2. *incana.*
Ethulia 1. *tomentosa.* Linn. syst. nat. tom. ii. 536. & Mantiss. pl. pag. 110.

POLYGAMIA SUPERFLUA.

Artemisia 1. *vulgaris*, by the *Chinese* called Gnaï.
2. *Chinensis.* Linn. sp. pl. 1190.
3. *minima.* ibid.
Carpesium 1. *abrotanoides.* See tab. x.

Baccharis

SINENSIS.   361

Baccharis 1. *Indica*, or the *Kate-gnai* of the *Chinese*.
Conyza 1. *Chinenfis*.
     2. *hirfuta*. The *Chinese* call this plant *Vreelatfoy*, or *Kang-gan-faw*.
Senecio 1. *divaricatus*.
After 1. *Indicus*.
    2. *Chinenfis*. Chinese After. Linn. spec. pl. 1232.
Solidago 1. Chinenfis, caule procumbente, ramis alternis, foliis radicalibus linearibus. *Ofbeck*.
Chryfanthemum 1. *Indicum*, by the *Chinese* called *Kock-faw*.
Sigefbeckia 1. *Orientalis*. The *Chinese* name is *Khimag*.
Verbefina 1. *Chinenfis*, by the *Chinese* called *Kaling-faw*.
     2. *proftrata*.
     3. *calendulacea*.

MONOGAMIA.

Lobelia 1. *zeylanica*.
Impatiens 1. *Chinenfis*.
     2. *balfamina*.

GYNAN-

GYNANDRIA.

DIANDRIA.

Epidendrum 1. *ensifolium.*

DECANDRIA.

Helicteres 1. *angustifolia,* by the *Chinese* called *Kay-maw.* See tab. v.

MONOECIA.

TRIANDRIA.

Phyllanthus 1. *Niruri.*

TETRANDRIA.

Urtica 1. *nivia.*
Morus 1. *alba.*

PENTANDRIA.

Xanthium 1. *Orientale.* Linn. sp. pl. 1400.
Amaranthus 1. *tristis,* called *In-soy* by the *Chinese.*
2. *cruentus.* Linn. sp. pl. 1406.

POLYAN-

SINENSIS. 363

POLYANDRIA.

Sagittaria 1. *trifolia.* Linn. sp. pl. 1410.
2. *fagittifolia,* called *Succoyee-faw.*

MONADELPHIA.

Thuya 1. *orientalis.*
Croton 1. *febiferum,* by the *Chinese* called *O-ka-o.*

SYNGENESIA.

Trichofanthes 1. *Anguina.* Linn. sp. pl. 1432.
Cucurbita 1. *lagenaria,* by the *Chinese* called *Po-o.* Parents hang the fruit of this plant to their children's necks, to prevent their being drowned.
2. *Chinensis,* Osbeck.
Cucumis 1. *acutangulus.* Linn. spec. pl. 1436.
Bryonia 1. *cordifolia.*

GYNANDRIA.
Andrachne 1. *fruticofa.*

DIOECIA.

DIOECIA.

Pentandria.

Zanthoxylum 1. *trifoliatum*, called *Lack-faw* by the *Chinese*.

Hexandria.

Smilax 1. *saffaparilla*.
      2. *China*, is by the *Chinese* called *Long-fan-tao*.

Dioscorea 1. *alata*. Yams. Their *Chinese* name is *Idaï-sio*; but Captain *Eckeberg* says, the *Chinese* call them *Oo-taw*.

POLYGAMIA.

Monoecia.

Musa 1.   *paradisiaca*. Plantain-tree. Is called *Tsey* by the *Chinese*.
      ——— β. Cliffortiana. Linn. sp. pl. 1477.

Andropogon 1. *Schænanthus*.
      2. *Ischæmum*.
      3. *fasciculatum*.

                     Holcus

SINENSIS.

Holcus 1. *latifolius.*
Apluda 1. *mutica.*
Ischæmum 1. *aristatum.*
Mimosa 1. Chinensis, inermis, stipulis foliolo longe majoribus, semicordatis. *Osbeck.*
Panax 1. quinquefolium. Ginseng. By the *Chinese* called *Jansom*, or *Jansam.*

TRIOECIA.

Ficus 1. *Indica.* Banian-tree.
2. *pumila.* Linn. spec. pl. 1515.

CRYPTOGAMIA.

FILICES.

Onoclea 1. *sensibilis.*
Ophioglossum 1. *scandens*, by the *Chinese* called *Kayin-sé.*
Acrostichum 1. *punctatum.* Linn. spec. pl. 1524.
2. *dichotomum.* ibid.

Pteris 1. *vittata.* See tab. iv.
     2. *femipinnata*, by the *Chinefe* called *Kalao.* See tab. iii. fig. 1.
Blechnum 1. *Orientalis.*
Polypodium 1. *varium.*
     2. *criftatum.*
     3. *Barometz.*
Adiantum 1. *flabellulatum*, by the *Chinefe* called *Siagmaoquang.*
     2. *chufanum.* Linn. fp. pl. 1558.
Trichomanes 1. *Chinenfe.* See tab. vi.

M u s c i.

Lycopodium 1. *nudum.*
     2. *cernuum.*
     3. varium. *Ofbeck.*

A l g æ.

Jungermannia 1. Chinenfis. *Ofbeck.* See Dill. Mufc. t. lxix. fig. 4.
Lichen 1. criftatus.
     2. Chinenfis. *Ofbeck.*
     3. Euphorbiæ, foliaceus, pulverulentus. *Ofbeck.*

Fucus

SINENSIS.

Fucus 1. *Tendo.* Linn. fp. pl. 1631.
Byffus 1. *Flos Aquæ.*

F U N G I.

Agaricus 1. Chinenfis. *Ofbeck.* Confer *Fungus* Kæmph. Amœn. 832.
Boletus 1. *Favus.* Linn. fp. pl. 1645.

INDEX.

INDEX.

The common Figures denote the Page; the Roman Numerals the Volume: where no Roman Numerals are put, the first Volume is meant.

A.

ABRUS precatorius,	384
Acanthus ilicifolius,	138
Acanziles *or* Alcachofas, *see Cynara Scolymus.*	
Achyranthes aspera,	336
——— *Chinensis,*	329
——— *lappacea,*	*ibid.*
Acrofs the way, an Isle near Java, so called,	133
Adelphozion,	123
Adiantum flabellulatum,	II. 7
Adonis annua,	73
Agaricus Chinensis,	356
Agave Americana,	52
Agrostis Indica,	346
Aira feminibus hirsutis,	354
Albatros, see *Diomedea exulans.*	
Albula Chinensis,	385
	Allium

Allium subhirsutum,	62
——— *triquetrum*,	66
Almanacks, Chinese,	291
Alopecurus hordeiformis,	376
Alsine media,	19
Alum,	244
Amaranthus tristis,	350
American aloë, see *Agave Americana*.	
Ammania baccifera,	387
Ammi Hispanicum,	75
Amomum Zerumbet,	II. 61
Anagallis latifolia,	56
——— *monelli*,	73
Anas Chinensis,	II. 33
——— *nigra*,	120
Anchusa angustifolia,	74
——— *officinalis*,	59
Andrachne fruticosa,	368
Andropogon bicorne?	59
——— *fasciculatum*,	346
——— *Ischæmum*,	ibid.
——— *Schoenanthus*,	ibid.
Anemone palmata,	59
Anethum fœniculum,	55
Angeri point, on Java,	132
Anthemis valentina,	74
Anthoxanthum odoratum,	83
Anthyllis tetraphylla,	67
Antirrhinum arvense,	62
——— *orontium*,	67
——— *punctatum*,	66
Apis lævis, flavo fulvoque varia,	II. 10
——— *rufa, abdomine fusco*,	148
——— *violacea*,	71
Apluda mutica,	350
Arachis hypogæa,	377
Aralia Chinensis,	378
	Architecture,

INDEX.

Architecture, Indian,	II. 177
Areca Cathecu,	257
Arenaria rubra,	74
Aristida adscensionis,	II. 98
Aristolochia rotunda,	55
Armenians, at Suratte,	II. 202
Aromas, see *Mimosa Farnesiana*.	
Arrack,	316
Artemisia vulgaris,	394
Artichokes, see *Cynara Scolymus*.	
Arum arisarum,	51
———— *maculatum*,	56
Arundo Bambos,	276
———— *Donax*,	55
Ascension Island, in the Atlantic Ocean,	II. 77
Asclepias gigantea,	140
Asia, preserved Bamboo roots,	310
Asparagus acutifolius,	55
———— *aphyllus*,	ibid.
———— *falcatus*,	ibid.
———— *officinalis*,	ibid.
Asphodelus fistulosus,	59
———— *ramosus*,	ibid.
Asplenium nidus,	II. 49
Asses, common in Spain,	38, 39
———— flesh, eaten by the Tartars in China,	II. 308
Aster Indicus,	378
Astragalus Bœticus,	82
Atriplex portulacoides,	55
Averrhoa bilimbi,	306
Avicennia tomentosa,	333
Ayqua,	297. 306

B.

Baccharis Indica,	394
Bæckea frutescens,	372
Balistes Chinensis,	177

INDEX.

Balistes monoceros,	173
——— *nigropunctatus*,	176
——— *ringens*,	II. 93
——— *scriptus*,	174
——— *vetula*,	II. 92
Bamboo reed, see *Arundo Bambos*.	
——— roots, see Asia.	
Banca, a large Island near Sumatra,	164
Bancshall,	185
Banians,	II. 178
——— tree, see *Ficus Indica*.	
Bantam, point of,	162
——— queen of,	160
Barbers in China,	230
Barleria cristata,	362
Bartramia Indica,	376
Basella rubra,	II. 12
Batavia, capital of Java,	161
Bats?	161
Beans, early growth of,	52
Bellis annua,	65
Benjamin, or Benzoin, a gum,	260
Besant'yes, see *Holothuria physalis*.	
Beta vulgaris,	59
Bill of lading of the Swedish Indiaman,	II. 38
Birds nests,	258
Biscutella didyma,	56
Blatta orientalis,	170
Blechnum occidentale,	357
Blindness of the Chinese,	319
Bocca tiger,	180
Boletus caulescens,	II. 61
Bonnet fish, or Bonito, see *Scomber pelamis*.	
Bonzes,	240. 286
Booby, see *Pelecanus piscator*.	
Books,	233
Borax,	244
	Borrago

Borrago officinalis, 57
Bottle gourds, see *Cucurbita lagenaria*.
Bramins, II. 180
Brandy, Chinese, 315
Brassica Chinensis, 313
Briza elegans, II. 6
―― *media*, 83
Bryonia cordifolia, 374
Bryum murale, 20
Buprestis maxima (gigantea *Linn*.) 331. 384
Burnet, see *Poterium*.
Buxoides aculeata, 394
Byssus candelaris, 61

C.

Cacalia incana, 378
Cactus Opuntia, 54
Cadiz, bay of, 9
―― city of, *ibid*.
―― exchange of, 36
―― garden fruits sold there, 33. 50
―― houses in, 17
―― inhabitants of, 22, 23
―― *miol'ya*, a landing place, 10
―― public buildings of, 24, 27
Calamus rotang, II. 48
Calendula officinalis, 58
Calla Javanica, II. 61
Callvanses, see *Dolichos Sinensis*.
Cambogia or Gamboge, 260
Camellia Japonica, II. 17
Camphire, 253
Cana, see *Arundo donax*.
Canaria, the chief of the Canary Islands, 87
Canary Birds, see *Fringilla Canaria*.
―― Islands, 87
Cancer adscensionis, II. 97

Cancer arenarius, II. 219
―――― Chinensis, 182
―――― eremita, II. 52
―――― minutus, II. 116
―――― oryzæ, 357
―――― pelagicus, II. 115
Cangrejo, see *Sepia loligo*.
Canibas, an isle, 125
Canis aureus, the Jackcall, II. 198
Canna Indica, 330
Cantharis Chinensis, see *Lampyris Chinensis*.
Canton, city of, 214
―――――, province of, ibid.
Cape Pigeons, see *Procellaria Capensis*.
Cape Vincent, a promontory in Portugal, 8
Capsicum frutescens, 18, 209
Carabus totus niger, 65
Cardillos, see *Cynara scolymus*.
Carduus Syriacus, 47
Carex cæspitosa, 75
Carpesium abrotanoides, 329. II. 17
Caryota urens, II. 48
Casaguillas, a Spanish dress, 12
Cassia procumbens, 336
―――― sophera, 330
Cassida cinerea, 359
―――― nigra, oblonga, 337
Cassytha filiformis, 395
Catesbea Javanica, 139
Celosia argentea, 336
―――― cristata, 209
Centaurea pullata, 56
―――――― sphærocephala, 56. 83
Cerastium viscosum, 48
Cerbera manghas, 138
Cerinthe major, 74
Cervus (Javanicus), II. 54

Chamærops

INDEX.

Chamærops humilis, 55
Chætodon faxatilis, II. 53
Cheiranthus cheiri, 69
———— *incanus,* 19
———— *trilobus,* 51
Chenopodium ambrofioides, 55
———— *hybridum,* 19
China, agriculture of, II. 273
—— fertility of, II. 271
—— populoufnefs of, 272
—— religion of, 278
—— rice-fields of, II. 278
—— *root,* fee *Smilax China.*
—— foil of, II. 278
—— weather of, II. 282
Chinefe, 266
———— drefs of men, 267
———————— of women, 270
———— mercantile genius of, II. 242
———— paintings, 242
Chiton læve, 84
——— *marginibus dorfi fpinofis,* II. 60
Chryfanthemum coronarium, 74
———————— *Indicum,* II. 6
———————— *fegetum,* 74
Cicada Chinenfis, 331
Cinnabar, 245
Ciftus fumana, 66
—— *hirtus,* 67
—— *falicifolius,* 66
—— *falvifolius,* 67
—— *tuberaria,* 66
Citrus aurantium, 329
—— *decumana,* 150
—— *medica,* 208. 306
—— *Sinenfis,* 307
Clematis Chinenfis, 329

Clerodendron

INDEX.

Clerodendron fortunatum,	369
Clupea myſtus,	II. 25
——— thriſſa,	II. 26
——— tropica,	II. 103
Clypeola jonthlaſpi,	56
Coccinella quadripuſtulata,	368
——— ſeptempunctata,	64. 359
Columba turtur,	158
Columnea Chinenſis,	371
Commelina Chinenſis,	393
——— communis,	ibid.
Comprador,	179
Conferva bulboſa,	61
Conojito, ſee Fumaria officinalis.	
Convallaria Chinenſis,	353
Convolvulus althæoides,	82
——— batatas,	311
——— hederaceus,	326
——— hirtus,	376
——— pes capræ,	139
——— reptans,	313
Conus (Chinenſis),	303
Conyza Chinenſis,	386
——— hirſuta,	374
——— ſaxatilis,	70
Copper,	243
Cordia myxa,	II. 58
Cork tree, ſee Quercus ſuber.	
Coronilla juncea,	67
Corrigiola littoralis,	83
Corypha umbraculifera,	II. 58
Coryphæna equiſelis, Dorado,	II. 118
——— hippurus, Dolphin,	117. II. 117
Coſtus dulcis,	259
Cottons,	241
Cotyledon umbilicus,	20
Cratægus oxyacantha,	82

Crepis

INDEX.

Crepis barbata,	48
——— fœtida,	83
Crinum Asiaticum,	143
Crithmum maritimum, Samphire,	46
Crocus bulbocodium,	58
Crotolaria juncea,	336
Croton sebiferum,	II. 5
Croziers, or Southern Crofs, a conftellation,	106
Cryptanthus Chinensis,	345
Cucurbita lagenaria,	150
——— pepo,	ibid.
Cupressus sempervirens,	18
Curcuma Chinensis,	329
Cycas circinnalis,	259
Cynara humilis,	74
——— scolymus,	51
Cynoglossum cheirifolium,	58
Cynosurus Ægyptius,	376
Cyperus dichotomus,	371
——— haspan,	376
——— iria,	371
——— odoratus,	361
Cyprinus Cantonensis,	188
——— pelagicus,	II. 113

D.

Danish Island, in the river Tiger,	187
Daphne Gnidium,	55
——— Indica,	II. 6
Datchin,	262
Delphinus Chinensis,	II. 27
——— Orca, Grampus,	7
——— Phocæna, Porpeffe,	12
Dermestes, subrotunda atra,	II. 66
Diomedea Adscensionis,	II. 89
——— exulans, Albatros,	109
Dioscorea alata, Yams,	311
Dogfish,	

INDEX.

Dogfish, greater, see *Squalus canicula.*
Dolichos maximus scandens, 394
——— Sinensis, 304
——— Soya, 253
Dolphin, see *Coryphæna hippurus.*
Dorado, see *Coryphæna equiselis.*
Doronicum bellidiastrum, 59
Dracæna ferrea, II. 14
Ducks, hatched in China, II. 312
Dunkirk, II. 158
Dwarf-mallow, see *Malva rotundifolia.*
Dyers, 230

E.

Ebony, 227
Echeneis remora, 103
Echium Creticum, 74
Echinops ritro, 59
Elephants, docility of, II. 213
——————— gratitude of, II. 198
Emberiza familiaris, 157
Epidendron amabile, II. 50
——————— ensifolium, II. 15
Eriocaulon sexangulare, 387
Erythrina corallodendron, 141
Evolvulus alsinoides, 392
Euphorbia esula, 60
————— exigua, ibid.
————— falcata, ibid.
————— helioscopia, 47
————— myrsinites, 60
————— neriifolia, 329
————— origanoides, II. 98
————— paralias, 42
————— peplus, 60
————— serrata, 84
Exocœtus volitans, 90

Factory

F.

Factory at Canton,	204. 210
Falkenberg, a town in Sweden,	3
Fay-ye, see *Gobius pectinirostris.*	
Fayal, one of the Azores,	II. 120
Fdau-fu,	218. 305
Fennel, see *Anethum.*	
Feol harbour in the Gothenburgh rocks,	2
Ferro, one of the Canary Islands,	87
Fiador,	211
Ficus Indica,	215. 381. II. 171
Fishery, in China,	II. 317
Flagellaria Indica,	II. 59
Flying fish, see *Exocœtus.*	
Fœroe Islands belonging to Denmark,	6
Fortaventura, one of the Canary Islands,	87
Frederick-Henry, a hidden rock,	II. 44
French Island, in China,	347
Fringilla Canaria,	18
Fritillaria meleagris,	83
Frutex baccis albis,	328
Fucus divaricatus,	II. 122
—— *lendigerus,*	II. 99
—— *maximus,*	II. 73
—— *muscoides,*	II. 99
—— *natans,*	II. 109
—— *vesiculosus,*	II. 122
Fumaria officinalis, Fumitory,	55
Funchal, a town and port in Madeira,	II. 160
—— ladies of,	II. 162
Fu-yenn,	216

G.

Galgant,	256
Galium aparine,	55
Gam-boge, or Gum-gutta,	260
	Games,

Games, Chinese,	II. 247
Gamon, see *Asphodelus ramosus*.	
Gannets, see *Pelecanus bassanus*.	
Genista Anglica,	78
Gentoos, or Malabarians, at Suratte,	II. 177
———— manners of,	II. 180
———— women of,	II. 178
———— their women's dress,	II. 186
Gerardia glutinosa,	370
Geranium cicutarium,	56
———— *gruinum*,	66
———— *molle*,	58
Ginseng, see *Panax quinquefolium*.	
Gnao, see *Nymphæa nelumbo*.	
Gobius eleotris,	II. 32
———— *niger*,	201
———— *pectinirostris*,	200
———— *tropicus*,	II. 102
Gold,	243
Goldsmiths,	226
Gomora, one of the Canary Islands,	87
Gomphrena globosa,	209
Goose grass, see *Galium aparine*.	
Gossypium herbaceum,	349
Gothenburgh, a Swedish town, and harbour for India ships,	1
Gracula religiosa,	157
Grampus, see *Delphinus orca*.	
Granate mountain, in Spain,	8
Gratiola virginianoides,	329
Grilleria, cage for locusts,	71
Grillos, Spanish locusts, kept in cages,	ibid.
Gryllus viridis, *Whom-ma*,	377
Guayava, see *Psidium Guajava*.	
Guettarda speciosa,	II. 57
Gulls,	

INDEX.

Gulls, herring, see *Larus fuscus.*
—— white, see *Larus canus.*
Gungung, 186, 187

H.

HAppa, or Hoppo, 216. 359
Hatters in China, 235
Hedera helix, 70
Hedyotis herbacea, II. 4
Hedysarum biarticulatum, 378
—— *coronarium,* 77
—— *Gangeticum,* 330
—— *hederocarpon,* 354
—— *lagopodioides,* 346
—— *maculatum,* II. 8
—— *pulchellum,* 374
—— *styracifolium,* II. 8
—— *triflorum,* 353
—— *triquetrum,* 374
Heracleum sphondylium, 82
Hernandia sonora, II. 63
Hibiscus ficulneus, 328
—— *mutabilis,* II. 10
—— *populneus,* II. 52
Higuera del inferno, see *Ricinus communis.*
Hippobosca, 129
—— *nigra,* II. 97
Hippocrepis comosa, 67
Hirundo rustica, 91
Ho-a-khe, 232
Holcus latifolius, II. 8
Holly, see *Ilex aquifolium,*
Holothuria physalis, II. 74
Hoopoe, see *Upupa epops.*
Humulus lupulus, 336
Husbandry, honoured in China, 296
Hyacinthus monstrosus, 56

Hyacinthus

INDEX.

Hyacinthus serotinus, 56
Hyoseris hedypnois, 75
——— *radiata,* ibid.
——— *rhagadioloides,* ibid.
Hyoscyamus albus, 83
Hypericum Chinense, II. 2
Hypnum Javanense, II. 49
Hypochæris maculata, 82
——— *radicata,* 59

I. J.

Jackall, see *Canis aureus.*
Japanners, 229
Jasmine sphinx, see *Sphinx atropos.*
Jasminum Azoreum, II. 51
Java, Great, one of the Sonda Isles, 126. 160
——— head, a promontory on Java, 130
——— Little, or Baly, an Isle near Great Java, 160
——— monkies, see *Simia aygula.*
——— sparrows, see *Loxia oryzivora.*
Ilex aquifolium, 54
Illecebrum paronychia, 58
Impatiens balsamina, 209
——— *Chinensis,* 344
Indigo, 256
Indigofera tinctoria, 335
Ink, Indian, 245
Joanna, or St. Joanna, an Isle near Madagascar, II. 166
Joiners in China, 226
Ipomoea quamoclit, 210. 336
Iris Xiphium, 58
Iron tree, see *Dracæna ferrea.*
Ischæmum aristatum, 376
——— *muticum,* 140
Isla, a town in Spain, 78
Islands, seven, near Java, 160

Juncus

Juncus acutus,	48
Jungermannia Chinensis,	355
Junks,	195
Jussiæa repens,	II. 17
Justicia procumbens,	381
—— *purpurea*,	372
Ixora coccinea,	335

K.

K Amm-katt,	306
Kann, see Katty.	
Ka-o-lin,	232
Kas,	262
Katong qua,	374
Katty,	262
Kay-in,	374
Kilong,	229
Kitchen-gardens of the Chinese,	II. 298
Kobi,	261
Krakatoa, an Island near Java,	133
Kulier,	213

L.

L Aan-fa,	II. 14
Lacerta *Chinensis*,	106. II. 67
Lack-tao,	304
Laholm, a town in Sweden,	3
Lai, see Kas.	
Lamium amplexicaule,	58
Lampyris Chinensis,	361
Lancerota, one of the Canary Islands,	87
Lanfa, or Leenfa,	209
Lang-an,	309
Language, Chinese,	II. 237
Lanius schach,	367
Lantoa, an Isle in the Chinese sea,	174

Lapis

INDEX.

Lapis lazuli,	244
Larus canus,	9
—— *fuscus,*	ibid.
Lat-yee,	308
Latt-sa,	II. 6
Lavendula stoechas,	66
Laurus camphora,	253
Lawsonia inermis,	354
Laytang,	262
Lead,	244
Lemt'yes, small lemons, see *Citrus medica.*	
Lemur catta,	II. 168
Lepas anatifera,	121
Leucojum autumnale,	67
Ley-kao,	377
Libellula Chinensis,	381
—— *fusca,*	171
Lichen Chinensis,	356
—— *cristatus,*	51
—— *euphorbiæ,*	378
—— *marinus,*	II. 52
—— *parietinus,*	20
—— *physodes,*	59
—— *pulverulentus,*	II. 49
—— *roccella,*	10
Lingen, an Isle near Sumatra,	II. 43
Ling-kamm, or Leng-ka,	305
Linting, an Isle in the Chinese sea,	178
Linum usitatissimum,	59
Literature, Chinese,	277
—————— Spanish,	28
Lobelia Plumierii,	II. 57
Lobelia Zeylanica,	391
Locusts, Chinese,	377
Lophius histrio,	II. 112
Lotus cytisoides,	48
Loxia cardinalis,	19

Loxia

Loxia oryzivora,	158
—— *violacea*,	19
Lucipara, an Island near Sumatra,	163
Lupinus albus,	74
—— *hirsutus*,	ibid.
—— *luteus*,	ibid.
—— *varius*,	ibid.
Lycium barbarum,	II. 16
—— *Europæum*,	55
Lycopodium cernuum,	356
—— *nudum*,	ibid.
—— *varium*,	ibid.
Lycopsis vesicaria,	59

M.

Macao, a Portuguese town in China,	178
Macauco, see *Lemur Catta*.	
Mace,	262
Madagascar,	II. 166
Madeira,	87
—— grapes of,	II. 162
Madrepora organum,	II. 47
Magellanic clouds, a constellation,	112
Magpies, grey-spotted Chinese,	377
Mahie, a French settlement on the coast of Malabar,	II. 211
Mahometans at Suratte,	II. 184
Malabarians, or Gentoos,	II. 177
Malmucks,	108
Malva Mauritiana,	82
—— *rotundifolia*,	47
Mammea Asiatica,	II. 62
Man of war, see *Pelecanus Aquilus*.	
Mandarin,	181
—— fish,	II. 26
—— —— little,	II. 31
Mangifera Indica, } Mango,	308

INDEX.

Mangulor town, on the coast of Malabar, II. 209
Maranta galanga, 256
Marrubium vulgare, 58
Matricaria chamomela, 56
Mayota, II. 166
Medicago polymorpha, 50
Melastoma octandra, 341
——— Malabarica, 354
Melia parasitica, II. 63
Meloë majalis, 64
——— variegata, 84
Memecylon capitellatum, 140
Mercurialis annua, 45
——— tomentosa, 73
Merops viridis, 147
Mes, see Mace.
Michelia champacca, 148
Mill beetles, see *Blatta orientalis*.
Millepora, 47
Mimosa Chinensis, 378
——— Farnesiana, 69
Mintao, 375
Mirabilis odorata, 326
Mohilla, II. 166
Mollugo pentaphylla, 387
Monarda Chinensis, 391
Monopin, a mountain on the isle of Banca, 164
Monsoons, II. 42
Moquaifa, 209
Morinda citrifolia, II. 56
——— umbellata, 363
Mother of pearl, 265
Mules, used in Spain, 35
Musa paradisiaca, plantain, 151, 308
Musca nivea, II. 97
——— vulgatissima, ibid.
Musick, Malabarian, II. 190
Musk,

Musk, 245. 384
Mussænda frondosa, 363
Mustard, oriental, 309
Myosotis apula, 81
———— *scorpioides arvensis,* 56

N.

Nanka, or Polo Nanka, an isle near Sumatra, 165
Narcissus tazetta, 209
Nardus articulata, 346
———— *ciliaris,* 353
Nauclea orientalis, 355. 395
Nerium oleander, 44
New Bay, in Java, opposite New Island, 132
—— Island, between Java and Sumatra, 131
Nicotiana paniculata, 150
Northcaper, see *Delphinus orca.*
Nyctanthes hirsuta, 329
———— *orientalis,* 209
Nymphæa nelumbo, 310

O.

O*Cimum gratissimum,* 376
Oldenlandia umbellata, 386
Olea Europea, the olive tree, 15
Oniscus asilus, 65
Onoclea sensibilis, 142. 271
Ononis repens, 42
Ophioglossum scandens, 375
Opium used by the Chinese, II. 247
———————— Javanese, II. 261
Ophrys insectifera β. *arachnites,* 72
———————— α. *myodes,* 75
Oranges, China, 307
Orchis fuscescens, 61
Origanum Creticum, 33
Ornithogalum umbellatum, 67

Ornithopus

Ornithopus compressus,	67
Orobanche major,	78
——— *ramosa,*	ibid.
Orselle, see *Lichen roccella.*	
Oryza sativa,	350. 254
Osbeckia Chinensis,	342, 343
Oxalis corniculata,	389
Oysters,	II. 30

P.

PAckfanny, see *Albula Chinensis.*	
Pack-la, Chinese olives,	309
Pagodas,	238. II. 231
Palankin,	218
Palma, a Canary Island,	87
Palmetto, see *Chamærops.*	
Panax quinquefolium, Ginseng,	222
Panicum alopecuroideum,	375
——— *arborescens,*	330
——— *brevifolium,*	346
——— *crus galli,*	59
——— *dissectum,*	346
——— *glaucum,*	374
——— *patens,*	346
Papaver Rhœas,	56
Papilio Agamemnon,	332
——— *Almana,*	ibid.
——— *Aonis,*	ibid.
——— *C Aureum,*	ibid.
——— *Chrysippus,*	ibid.
——— *Deipholus,*	331
——— *Demoleus,*	332
——— *Dissimilis,*	331
——— *Euippe,*	332
——— *Helena,*	331
——— *Hyale,*	61
——— *Leucothoe,*	332

Papilio Lintingenfis, 179
——— *Midamus,* 332
——— *Mineus,* ibid.
——— *Orythia,* ibid.
——— *Pammon,* ibid.
——— *Philoctetes,* ibid.
——— *Plexippus,* ibid.
——— *Rumina,* 65
——— *Similis,* 331
——— *Troilus,* 332
——— *Tryphe,* ibid.
Parietaria Lufitanica, 19
Paron, fee *Juncus acutus.*
Parthians, or Parfees, at Suratte, II. 183
Partridge, red-legged, fee *Tetrao rufus.*
Passerina hirfuta, 63
Passiflora cœrulea, 18
Patiallingas, fmall merchant-fhips in the Indies, 159
Pavetta Indica, II. 51
Paulinia Afiatica, II. 9
Pekul, 262
Pelecanus aquilus, man of war, 90. II. 87
——— *baffanus,* II. 71
——— *onocrotalus,* pelican, II. 87
——— *pifcator,* booby, 90. 127
Pepper Bay, in Java, 132
Perca Adfcenfionis, II. 95
——— *Chinenfis,* II. 25
Periploca Græca, 336
Petun-tfé, 232
Phaëton æthereus, tropic-bird, 90. II. 85
Phalæna atlas, 330
Phlomis purpurea, 55
Phyllanthus Niuri, II. 2
Phyfalis, 57
Phytolacca Javanica, II. 59
Piedra Blanca, a rock in the Chinefe fea, 172

Piedra del Puerco,	258
Pinang,	257
Pinus pinea, Spanish Pine,	37
Piper betle,	314
Pistacia lentiscus,	78
Plantago coronopus,	82
Plantain tree and fruit, see *Musa paradisiaca*.	
Plays, Chinese,	323
Pleasure-gardens of the Chinese,	II. 305
Poa angustifolia,	378
—— *Chinensis*,	330
—— *tenella*,	ibid.
Policy of the Chinese,	II. 252
Polo-toya, an isle near Sumatra,	166
Polygala ciliata,	356
Polygonum barbatum,	353
———— *Chinense*,	330
———— *orientale*,	353
Polypodium Barometz,	356
—— —— *cristatum*,	ibid.
———— *parasiticum*,	II. 61
———— *varium*,	II. 9
Populus alba,	15
Porcellane,	231
Porcos, rocks near Cadiz,	9
Porpess, see *Delphinus phocæna*.	
Porto Santo, a Canary isle,	87
Portulaca oleracea,	II. 99
Poterium sanguisorba,	83
Prince Island, in the Straights of Sonda,	132
Proas, Javanese boats so called,	148
Procellaria æquinoctialis, storm-finch,	113
———— *Capensis*, Cape Pigeons,	109
Psidium guajava,	309
Psittacus Alexandri,	156
—— *galgulus*,	154

Psittacus

Pfittacus garrulus, 18
Pteris femipinnata, 375
——— *vittata*, 381
Puerto de Santa Maria, a town near Cadiz, 10
——— Real, a town near Cadiz, 9
Punica granatum, pomegranate, 57

Q.

Quaifa, II. 14
Quail, Chinese, see *Tetrao Chinensis*.
Queda, a town in the Straights of Malacca, II. 216
Quercus fuber, cork-tree, 37
Quickfilver, 245

R.

R *Ana Chinensis*, 299
Ranunculus aquatilis, 60
——————— *bulbofus*, 59
——————— *muricatus*, 83
Ravens, Chinese, with white necks, 377
Refeda glauca, 56
——— *lutea?* 83
Retamas, see *Spartium monospermum*.
Rhamnus lineatus, 353
——— *æ nopolia*, 386
——— *thea*, 375
Rhubarb, 254
Rhus Chinense, 375
——— *Javanicum*, ibid.
Rice, 254
Ricinus communis, 57
Riff, a Swedish harbour in the Gothenburgh rocks, 2
Ro, see *Cistus falvifolius*.
Robbers in China, 322
Rosemary, abundant in Spain, 33
Rosewood, 228
Rota, a town near Cadiz, 10

C c 4 *Rubus*

Rubus fruticosus,	75
Ruellia crispa,	390
———— *ringens,*	370
Rumex acetosa,	60
———— *spinosus,*	50
Ruta graveolens,	67

S.

Saccharum officinale,	350
———— *fluviatile,*	199
Sagittaria bulbis oblongis,	334
Sagu, or sago,	259
Saintfoin, see *Hedysarum coronarium.*	
Salicornia fruticosa,	75
Salsola fruticosa,	74
———— *kali,*	33
Saltamatos, large locusts,	64
Salvia verbenaca,	58
Sambucus nigra,	II. 8
Samm-nimm, see *Averrhoa bilimbi.*	
Sampanes,	190
———— duck,	194
———— dung,	196
———— fishermens,	193
———— mandarin,	195
———— of burthen,	194
———— passenger,	190
Samphire, see *Crithmum.*	
Samsu,	235. 315
Sanguis draconis,	259
Santa Cruz, a town on Teneriffe,	88
Santal wood, or *Santalum album,*	260
Satureja capitata,	66
Scarabæus bilobus,	65
———— *sacer,*	48
———— *typhœus,*	65
Schœnus mucronatus,	48
Scilla Peruviana,	84
	Scilly

Scilly Iflands,	II. 122
Scirpus Chinenfis,	354.
—— *glomeratus,*	326
Scolopendra pedibus utrinque viginti,	II. 30
Scomber glaucus,	II. 94
—— *pelamis,* bonito,	90. 94
—— *thynnus,* tunny,	90. 98
Scorpiurus falcata,	75
Scoter, fee *Anas nigra.*	
Scrophularia fambucifolia,	75
Scutellaria Indica,	II. 3
Scyllæa pelagica,	II. 114
Sea purflane, fee *Atriplex portulacoides.*	
Sect of Tao-tfa, ⎫	
—— Fo or Foé, ⎬ fee China (religion of).	
—— Confucius, ⎭	
Selleria, fee *Tophus.*	
Sempervivum arboreum,	45
Senecio communis,	46
—— *divaricatus,*	378
Sepia loligo,	92
Serapias lingua,	80
Sertularia confervæformis,	II. 30
Shaddock, fee *Citrus decumana.*	
Shaupann,	228
Sherardia arvenfis,	59
—— *fruticofa,*	II. 99
Shoemakers in China,	233
Sida cordifolia,	141
—— *fpinofa,*	329
Sigefbeckia orientalis,	374
Silene conoidea,	56
—— *pendula,*	59
Silk, raw,	241
—— ftuffs,	*ibid.*
Simia aygula,	151
Sifymbrium irio,	46
	Sifymbrium

INDEX.

Sisymbrium sylvestre, 61
Sitta Chinensis, II. 12
Siuu, Chinese truffles, 312
Smilax aspera, 78
—— *China,* 255
—— *sassaparilla,* II. 10
Snail-trefoil, see *Medicago.*
Solanum diphyllum, 328
—— *Indicum,* 379
—— *nigrum,* 57
Solidago Chinensis, 393
Sonchus oleraceus, 19
Sophora alopecuroides, II. 56
Sovaja, a kind of corn, 32. 49
Soya, see *Dolichos soya.*
—— see *Hedysarum coronarium.*
Spartium junceum, 81
—— *monospermum,* 42
—— *spinosum,* 67
Sparto, see *Stipa tenacissima.*
Sparus Chinensis, II. 31
—— *nobilis,* II. 26
—— *spinus,* II. 53
Spergula pentandra, 69
Spermacoce verticillata, 355
Sphagnum palustre, 5
Sphinx atropos, 133
Spices, 260
Squalus adscensionis, II. 91
—— *canicula,* 100
—— *catulus,* 114
St. *Helena,* an English isle in the Atlantick, II. 76
St. *Joseph's flower,* see *Allium triquetrum.*
St. *Lucar,* a town near *Puerto de Santa Maria,* 67
St. Paul and Amsterdam, two rocks in the Indian sea, 119
St. Pedro, a rock on the coast of Spain, 8

St.

INDEX.

St. Sebaftian, a caftle near Cadiz,	9
Stachys arvenfis,	58
—— *hirta*,	56
Statice armeria,	83
Stellaria arenaria,	59
Sterna nigra,	II. 42
Sticklack,	260
Stipa tenaciffima,	15
Storm-finch, fee *Procellaria æquinoctialis*.	
Sugar,	246
Sumatra, one of the Sonda Iflands,	163
Sunfpurge, fee *Euphorbia heliofcopia*.	
Suratte, a town on the coaft of Malabar,	II. 170
—— cattle of,	II. 173
—— inhabitants of,	II. 177
—— ftreets of,	II. 175
—— trade of,	II. 194
—— weights and coins of,	II. 195
Swallow, fee *Hirundo ruftica*,	
Swine, Chinefe,	II. 309
Syan pan,	265
Syngnathus argenteus,	II. 107
————— *pelagicus*,	II. 113

T.

Tale,	262
Tamarinds, }	309
Tamarindus Indica, }	
Tanacetum balfamita,	69
Tan-noao, fee *Gobius niger*.	
Targionia hypophylla,	55
Tayfun, ftorm fo called by the Chinefe,	169
Taylors in China,	234
Tea,	246
—— ankay,	247
—— bing,	250
—— bohea,	248

Tea

Tea, brown,	247
—— gobe,	250
—— honam,	247
—— hyson,	250
—— kuli,	247
—— linkisam,	249
—— padre futchong,	ibid.
—— pecko,	250
—— singlo,	ibid.
—— futchong,	248
—— tao-kionn,	ibid.
—— tio,	250
Tel, see Tale.	
Tenebrio muricatus,	65
Teneriffe, one of the Canary isles,	87
——————— Pico of,	88
Terraces, hills divided into,	II. 290
Testudo mydas,	II. 80. 89
Tetradapa Javanorum, see *Erythrina corallodendron.*	
Tetrao Chinensis, Chinese quail,	303
—— *rufus,* red-legged partridge,	18
Tetrodon ocellatus,	364
Teucrium fruticans,	67
——————— *iva,*	55
Thlaspi bursa pastoris,	56
Thuya orientalis,	209
Tiapp, a passport,	181
—— houses, customhouses in China,	197
Tillæa procumbens,	77
Tin,	244
Tintenaque, or tutanego,	243
Tobacco, dangerous to import into Spain,	13
——————— see *Nicotiana paniculata.*	
Tombs, magnificent,	II. 175
Tophus, particulis testaceis, argillâ & arenâ coadunatus,	14
Torenia Asiatica,	337

Torvicho

INDEX.

Torvicho, or tomillo, see *Passerina hirsuta*.	
Trachinus Adscensionis,	II. 96
Tragopogon Dalechampii,	57
Trapa natans,	305
Trees, Chinese, culture of,	II. 301
Trichomanes Chinense,	357
Tropic bird, see *Phaëton æthereus*.	
Trumpet weed,	II. 73
Tsang-to, or tsang-tack,	216
Tunny, see *Scomber thynnus*.	
Turdus canorus, or } *Turdus Chinensis*, }	II. 121
Turf, constituent parts of,	5
—— method of digging it in Halland,	3, 4
—— qualities of that in Halland,	4
Two Brothers, isles near Java,	162

U. V.

Valeriana Chinensis,	353
—— *cornucopiæ*,	51
Vargoe Hoala, a Swedish harbour,	2
Verbascum Osbeckii,	68
Verbena nodiflora,	363
Verbesina calendulacea,	356
—— *Chinensis*,	393
—— *lavenia*,	141
—— *prostrata*,	356
Veronica agrestis,	56
—— *anagallis aquatica*,	74
Vices of the Chinese,	II. 238
Vicia lutea,	57
Vientaro, see *Cerbera manghas*,	138
Vinca major,	56
Viscum baccis rubentibus,	353
Vitex negundo,	330
—— *trifolia*,	140

Ulex

Ulex Europæus,	78
Ulva lactuca,	II. 99
Umbrellos,	232
Volckameria inermis,	374
Upupa epops,	86
Urena Chinensis,	363
—— *lobata*,	354
—— *procumbens*,	387
—— *sinuata*,	141
Urtica dioica,	57
—— *nivea*,	215
—— *urens*,	57
Utricularia bifida,	II. 1

W.

Wake Robin, see *Arum maculatum*.
Waltheria Indica,	375
Wampu, a town in China,	185
Watches,	236
Welcome Bay, in Java,	132
Whomma, Chinese locusts,	377

Wo-aw-siong, see Bonzes.

X.

Xerez de la Frontera, a town in Spain, from whence the Xerez wine or sherry is brought,   34

Y.

Yams, see *Dioscorea alata*.
    Yansam or Yansom, see *Panax quinquefolium*.
Yedra, see *Hedera helix*.

Yerva

INDEX.

Yerva de Santa Maria, see *Tanacetum balsamita.*
—— mala, see *Nerium oleander.*

Z.

Z*anthoxylum trifoliatum,* 364
Z*ostera marina,* II. 122

F I N I S.

ERRATA.

VOLUME I.

Pag. 2. line ult. *for* Holland, *read* Halland.
3. 1. *for* was not common, *read* was common.
    7. *for* Holland, *read* Halland.
12. 7. *for* Cafa guillas, *read* Cafaquillas.
96. ult. *for* we paffed in, *read* we paffed under the fun, in.
107. 23. and ult. *for* ocres, *read* oeres.
145. antepenult. *for* wrought, *read* written.
146. penult. *for* which gives a luftre to their complexions, *read* which makes their hair look gloffy.
179. 22. *for* and kept near the fhip (or Bancfhal), *read* and kept either near the fhip or near the Bancfhal.
184. 18. *for* Centurion, *read* Anfon.
195. 19. *for* three mace peckuls, *read* three mace, the peckul.
223. 17. *for* Jartona, *read* Jartoux.
246. 3, 4. *for* Cochin, China, *read* Cochin-China.
261. 6. *for* ocre, *read* ocre.
263. 7. *for* ocre, *read* oere.
266. 2. *for* 20, *read* 10.
301. 15. *for* ocre, *read* oere.
362. 9. *for* Ablieyfa, *read* Abkeyfa.
371. 4. *dele* TAB. X.

VOLUME II.

115. 23. *for* brachiperus, *read* brachyurus.
121. 1. *for* Lhin. *read* Chin.
123. 2. *for* ftatia, *read* ftatice.
166. 13. *for* maflota, *read* mayota.
182. 7. muft, *dele the comma, and read* mufk.
187. penult. *for* put our heads on their left fhoulder, *read* put their heads on the left fhoulder of their friends.
188. 1. *for* then we, *read* then they.
    for ours, *read* thofe of their friends.
    2. *for* our, *read* their.
192. penult. *for* half a quarter, *read* half a quarter of a yard.
194. 6. *for* Camboya, agates, *read* Camboya-agates.
200. 4. *for* articularius, *read* cubicularius, or Alexandri.
204. 10. *for* all the factories belonging to the Englifh in the Eaft Indies have chaplains, *read* but a clergyman they think quite unneceffary.
205. 25. *for* worked on with faddles, *read* worked with paddles.
206. 1. *for* rails, *read* nails.
246. 18, 19. *for* finews of deer, *read* ftag's pizzles.
258. 11. *for* are, *read* are wound.

www.ingramcontent.com/pod-product-compliance
Lightning Source LLC
Chambersburg PA
CBHW020740020526
44115CB00030B/698